# CHANGE YOUR THINKING

**SARAH EDELMAN, PHD,** is a psychologist, trainer, and university lecturer. Through both her private practice and continuing education programs, she teaches people to use CBT as a self-help tool. She conducts workshops for mental health professionals, people working in government and private sector organizations, and the general public.

# CHANGE YOUR THINKING

Overcome Stress, Combat Anxiety and Depression,
and Improve Your Life with CBT

## Sarah Edelman, PhD

**DA CAPO PRESS**
A Member of the Perseus Books Group

CHANGE YOUR THINKING:
*Overcome Stress, Combat Anxiety and Depression, and Improve Your Life with CBT*

Copyright © 2002, 2006, 2007 Sarah Edelman

## Published by Da Capo Press
## A Member of the Perseus Books Group
## www.dacapopress.com

Originally published in somewhat different form in Australia in 2002 and 2006 by ABC Books under the title *Change Your Thinking: Positive and Practical Ways to Overcome Stress, Negative Emotions and Self-Defeating Behavior Using CBT*. This edition was published by arrangement with ABC Books.

Library of Congress Cataloging-in-Publication Data

Edelman, Sarah.
  Change your thinking : overcome stress, combat anxiety and depression, and
improve your life with CBT / Sarah Edelman.
    p. cm.
  Originally published: Australia : ABC Books,  2002.
  ISBN-13: 978-1-60094-052-1 (trade paper)
  ISBN-10: 1-60094-052-8 (trade paper)
  1. Cognitive therapy.  I. Title.
RC489.C63E34 2007
616.89'142-—dc22

                          2007016933

The information in this book is intended to help readers make informed decisions about their health and the health of their loved ones. It is not intended to be a substitute for treatment by or the advice and care of a professional health care provider. While the author and publisher have endeavored to ensure that the information presented is accurate and up to date, they are not responsible for adverse effects or consequences sustained by any person using this book.

EBM
15  14

Designed by Avril Makula, GRAVITY AAD
Printed in the United States of America

To my mom and dad

# Contents

**66** I think these difficult times
Have helped me to understand better than before
How infinitely rich and beautiful life is in every way
And that so many things one goes around worrying about
Are of no importance whatsoever **99** Karen Blixen

# Introduction

*There is nothing good or bad, but thinking makes it so.*

HAMLET

Have you ever worked yourself into a state chewing over some issue and then later realized that it was not really that important after all? Perhaps a part of you even acknowledged at the time that it was not such a big deal, but once those thoughts took hold, your emotions seemed to develop a life of their own.

Or maybe you have experienced a time when you were feeling upset about a particular issue, and you talked it over with friends. They said some things that you had not thought about before, and when you took on board some of their points, you felt much better. Talking to your friends showed you another way of thinking about your situation, and when you started to think differently, your feelings changed.

Every day we experience situations that demonstrate this simple principle—the way we think determines the way we feel. Things go wrong; people act selfishly; disappointments happen. Whether or not we get upset by them, and the degree of our distress, depends largely on the way that we think about them. Sometimes we can make ourselves feel pretty miserable, even when our life circumstances are not all that bad, simply by thinking in a negative, self-defeating way. While we may blame other people or our life circumstances for making us feel angry, frustrated, resentful, anxious or despondent, the truth is that our **cognitions**—thoughts and beliefs about a situation—largely determine how we feel and behave.

This is good news because while we may not be able to change other people or our life circumstances, we can change the way we think about them. And if we can learn to think in a more balanced way, we can stop upsetting ourselves every time a problem arises. Changing the way we think about a situation will change the way we feel. This simple tenet is a key principle of **cognitive behavior therapy**—a psychological approach that is used in clinical psychology and stress management programs all over the world. (The word "cognitive" means using thoughts. Therefore a cognitive therapy is one that helps us to examine and change the way that we think.)

In the last two decades, cognitive behavior therapy (or CBT for short) has emerged as the dominant method used by mental-health professionals to treat most psychological problems. This is because hundreds of studies conducted by researchers around the world have shown that CBT is effective in the management of a wide range of psychological conditions. These include anxiety, depression, panic attacks, insomnia, phobias, relationship problems, shyness, substance abuse, sexual dysfunction, post-traumatic stress and social phobia. CBT has also proven very helpful in the management of common daily life problems—from minor hassles (e.g., running late for an appointment) to major psychological challenges (e.g. losing a job). While it was originally developed for the treatment of particular psychological disorders, CBT strategies are now used by large numbers of people to help them feel happier and more in control of their lives. Because the principles of CBT are easy to learn, it is highly suitable for use as a self-help tool in the management of day-to-day stress.

This book will teach you about cognitive behavior therapy and how to apply the principles to your daily life situations. You will learn to recognize some of your own patterns of thinking that create unnecessary distress, and how to respond to potentially stressful situations in a helpful way. This may involve modifying some of your behaviors, as well as changing some of your thoughts and beliefs. Applying these techniques will enable you to avoid getting upset in all sorts of situations, and as a result you are likely to feel happier and more in control.

Please note that if you suffer from a particular psychological disorder (e.g., major depression, obsessive-compulsive disorder, generalized anxiety disorder, eating disorder, bipolar disorder), it is important that you receive more specific treatment from a qualified mental-health professional. While self-help books such as this one can help to reinforce some of the information that you receive during counseling sessions, no book is a substitute for therapy. If, in addition to your therapy, you would like to read more about CBT approaches to managing your particular problem, see Recommended Reading at the end of this book. (If you would like assistance in finding a psychologist in your area, the American Psychological Association provides a referral service—see details at the end of this book.)

# ONE

# Cognitive Behavior Therapy (CBT)

We are what we think.
All that we are arises with our thoughts.
With our thoughts we make the world.

BUDDHA

## HOW IT ALL STARTED

Compared to other fields of study, psychology is a young discipline. It came into existence in 1879, when Wilhelm Wundt founded the first scientific laboratory at Leipzig University, Germany. At that time, psychology focused on the study of learning, memory, perception and sensory processes. Cognitive Behavior Therapy is younger still. It was born in the 1960s and early 1970s, and only became widely adopted as a "model" for the treatment of psychological problems in the last two decades. Perhaps the best-known pioneer in the field of psychology was Viennese psychiatrist Sigmund Freud, whose theories were developed at the end of the nineteenth century. Freud emphasized the role of unconscious mental processes in determining how we feel and behave. A central theme in Freud's theories was that psychological problems stem from our early childhood experiences and unconscious mental conflicts. To resolve psychological distress, Freud believed that individuals needed to gain insight into their unconscious conflicts by recalling and making sense of their early childhood experiences. Freud's therapy is called psychoanalysis and was widely used by mental-health practitioners during much of the twentieth century, and it is still used today.

In the last forty years, various experts in the field have challenged some of Freud's theories. One of the strongest criticisms of Freud's approach to therapy is that it does not stand up well to empirical testing (testing through carefully controlled studies). To date there is little objective evidence that psychoanalysis enables people to overcome psychological problems such as major depression or anxiety disorders. Defenders of

Freud's approach argue that people must have insight into the reasons for their current problems before they are able to overcome them. However, Freud's detractors point to the large number of studies that suggest that psychological problems can be overcome by changing perceptions and behaviors, without extensively revisiting early childhood experiences. While the experts continue to debate the usefulness of many of Freud's ideas, it is widely agreed that his focus on the unconscious mind was a major and important contribution to modern psychology.

In the 1950s, a new form of psychology called **behaviorism** emerged in the United States of America and in Britain. The principles of behaviorism were initially developed through work with laboratory animals and were subsequently tested with humans. Behaviorism was based on the idea that psychological problems are caused by faulty learning, and that most problems can be resolved by teaching people to change some of their behaviors. The use of rewards and punishments were often used to encourage people to modify their behaviors (such as confronting a feared situation rather than avoiding it). Behaviorism proved to be effective in the treatment of some anxiety disorders and childhood problems; however, it was not all that successful in the treatment of depression and other psychological problems. A major contribution of behaviorism was its commitment to empirical testing—the effects of the therapy were evaluated in carefully designed studies, and the findings were reported in clinical journals. Empirical testing is now widely used in psychology for evaluating the usefulness of different psychological treatments.

## COGNITIVE BEHAVIOR THERAPY (CBT)

Two of the most influential pioneers in the development of CBT were clinical psychologist Albert Ellis and psychiatrist Aaron Beck. Both Ellis and Beck started their careers as psychoanalytic therapists, focusing on their patients' past experiences as a way of trying to help them to get better. However, both ultimately rejected Freud's theory that remembering and understanding past experiences is the key to recovery. In the early 1960s, Ellis started to focus on the role of thoughts and beliefs in causing psychological problems. He argued that people often upset themselves by thinking irrationally, and that a lot of psychological problems can be resolved by teaching people to think in a more rational way. His model of psychology was initially called Rational Therapy, but its name was later changed to Rational Emotive Therapy (RET), to acknowledge that the aim of the therapy was to apply rational thinking to change emotional responses. In the 1990s, the name was changed to **Rational Emotive Behavior Therapy (REBT)**, to acknowledge the fact that behaviors also play an important role in determining how we feel, and that the therapy targets behaviors as well as beliefs. Today, REBT is widely used by mental-health practitioners around the world. Many of the techniques that are described in this book are based on REBT.

Aaron Beck made his initial contribution to the development of CBT in the area of depression. He observed that people who are depressed have faulty or distorted thinking patterns. These patterns stem from what he called **schemas**—core beliefs that bias the way we perceive and interpret our experiences. Beck described schemas as being like templates that we use to make sense of our life experiences. Negative schemas like "I am inferior to other people," "people can't be trusted," "I will be abandoned" or "the world is a dangerous place" give rise to faulty thinking in day-to-day situations, and therefore contribute to depression, anxiety and other psychological problems. Beck used the term **maladaptive thinking** to describe cognitions that give rise to unnecessary distress. Like Ellis, Beck maintained that the aim of therapy should be to help people recognize and change their faulty thinking patterns and self-defeating behavior.

While Ellis used the term "irrational beliefs" to describe cognitions that give rise to upsetting emotions, other authors have used words like "negative thinking," "unhelpful cognitions," "unrealistic thoughts," "faulty thinking" and "self-defeating cognitions" to much the same effect. The various terms are used interchangeably throughout this book to convey the idea of thoughts and beliefs that make us feel bad.

Cognitive behavior therapy is made up of a number of techniques and approaches that have been developed from the contributions of clinicians and researchers all over the world. In addition to Ellis and Beck, important contributors include Joseph Wolpe, Arnold Lazarus, Donald Meichenbaum, Arthur Freeman, Christine Padesky, Paul Salkovskis, Judith Beck and many others. The techniques that are adopted for use by CBT practitioners have been tested in clinical trials, and their effects have been measured and compared to other treatments and placebo pills. Cognitive behavioral techniques used in clinical psychology continue to evolve over time, as they are developed and evaluated through clinical trials. While there are differences in some of the techniques and terminology used by various schools of CBT (e.g., followers of Beck versus Ellis), all CBT approaches use two types of strategies:

**Cognitive strategies** involve learning to recognize the thoughts, beliefs and attitudes that make us feel bad, and reframing them into more realistic, psychologically healthy ways of thinking.

**Behavioral strategies** involve undertaking certain behaviors that help us to change the way we think and feel. These include experimenting with new behaviors, such as confronting rather than avoiding situations that we fear or abandoning perfectionist behaviors; using assertive communication; practicing deep-relaxation techniques; problem solving; goal setting; utilizing social support; and activity scheduling.

The emphasis of CBT is on present thinking rather than past experiences. This is not to say that our childhood experiences do not influence the way that we think and feel—

there is no doubt that they do. Neglect, trauma, and physical or psychological abuse in early childhood often contribute to problems later on in life. However, not all psychological problems are the result of bad parenting. We know, for instance, that people who had pretty normal childhoods still sometimes develop psychological problems. Conversely, those who had unhappy childhoods can still grow into well-adjusted adults. Whatever our childhood experiences, there is little evidence that therapies that focus predominantly on childhood history enable people to overcome their current psychological problems, such as depression, anxiety disorders or other disorders. In fact, excessively focusing on past injustices or parental neglect can be self-defeating if it discourages people from actively working to resolve their current problems. While it is often helpful to acknowledge the difficulties that we faced in early childhood, the key to recovery lies in the things that we can do from now on.

## COGNITIONS—THOUGHTS AND BELIEFS

We have already seen that cognitions are made up of our thoughts and beliefs, but what is the difference between the two? While they are related, thoughts and beliefs are not the same thing. Thoughts are transient and often conscious. We have thousands of thoughts each day, and we can often—but not always—identify what we are thinking about if we stop and try. Our thoughts influence the ways that we feel and behave.

Beliefs are stable and often unconscious assumptions that we make about ourselves, other people and the world. Although we can sometimes consciously think about our beliefs, and even question whether they are rational or valid, we do not do this most of the time. Our beliefs influence the way that we think, feel and behave.

> Bob narrowly avoids a car accident when another motorist fails to give way to him.
> As he gestures angrily at the other driver, Bob thinks to himself, "Stupid idiot!"

Bob's thoughts are easy to identify—"Stupid idiot!" But what about the beliefs that gave rise to them? Like many people, Bob believes that others should always do the right thing—and, in particular, they should obey the road laws. In fact, it was this belief, and not the other person's poor driving, that made Bob feel angry. If Bob only held a preference that people should obey the road laws rather than a strong belief that they must always do so, Bob would have responded with brief irritation rather than anger. Similarly, if you believe that all people must drive well and always obey the road laws, chances are you are going to get very upset on occasions when they do not. On the other hand, if you believe that most people drive reasonably well most of the time, but that sometimes some people don't, this experience is much more likely to leave you feeling annoyed rather than furious.

While it is totally reasonable to want people to do the right thing, the belief that others should always do the right thing gets us into trouble (see chapter 2).

## COGNITIONS CREATE FEELINGS

Feelings are emotions. We all have them—we all know how it feels when we are happy, sad, excited, angry, embarrassed, grateful, disgusted or delighted—but it is hard to define exactly what feelings are. We can say that most feelings are either pleasant or unpleasant, and that much of our behavior is motivated by the desire to avoid unpleasant feelings and to experience more pleasant ones. Our feelings are largely determined by our cognitions. Whether we feel delighted, disappointed or depressed at any particular time depends on our thoughts and beliefs in relation to our situation.

| COGNITION | FEELING |
|---|---|
| Something bad might happen. | anxiety |
| They did a bad thing and they shouldn't be able to get away with it. | anger |
| I did a bad thing, and I deserve to be punished. | guilt |
| Things are going really well for me. | contentment |
| I have lost something that I value. | sadness |
| The world is a bad place, I am a worthless person, and the future is hopeless. | depression |
| I did an immoral thing, and people think badly of me. | shame |
| Things are not going the way that they should. | frustration |
| Something good is going to happen. | excitement |
| That is revolting. | disgust |
| I am inferior to others. | inadequacy |
| I am a bad person. | self-loathing |
| That's not what I expected. | surprise |

## COGNITIONS AFFECT OUR BEHAVIORS

Not only do our cognitions determine the way we feel, they also play an important role in the way we behave. Our cognitions can motivate us to do things that are consistent with our goals, such as keep in touch with friends, exercise regularly, pursue our interests or solve a problem. On the other hand, cognitions can give rise to self-defeating behaviors, such as procrastination, abusing a loved one, isolating ourselves or neglecting our health. Cognitions give rise to helpful or unhelpful behavior.

We have already seen that modifying negative or unhelpful cognitions can help us to feel better. In addition, changing certain cognitions can motivate us to behave in ways that are life-enhancing or consistent with our goals. Interestingly, the relationship also works in reverse. Just as our cognitions affect our feelings and our behaviors, so too our behaviors can affect the way we think and feel.

| COGNITION | BEHAVIORS |
|---|---|
| I must be loved and approved of by everyone. | Excessively try to please others; avoid assertive behavior. |
| I must do things perfectly. | Procrastinate; slow, inefficient performance. |
| Making mistakes is an opportunity to learn—it's not a catastrophe. | Willing to try again—several times, if necessary—to reach goals. |
| People should do what I believe is right. | Unfriendly or hostile towards those who do not meet expectations. |
| I am likeable and worthwhile. People respond positively towards me. | Willing to reach out to people, initiate friendships and take social risks. |
| My life should be easy—I shouldn't do things that are difficult or not enjoyable. | Avoid activities that are difficult or unpleasant, even if they are for the best. |
| I am incompetent. | Avoid trying to learn new things. |
| I must have someone stronger than myself whom I can rely on; I can't cope on my own. | Stay in unhealthy, loveless or destructive relationships; tolerate abusive treatment. |
| I can get anything I want if I'm willing to work hard towards it. | Willing to spend time and effort in working towards goals. |
| If I want something, I must have it immediately. | Engage in addictive behavior, such as drinking alcohol, smoking, taking drugs, poor diet, etc. |
| Everyone is trying their best. No one deserves to be judged or condemned. | Get on well with most people. |
| I am flawed; I am not OK. | Self-conscious in social interactions; avoid eye contact; avoid taking social risks. |

## BEHAVIORS AFFECT COGNITIONS AND FEELINGS

Our behaviors can influence our feelings in two ways. Firstly, certain behaviors have a direct mood-enhancing effect. Secondly, some of our behaviors influence the way we feel indirectly, through their effect on our cognitions.

### The direct mood-enhancing effect of behavior

We have all experienced situations where changing our behavior made a difference to our mood. Perhaps at a time when you were feeling down, you made a decision to call a friend, and doing so made you feel better? Or perhaps you did some physical exercise, played some music or became absorbed in an interesting project? Actions such as these can lift our spirits because they are inherently pleasurable and they distract us from our negative thoughts. Doing things that give us a sense of achievement or purpose can also lift our spirits. Going to work or engaging in regular activities can help us to feel good. So can cleaning out a cupboard, painting a room, writing a letter, or finishing an outstanding job (see chapter 8).

**The indirect effect of behavior on the way we feel—via cognitions**

Many of our behaviors serve to reinforce our existing cognitions. For instance, avoiding social contact with other people can reinforce the belief that we are not OK or that people do not like us. This in turn may lead to feelings of loneliness, depression or poor self-esteem. Behaving unassertively much of the time may reinforce the belief that it's not acceptable to ask for what we want. This may cause us to feel frustrated and resentful at times. Choosing to avoid situations that we fear reinforces the belief that those situations are highly threatening. As a result, we feel extremely anxious whenever we need to confront those situations. Trying to do things perfectly all the time reinforces the belief that everything we do must be perfect. As a consequence, we become anxious or immobilized in situations where we believe that we may not do a perfect job.

## CHANGING OUR BEHAVIOR CAN CHANGE THE WAY WE FEEL

Changing some of our behavior can help us to think differently about our situation, and feel better as a result. For instance, initiating social contact with certain people may help to challenge the belief that we are incapable of making friends, and our new cognition ("I can make friends when I make the effort") may cause us to feel better about ourselves. Confronting some of the things that we fear—the dreaded social function, the speech or that unpleasant phone call—can lead us to stop perceiving those situations as highly threatening, and our revised cognitions ("I can handle it—it's not so bad") help to reduce our anxiety in those situations. Completing some tasks less than perfectly can help us to recognize that things don't have to be perfect, and this revised belief frees us from unnecessary anxiety. Communicating assertively in order to resolve a conflict can lead us to realize that we are capable of solving certain problems, and to feel happier as a result. Doing certain things that we keep putting off (e.g., doing your tax return, having the in-laws for dinner) can help us to recognize that they are not so bad after all, and so reduces our guilt and frustration and increases our confidence. And, believe it or not, being nice to someone that we dislike can enable us to perceive them more charitably, and feel more comfortable in their presence. All of these behaviors can help us to feel better through their influence on our cognitions (see chapter 3).

## WHERE DO OUR COGNITIONS COME FROM?

As cognitions play such an important role in the way we feel and behave, it would be reasonable to ask, "Why do I have these cognitions? And why is it that some people think rationally most of the time, while others have lots of negative and self-defeating thoughts so frequently?" The answers lie in the many different influences that shape our perceptions over the course of our lives. These include:

> ➤ our early childhood experiences—the messages that we received from our parents, teachers, peers, siblings, etc.
> ➤ the people with whom we have associated throughout our lives, including partners, significant friends, family members and work colleagues
> ➤ our life experiences, including our achievements, losses, failures, successes and rejections
> ➤ the information that we acquired from reading, courses and educational institutions
> ➤ the accumulated messages that we receive from society via television, billboards, magazines, newspapers and movies
> ➤ our innate temperament and biological predisposition.

## Biological predisposition?

While there is no gene for negative thinking, biological factors can influence the way we respond to situations, and ultimately the way we learn to think. For instance, some people have an inherent predisposition towards becoming anxious. As a result, they tend to focus on potentially threatening events, experience more intense physiological arousal and are more likely to perceive situations as potentially harmful. Similarly, people who have a predisposition towards depression are more likely to perceive themselves and their experiences in a negative way. People who are predisposed towards shyness (yes, shyness is also influenced by our genes) may be more sensitive to messages that they receive from others, and therefore may tend to perceive rejection or disapproval in some of those messages.

While our biology can influence our psychological predisposition, this does not mean that negative feelings are unavoidable. People who have a biological disposition towards heart disease need to work harder than others at maintaining a healthy diet, getting regular exercise and reducing their cholesterol levels. Similarly, those with a biological disposition towards a particular psychological problem need to put more effort into managing their emotions compared to others who don't have that disposition. Learning to apply CBT strategies can help us to manage that disposition and substantially reduce the frequency and intensity of distressing episodes. In addition, when psychological problems emerge, applying CBT strategies can reduce the severity of the problem and enable faster recovery.

## What about the messages we get from society?

Many of the messages that we get from society via the mass media contribute to unhappiness by influencing our beliefs. Images portrayed on television, the movies, in magazines and in advertising focus on the importance of things like:

➤ having a high-status, well-paid job
➤ being slim, young and attractive
➤ achieving wealth, career success and popularity
➤ having happy harmonious relationships with family and friends.

People buy into these messages to different degrees. Many people believe that to be successful they must have a highly paid job and own expensive consumer items or that they must be slim and youthful in appearance or that they must have lots of friends. The more strongly we hold beliefs such as these, the more likely we are to feel unhappy at times when reality fails to live up to our expectations. So for example, if you believe that you must have happy, harmonious family relationships, but in reality your family relationships are dysfunctional, the belief that things must not be this way makes you feel bad. While there is no problem with preferring to have happy family relationships, beauty, friends, achievements or material wealth, believing that things must be a certain way is guaranteed to create unhappiness. (In fact, advertisers depend on this to help them sell their products.)

The good news is that thoughts and beliefs can be changed. Hundreds of studies have demonstrated that people can modify their cognitions, and feel much better as a result. This process involves recognizing the particular cognitions that make us feel bad in the first place, challenging the irrational or negative aspects of our thinking, and finally, developing more reasonable and balanced ways of thinking about our situations. Clearly, some patterns of thinking are more deep-seated, and therefore harder to alter than others, and changing these cognitions requires a lot more effort and reinforcement. Behavioral disputing strategies are particularly valuable for shifting deep-seated beliefs that are otherwise difficult to budge (see chapter 3).

## CBT IS NOT JUST "POSITIVE THINKING"

If you are a reader of popular psychology and inspirational self-help books, you have probably come across books that suggest using affirmations to help you to be more positive. Typical affirmations include:

➤ Every day, in every way, I'm getting better and better.
➤ I am prosperous and I am a winner.
➤ My world is full of abundance.
➤ Things are working out to my highest good.
➤ The universe lovingly takes care of me.
➤ I love myself and I approve of myself.

Many people use statements such as these to help them adopt new ways of thinking, but do they really work? The answer depends on whether or not you believe them to be true. Affirmations can help to reinforce credible concepts.

> *Rodney, who feels depressed after performing badly at a job interview, might benefit from affirming, "It's not a disaster," "This is a good learning experience" or "Rome wasn't built in a day."*

On the other hand, reciting empty statements that don't feel true does not magically imprint them on our unconscious mind and make them real.

> *Pete has made some poor investment decisions, which caused him to lose a substantial sum of money. His tendency to equate self-worth with financial success has affected his self-esteem, and as a result, Pete has become difficult to live with. Consequently his relationship with his wife has become severely strained. For Pete, reciting affirmations such as "Things are working out for my highest good" or "I am prosperous and I am a winner" is not likely to be helpful because he doesn't believe them to be true.*

Such affirmations are wishful rather than positive thinking, and repeating them, even hundreds of times, is unlikely to make them credible. In CBT the emphasis is on developing healthy, realistic cognitions. So it may be useful for Pete to repeat statements that remind him of a more positive but realistic perspective, such as:

> ➤ It would be nice to be perfect, but it's human to make mistakes.
> ➤ I've learned from this experience—I'll do it better next time.
> ➤ I can cope with this, one step at a time.
> ➤ In the end, the consequences are not really so disastrous.

Some writers have suggested affirmations can be more easily internalized if you tape-record them on a loop tape, and play them all night. This works on the theory that even though we are asleep, our unconscious mind hears every single word. Wouldn't it be great if life were that simple? Unfortunately, there is no evidence that statements repeated during sleep automatically sink into our unconscious mind.

## APPROPRIATE VERSUS INAPPROPRIATE FEELINGS

The aim of CBT is not to eliminate all upsetting emotions, but to respond to situations appropriately. There are some situations in which it is perfectly appropriate to feel sad, regretful, annoyed or disappointed. If we lose something that we value, it is appropriate to feel sad. If we fail to achieve a particular goal, it is appropriate to feel disappointed. If we do something that we subsequently discover has been hurtful to another person, it is appropriate to feel regret. If someone else does something that we consider to be unfair, it is appropriate to feel annoyed. Psychologically healthy responses are those in which our emotions are reasonable, given the situation in which we find ourselves. Accordingly, we experience regret rather than extreme guilt, disappointment rather than shame, concern rather than intense anxiety, sadness rather than depression, annoyance rather than extreme anger.

> 66 Emotions are either appropriate or inappropriate. When you feel sorry and annoyed and regretful and disappointed when something has gone wrong in your life or you have been dealt with unjustly, it's very sane ... "Appropriate feelings" means appropriate to your desires to survive and be happy. Inappropriate negative feelings are emotions such as depression, anxiety, despair and worthlessness, which tend to make obnoxious conditions and frustrations worse, rather than help to overcome them. 99 ALBERT ELLIS

In some situations, it is appropriate to experience grief. The death of a loved one, the loss of one's home, the diagnosis of a serious illness or even the loss of a long-held dream will generate substantial pain and grief for most people. The pain of a significant loss can sometimes last for years, and although time eventually heals or at least lessens our pain, the scar often remains. Unfortunately, there is no easy way to shortcut the process of grief. However, even in situations that are inherently painful, negative thinking can generate additional, unnecessary suffering.

> *Gabriel is grieving for the loss of his wife, who died of cancer two years ago. While his grief is an appropriate response to the loss of his wife, his guilt and anger are not. By blaming himself for not having been a better husband, and blaming the doctors who treated his wife for not having been able to save her, Gabriel creates additional suffering that serves no useful purpose. His anger and guilt only intensify his pain and make his grief more difficult to bear.*

## THE ABC MODEL

When problems arise in the course of our daily lives, most of us instinctively presume that it is the things that happen to us that make us feel the way we do. So for instance, when we feel angry or sad, we assume that other people make us feel that way, and when we feel anxious, frustrated or depressed, we tend to blame our life circumstances.

However, as Ellis pointed out, events and people do not make us feel good or bad—they just provide a stimulus. It is actually our cognitions that determine how we feel in any given situation.

To illustrate this, Ellis devised the ABC model, where:

> A stands for "antecedent" (the situation that triggers our response).
> B stands for "beliefs" (our cognitions about the situation).
> C stands for "consequences" (the way that we feel and behave).

While we tend to blame A (the antecedent) for C (the consequences), it is actually B (our beliefs) that make us feel the way we do. Let's look at a simple example:

Imagine that you are running late for an appointment, and that you are feeling anxious.

> A: antecedent—running late for an appointment
> C: consequences—anxiety, fretting, reckless driving

You are feeling anxious (C) not because you are running late (A), but because of your beliefs (B) about punctuality and the consequences of running late. Typical beliefs that make people feel anxious in this situation include, "I must always be punctual. People won't like me if I arrive late. I must have everyone's approval all of the time, and it would be awful if they thought badly of me."

## INTRODUCING D: DISPUTE

Ellis used the term **dispute** to describe the process of challenging the way we think about situations. Once we identify the thoughts and beliefs that make us feel bad, our next step is to dispute them. For instance, to dispute the beliefs that make us feel anxious when we are running late, we might tell ourselves, "My past experiences have taught me that even when I'm running late, I usually still get there on time or just a little late. Even if I arrive a bit late, it's unlikely to have major negative consequences. I prefer to be punctual, and I usually am, but if I am late on this occasion it's not likely to have catastrophic consequences."

Disputing our beliefs in this way helps us to experience more appropriate emotions—concern rather than intense anxiety. It also encourages us to behave more appropriately—in this case, to avoid reckless driving.

Disputing unhelpful thoughts and beliefs is the most important aspect of cognitive behavior therapy. Learning to dispute and ultimately change, the cognitions that make us feel bad is the key to avoiding and releasing many upsetting emotions. However, before we can do this, we need to recognize the beliefs and patterns of thinking that create upsetting emotions in our own daily experiences.

# IN SUMMARY

➤ Cognitive behavior therapy is based on the tenet that cognitions—our thoughts and beliefs—largely determine the way we feel. Many distressing emotions such as anger, anxiety, depression, guilt and low self-esteem are caused by cognitions that are negative or self-defeating.

➤ The focus of CBT is on developing realistic cognitions in order to minimize our experience of upsetting emotions. We can do this either directly, by challenging the thoughts and beliefs that make us feel bad or indirectly, by changing some of the behaviors that influence and reinforce our negative cognitions.

➤ The aim of CBT is not to eliminate all distressing emotions, but to help us respond appropriately to potentially stressful situations.

➤ CBT differs from notions of positive thinking in that we aim to develop realistic rather than wishful thinking.

## TWO

# Recognizing Faulty Thinking

*If you're pretty crazy then you're in good company because the human race as a whole is out of its goddamn head. Now all of you, of course, know this about others—about your mother and father and sister and brothers and friends and wives and husbands. You know how nutty they are. Now the problem is to admit this about yourself, and then to do something about it.*

ALBERT ELLIS

If we brought together the happiest ten percent of people in the world, what do you think they would have in common? Lots of money? Good looks? Career success? Fame and admiration from others? Wrong! The happiest people in the world are those who have the most flexible attitudes. Of all the people you consider to be genuinely happy (most of us can count them on one hand), are any of them rigid, demanding or uncompromising? Do they get upset when things do not go their way? Do they exaggerate the consequences when things go wrong?

A key characteristic of happy people is their ability to bend with circumstances when necessary. This does not mean that they are weak or apathetic. In fact happy people are often keen to work towards the things that they want. But, they are also willing to accept that some things are beyond their control, and do not demand that things should be different. When you think about it, much of the distress that we experience in our daily life stems from rigid, irrational beliefs about how things should be.

## IRRATIONAL BELIEFS

Albert Ellis observed that people by their very nature are inclined to think in ways that are irrational and self-defeating. He noted that some people are particularly predisposed towards becoming upset because they habitually think in irrational ways. According to Ellis, our thinking is irrational if it goes against our innate desire for happiness and survival. So, if holding a particular belief makes you experience inappropriate anger, frustration, anxiety, depression or low self-esteem or thwarts your ability to experience good health and long life, then according to Ellis's definition the belief is irrational. This includes beliefs that cause us to engage in self-defeating behaviors such as procrastination, addictive behaviors, remaining in abusive relationships and neglecting our physical health. Ellis described many irrational beliefs that contribute to unhappiness and psychological distress, including the common irrational beliefs listed below.

| COMMON IRRATIONAL BELIEFS | CONSEQUENCES |
|---|---|
| I must be loved and approved of by everyone. | anxiety, unassertive behavior, depression, poor self-esteem |
| I must be competent, adequate and achieving in every respect. | anxiety, self-downing, depression, frustration, shame, procrastination |
| The world should be a fair place and I should always be treated fairly. | anger, resentment, frustration, depression |
| People should have the same values and beliefs as me, and they should do things the way I would do them. | anger, resentment, poor relationships |
| Certain people are bad, and they should be blamed or punished for their misdeeds. | anger, resentment, hatred, depression |
| When I do something badly, I am a bad person, a failure, an idiot. | poor self-esteem, frustration, depression |
| The world should provide me with what I need. Life should be comfortable. I shouldn't have to suffer. | frustration, depression, despair or be inconvenienced. |
| It is awful when things don't go the way that I would like. | frustration, anger, depression, anxiety |
| It's easier to avoid problems than to confront and deal with them. | procrastination, unresolved problems, relationship tensions, helplessness |
| Human unhappiness is caused by life circumstances, and it's impossible to be happy when things are not going well for me. | helplessness, hopelessness, failure to take responsibility, despair |
| If there is a chance that something bad might happen, I should dwell on it now. | anxiety, rumination |
| There is a correct solution to every problem, and it's awful if I can't find it. | indecision, procrastination, anxiety |

While these are some of the common irrational beliefs, there are literally hundreds of others that could be added to the list. Throughout this book we will look at many other beliefs that contribute to upsetting emotions.

# TYRANNY OF THE SHOULDS

One thing that many irrational beliefs have in common is that they are absolutist. In other words, we believe that things "should" or "must" be a certain way, rather than simply wishing or preferring them to be that way. Ellis called this lack of flexibility "demandingness" because we mentally demand that certain things must or must not happen. Others refer to this type of thinking as the **tyranny of the shoulds**—a term first coined by American psychiatrist Karen Horney in 1939. **Shoulds** are the rules or beliefs that we hold about the way things must be. Some of our shoulds focus on our own behavior and performance, while other shoulds focus on the way we believe that other people ought to behave and how the world should be. Of course, not everyone has lots of shoulds, but most people have some beliefs that are inflexible.

Many of the following shoulds get people into trouble. Can you identify any that cause you to feel bad at times?

- ❑ I should always do a perfect job.
- ❑ I should never make mistakes.
- ❑ I should always be productive in the use of my time.
- ❑ My life should be easy and hassle-free.
- ❑ I should always be treated fairly.
- ❑ I should always be in control over events in my life.
- ❑ Other people should always do the "right" thing.
- ❑ Other people should like and approve of me.
- ❑ I should be slim, youthful and attractive.
- ❑ I should be competent and effective in everything that I do.
- ❑ I should be doing and achieving more than I am.
- ❑ I should always be totally independent.
- ❑ I should always be positive, bright and cheerful.
- ❑ I should be married or in a committed relationship.
- ❑ I should have a harmonious, loving, supportive family.
- ❑ I should be a perfect parent.
- ❑ I should be sexy and have a high libido.
- ❑ I should be working.
- ❑ I should have a high-status job.
- ❑ I should be making lots of money.
- ❑ I should be witty, interesting and fun to be with.
- ❑ I should be like other people.
- ❑ I should have lots of friends.
- ❑ I should be as smart as the cleverest people I know.

❑ I should always say "yes" to requests from others.
❑ I should never be afraid or insecure.

These beliefs can make us miserable because our life experiences do not always match them. For example, the belief that "everybody must like and approve of me" will create problems when we come across someone who does not seem to like us. We may not be as youthful or slim as we would like to be or have a highly paid job or a happy marriage. We may not be as smart, witty or interesting as we would like. From time to time we make mistakes, people disapprove of us, our performance falters, hassles present themselves and friends let us down. The more strongly we believe that it must not be this way, the more likely it is that we will get upset.

It is not so much the content, but rather the rigidity of our beliefs, that makes us unhappy. Beliefs are not a problem when they are held as preferences. You will not upset yourself if you merely desire career success, good relationships, independence or a comfortable life, as long as you recognize that things do not have to be this way. It is also perfectly reasonable to prefer people to like us, to want them to do what we believe is right and to treat us fairly, as long as we are flexible enough to accept that things will not always be this way. Life constantly challenges us to be flexible. When things don't go the way we would like, we can make ourselves totally miserable by demanding that things should be different or we can choose to think in a more flexible way.

**A note of caution**—people often put too much emphasis on spoken words rather than their underlying meaning. Simply eliminating the use of the word "should" or "must" from your vocabulary does not make you a flexible thinker. It is not the words we use, but the things we believe that matter. Being flexible requires us to change our cognitions—not just our vocabulary.

## AWFULIZING

Ellis coined the term **awfulizing** to describe the common tendency to exaggerate the negative consequences of our life situations. Awfulizing (also often referred to as "catastrophic thinking" or "catastrophizing") means exaggerating the negative consequences—believing that something is awful or catastrophic, even though in most cases it only undesirable or unpleasant. As a result, we experience far greater distress than is appropriate for our circumstances. We may awfulize about many different issues, from minor hassles to more serious problems. Largely inconsequential events such as being kept waiting, having to spend time with someone we do not like, looking silly in front of others or forgetting an appointment can feel like a catastrophe when we perceive it that way. Even serious problems can become more distressing than they need to be when we exaggerate and dwell on their negative consequences.

Shoulds and awfulizing go hand in hand. We get upset when things do not go the way we believe they should because we assume that the consequences will be catastrophic.

> ➤ I must do it perfectly—it's terrible to make mistakes.
> ➤ People must like and respect me—it's awful to be disapproved of.
> ➤ I must find a partner—it's awful to be single.
> ➤ I should be slim—it's dreadful to be overweight.

When we learn to be more flexible in our thinking, we stop awfulizing as well.

## MONITOR YOUR THINKING

Our thoughts are like an inner voice, reflecting our perceptions of what is happening in our world. Ellis called this inner voice our "self-talk," while Beck referred to it as "automatic thoughts." Most of our thoughts are totally neutral or harmless: "I'd better let the cat in." "I wonder why Mom called?" "I must remember to pick up that package." "These shoes don't match this top." Some of our self-talk makes us feel good: "I did a really great job." "Hallie took her first steps today." "This is going to be a lot of fun!" "That dog is gorgeous." "They're such warm people." Conversely, some of our self-talk makes us feel bad: "What an idiot I am!" "I really screwed up badly." "I hate doing this!" "What a bore!" "What if they don't like me?" "He's late yet again. How typical!" Self-talk that is negative or self-defeating can be recognized because it usually precedes or accompanies upsetting emotions.

Tuning in to our thoughts is important, as it enables us to identify the cognitions that make us feel bad, and that are therefore worth challenging. For this reason it is helpful to monitor our thoughts—to think about what we think about. The best way to do this is to write down our thoughts every time we find ourselves feeling bad. Once we have done this, we can usually identify the beliefs that are associated with those thoughts.

> Sally has made arrangements to go out with her girlfriend on Saturday night; however, her friend called to cancel at the last minute. Now it's too late for her to make alternative plans. Sally feels upset over the thought of having to stay at home. She thinks to herself, "Everyone else is going out and having a good time, but I've got nowhere to go. It's so depressing."

While it is reasonable for Sally to feel disappointed at the last minute cancellation, is it necessary for her to feel so despondent? In fact, whether Sally feels indifferent, mildly disappointed, substantially annoyed or totally devastated will depend on her cognitions. Sally feels upset because she believes:

➤ Everybody goes out and has a good time on Saturday nights.
➤ I should always go out on Saturday nights.
➤ It's awful to have to stay home when other people are going out.

If Sally wants to stop feeling so miserable, she will need to become aware of her cognitions, and challenge some of the irrational aspects of her thinking (see chapter 3).

*Rosanne arranged to go overseas with her boyfriend, Martin, some time ago, but in the last two months she contracted mono and has been very unwell. Now, a week prior to the departure date, Rosanne lacks the strength or desire to travel. Rosanne feels anxious and guilty because she doesn't want to disappoint Martin. She thinks to herself, "This is a dreadful thing for me to do—Martin will be terribly disappointed. How can I let him down like this?"*

While it is reasonable for Rosanne to feel sorry at not being able to stick to her plans, it is not reasonable or helpful for her to feel so guilty and anxious. Rosanne's irrational beliefs include:

➤ Once I make plans I should always stick to them, no matter what.
➤ I should always put other people's needs before my own. I should never do anything that might disappoint others.
➤ It's unacceptable to cancel at this stage.

To feel less guilty, Rosanne will need to challenge some of her shoulds, and stop awfulizing about the situation. Of course, this is not to say that she should be indifferent to Martin's feelings and only do things to suit herself. In some situations it is good to go out of our way for other people, even when it is not very convenient. However, it is also important to be flexible. Things do not always work out the way that we would like, in spite of our very best intentions, and sometimes we are not able to meet our commitments. Although disappointing, the consequences are rarely disastrous.

*Jonathan has just completed his final year of high school. He has worked very hard all year, and has had his heart set on going to an Ivy League college. Upon receiving his final grades, Jonathan discovers that his grades were not high enough to get in. Jonathan feels devastated. He thinks to himself, "It's not fair. I worked so hard all year—all that sacrifice for nothing. What a waste of a year! My future is ruined."*

It is reasonable for Jonathan to feel disappointed at missing out on something he dearly wanted. It is appropriate for him to feel sad for a period of time, as he comes to terms with his disappointment and contemplates his future. However, the magnitude of Jonathan's despair is largely caused by inflexible beliefs about what he must achieve, and the consequences of not having achieved it. Jonathan's beliefs include:

> ➤ I must always succeed in the goals that I set for myself.
> ➤ If I don't get into a top school, my future is ruined.
> ➤ The consequences of not achieving my goal are catastrophic.
> ➤ Life should be fair—if I work hard towards something then I should always get it.

## CONSCIOUS AND UNCONSCIOUS COGNITIONS

Although we can often identify our thoughts simply by asking ourselves, "What am I telling myself right now?," sometimes it is not that clear. For instance, when Lara switches on the computer to start working on her essay she can feel her anxiety rising, but she is not aware of having any thoughts at all. Similarly, when Brian gets ready to head home from work on Friday afternoon, he can feel his mood plummet, although he is not aware of any particular thoughts. While we are not always conscious of our thoughts, we can usually identify what we are feeling—anxious, sad, guilty, embarrassed, worried, angry, or some other emotion. Whenever you have difficulty identifying your thoughts, focus on the emotion and ask yourself, "Why am I feeling this way right now? What is the meaning of this situation for me?" The table in chapter 1 (page 7) may help you to identify the thoughts that are associated with particular emotions.

In the above examples, both Lara and Brian can identify their thoughts after they take a little time to reflect on them. Lara's anxiety is caused by thoughts about all the work that she needs to do: "So much to do, and so little time." Brian's low mood is related to the fact that he has made no plans for the weekend—"Another weekend coming up, and I'll be alone again."

*Have you ever walked into a room of strangers and felt your anxiety rise? What might be the thoughts that create anxiety in this situation?*

## FAULTY THINKING

In Beck's *Cognitive Therapy of Depression*, he describes some of the logical thinking errors (sometimes called faulty thinking) that people frequently make when they are depressed.

While depression contributes to faulty thinking, virtually everyone makes thinking errors at times, and some people make them more frequently than others. Faulty thinking contributes to nearly all upsetting emotions, including depression, anxiety, guilt, anger, resentment, panic and poor self-esteem. The following are examples of common thinking errors.

## BLACK-AND-WHITE THINKING

This is the tendency to see things in a polarized way—either good or bad—while ignoring the middle ground. So for instance, you may evaluate people or situations as good or bad, positive or negative, success or failure. It is the inability to recognize that most situations are neither fantastic nor disastrous, but somewhere in between, that makes this type of thinking distorted. Black-and-white thinking is particularly common among people with perfectionist traits. In the example above, when Jonathan did not get high enough marks to enable him to study at this school of choice, he displayed typical black-and-white thinking: "Not getting into law means that I've ruined my future." By assuming that anything other than his first preference is totally unacceptable, Jonathan ignores the fact that he has many other options that may also lead to favorable outcomes.

*Ian had been working on a report for months, and after having finally submitted it, he discovered a minor error in one of the sections. Although the error does not have any significant consequences for the report's conclusions, Ian is devastated. "I really screwed up that report," he thinks despondently to himself. Ian is using classic black-and-white thinking: "Unless it is a hundred percent perfect, it's a disaster." The inability to see the middle ground—that in spite of a small error, he did a good job overall—causes Ian unnecessary distress and self-downing, and prevents him from feeling good about his achievement.*

✳

*Sasha has two categories for her acquaintances—good and bad. Whenever someone does something that she disapproves of, Sasha adds them to her "bad" list and no longer likes them. As time goes by, the number of people on her bad list grows. Sasha ignores the fact that everyone has both positive and negative traits, and that it is possible to like and accept people even when they are not perfect. No one is! Sasha's black-and-white thinking causes her to feel unnecessary resentment, and limits her ability to make friends and enjoy social relationships.*

## OVERGENERALIZING

When we overgeneralize, we draw negative conclusions about ourselves, other people and life situations, on the basis of limited evidence. Sometimes, just one experience is all it takes for us to start thinking in terms such as "always," "never," "everybody." For instance, "Whenever things start to look up, something bad always happens," "Every time I try to communicate I get nowhere," "I always mess things up," "I haven't achieved anything in the last ten years," "I'm a failure in my work and in my personal life."

> *Heather has had three long-term relationships in the last ten years, each of which eventually ended. After the third break-up, Heather concluded, "I'm not capable of having a relationship. I always get rejected. You can't trust men—they're all the same." Thinking this way made her feel depressed. While it is appropriate for Heather to examine some of the problems that existed in her previous relationships and to try to learn from her experiences, overgeneralizing about her past relationships makes her feel miserable and discourages her from trying again. It would be far more helpful for Heather to acknowledge that not all of her past relationships resulted in rejection (she had terminated some of the relationships herself), and not all of the men she had known were untrustworthy. She could also remind herself that although she had not yet found an ideal partner, there is no evidence that she is not capable of having a happy relationship.*

✳

> *Since her marriage broke up two years ago, Desiré has stopped communicating with most of her married friends. Her withdrawal began after someone had confided to her that one of her girlfriends thought that Desiré was flirting with her husband. After initially feeling incensed, Desire concluded, "Now that I am single, I am a threat to my female friends—they think that I am going to steal their husbands!" As a result, she decided to stop contacting her married friends. By overgeneralizing about her friends—assuming that all the women felt threatened by her presence—Desiré made herself bitter and sad, and deprived herself of friendships that she could have otherwise enjoyed.*

## PERSONALIZING

When we personalize, we feel responsible for things that are not our fault or we incorrectly assume that other people's responses are directed at us.

> *Maggie felt responsible because one of the guests at her dinner party was quiet all evening and did not appear to have a good time. In spite of her best efforts to include him, he did not join in much of the conversation, and Maggie felt that this was somehow her fault.*

*Rochelle felt offended by a neighbor who failed to acknowledge her when they passed each other in the street. It didn't occur to her that her neighbor was preoccupied with his own problems and didn't notice her walk by.*

✳

*Glenda's mother has been depressed ever since her husband died more than a year ago. Glenda feels guilty every time she speaks to her because she feels responsible for her mother's unhappiness. Although she is already doing everything she can to support her mother, Glenda nevertheless perceives that it is somehow her fault, and her responsibility to resolve her mother's grief.*

✳

*Kylie's husband has low libido, and Kylie takes it personally. "He obviously finds me unattractive," she thinks to herself. In fact, her husband's libido has dropped because of biological factors, including the natural effects of aging and blood pressure medication. In addition, Kylie's sensitivity on this issue causes her husband to experience performance anxiety, which dampens his libido even further.*

The challenge not to personalize is even greater when someone behaves rudely towards us.

*Frank felt offended when his boss spoke to him in an abrasive manner over some minor issue. Although initially he took it personally, Frank subsequently realized that his boss was under a huge amount of stress, and that his angry outburst reflected his own vulnerable state. As a result, Frank continued to be loyal and supportive of his boss—a response that was later acknowledged and appreciated.*

It is easy to feel indignant and write off someone who is rude or trade insults with them; it is harder to understand them. Recognizing that another person's reaction largely reflects their own personality or psychological state, and choosing not to take it personally, requires insight and flexibility. However, it inevitably generates benefits, such as avoiding unnecessary stress and promoting good relationships in the longer term.

## FILTERING

Negative beliefs about ourselves, other people and the world can bias the way we perceive many of our experiences. For instance, we may find ourselves focusing on just the negative elements of a situation, while ignoring all other relevant information. Our mind is quickly alerted to events that confirm our self-doubts, insecurities and fears, while we filter out information that does not support those cognitions. So, if you are anxious by nature, you hone in on evidence that the world is unsafe, while ignoring information that is inconsistent with this view. If you have poor self-esteem, you notice any events that suggest that you are incompetent or disliked, while ignoring evidence that you are competent and valued. And if you believe that the world is hostile and that people do not care, you will notice information that confirms this view, but filter out evidence that this is not the case.

Focusing on a particular detail while ignoring other objective information creates an unbalanced and unrealistic view that increases the likelihood of becoming upset.

> *Rita recently gave her first radio interview, and was subsequently told by the producer that it went really well, and all the more so given that it was her debut performance. Instead of being pleased with the positive feedback, Rita felt devastated. In her mind the comment focused on her inexperience, and implied that she was not very good at all. By selectively focusing on "debut performance" while ignoring the other feedback, Rita interpreted the comment as a criticism rather than a compliment.*

✳

> *Lana is a sales representative for a large pharmaceutical company. Although she is bright, articulate and very good at her work, Lana focuses on her weaknesses, and ignores her many strengths. As a result, she systematically discounts praise from her supervisor and work colleagues by assuming that "they're just saying these things to be nice." When Lana was recently told that her sales figures were the highest in the state, she put this down to good luck. "Anyone could have done it," she thought to herself. No matter how well she performs, Lana always finds a way of filtering out positive information and homing in on her weaknesses.*

## JUMPING TO NEGATIVE CONCLUSIONS

Many of us are inclined to draw negative conclusions in all sorts of situations, in spite of limited evidence to support those conclusions. We may assume the worst when things go wrong or interpret other people's comments or motives in the most negative light.

> *Jillian became despondent when the headlights and air-conditioning system in her new car failed just two weeks after purchase. While it was reasonable for her to feel annoyed, Jillian's thoughts—"I know this is going to go on and on; these sorts of problems just don't go away"—created excessive anxiety and sleepless nights. Her tendency to jump to negative conclusions in spite of limited evidence results in excessive anxiety in all sorts of situations.*

\*

*Nicki has not heard from her work colleague, Linda, for nearly two weeks. As they usually speak quite frequently, Nicki assumes that Linda must be angry with her because she intends to apply for a position that Linda is also interested in. The more she thinks about it, the more annoyed she becomes. Nicki remains angry for several days, until Linda finally calls her and explains that her daughter has been in the hospital.*

\*

*For her Honors thesis Rochelle is doing a project that involves surveying a large number of single mothers. She has sent two emails describing the nature of her research to a Web site for single mothers, hoping that they might be willing to inform suitable participants about her research. After receiving no reply, Rochelle concludes that they are obviously hostile to researchers and don't want to help.*

## MIND READING

This is a specific type of jumping to conclusions, based on the assumption that we know what other people are thinking. While sometimes our judgments are correct, in so many instances we get it wrong! Experience often shows that other people are nowhere near as judgmental or concerned about us as we presume.

*Simone had been unusually quiet during a catch-up with her old friend, Les. In the course of the evening, Les observed that she seemed quiet and asked whether she was OK. Simone interpreted this comment to mean that Les was bored with her company. She concluded that unless she is bright and chirpy, Les is not interested in spending time with her. Les, on the other hand, perceived Simone to be very distant that evening, and presumed that she must be feeling angry towards him. As he couldn't work out what he had done wrong, Les thought that she was judging him unfairly. As both engaged in mind reading, the two friends did not speak to each other again for almost a year.*

As so often happens when we jump to negative conclusions, not only do we feel bad, but we also behave in self-defeating ways.

*Len would very much like to have a girlfriend, but is horrified at his friend's suggestion to try Internet dating. "What if someone I know sees my profile on the Web site? They'll think I'm desperate!" he tells his friend. In addition, Len hates going to parties or social events because he assumes that people are looking at him and thinking that he is a loser. As is typical in these situations, no one actually notices Len or gives him any thought at all. However, Len's mind reading gives rise to self-defeating behaviors—he avoids opportunities that might enable him to get what he wants.*

✳

*Pam has a tendency to blush, which would not be a problem except for the fact that she assumes that other people notice and think that there is something wrong with her. Paradoxically, Pam's mind reading feeds her anxiety and keeps her blushing— which no one but Pam pays any attention to.*

Mind reading and perceived negative evaluation by others is a major contributor to social anxiety and social phobia. We often assume that people are judging us harshly when, in reality, most people outside of our immediate family and friendship group do not notice or give us much thought at all. We are just not that important in other people's minds, in the same way that they don't figure very much in ours.

## BLAMING

From time to time things go wrong in our lives, people let us down and unforeseen mishaps occur. While some people are particularly good at accepting disappointments and human imperfections, others tend to blame and condemn people for their faults. The problem with blaming is that it creates bitterness and resentment, and does not solve our problems. In fact, blaming people can be disempowering if it prevents us from taking action to change our situation.

*Mary has felt stuck in an unhappy marriage for the last twenty-five years, and has spent much of her adult life blaming her husband for all of her unhappiness. Unfortunately, blaming her husband has not helped Mary to resolve the problems within the marriage, but has simply made her bitter. At this stage of her life it would be far more useful for Mary to accept that her marriage has had its problems, and to start focusing on the things that she can do to improve her situation.*

✳

*Harold feels bitter and resentful after being sacked from the company to which he had given twenty-six years of loyal service. He blames the company for being totally callous and putting the interests of shareholders before the needs of its employees. Given the circumstances, it is appropriate for Harold to go through a period of grieving, which may involve some anger and sadness. However, as long as he continues to blame and criticize, it remains difficult for Harold to move on with his life. At some point, Harold needs to accept that lots of things aren't fair, and that it is better for him to plan for the future than to ruminate about the injustices of the past.*

66 Acceptance doesn't mean endorsement or saying that things are good. It means accepting bad reality and accepting that limited change is likely in the world right now. 99 ALBERT ELLIS

## LABELING

Everyone is fallible. We all make mistakes or do silly things at times and there are some things that we are just not good at. Sometimes we behave inappropriately, make stupid comments, do things that have a negative impact on other people, perform badly in our work, ignore symptoms of failing health, make unsound financial decisions or fail to achieve the things that we want.

The way that we think about our mistakes or perceived flaws determines whether or not we feel diminished by them. Sometimes it is rational and appropriate to tell ourselves, "That was a silly thing to do," "I made a big mistake" or "I'm not very good at this particular task." Thoughts such as these do not create problems because they focus on specific behaviors. In contrast, when we label ourselves as an idiot, a failure, ugly, no good, stupid, lazy, a loser or incompetent, we make gross generalizations about ourselves on the basis of specific behaviors or experiences. As a result we diminish our self-esteem and create other upsetting emotions such as guilt, shame, anxiety, self-loathing and depression. Labeling is the ultimate overgeneralization because it ignores the fact that people are a complex mixture of personal characteristics and behaviors, and we cannot be defined by just one or a few of these.

While some individuals are inclined to label themselves, there are others who use labels for other people: "That guy is a creep," "My boss is a jerk," "My sister-in-law is a bitch," "That politician is a sleaze-bag." Labeling others is just as illogical as labeling ourselves, since we sum up an entire person on the basis of particular behaviors or characteristics. Labeling is also self-defeating because it fuels anger and resentment, wastes our energy and makes it harder to get on with people. This does not mean that we should never judge people's actions. As with our own behaviors, it is totally reasonable to think that something was selfish, unfair or unethical or "what she did was very silly." However, it is important to distinguish between a person's actions and the person as a whole.

*Vince had an unpleasant exchange with his sister-in-law over a family matter, and he now perceives her as the enemy. Labeling her in this way produces a number of negative consequences, including stress for his wife, tension between families and social awkwardness whenever their paths cross. It also deprives his children of the opportunity to develop relationships with their cousins and to enjoy the benefits of an extended family.*

\*

*Christine spent six months working in a law firm with very poor work practices and an uncaring culture. Inadequate training and lack of access to advice caused Christine to slip up in some of her cases, and consequently she received negative appraisals from her supervisor. When Christine finally left the firm she perceived herself as incompetent and a failure. Labeling herself in this way further undermined her confidence, which in turn made it difficult for her to find another job.*

Whenever things do not work out, it is always useful to appraise the situation and objectively reflect on the reasons. Identifying the factors that contributed to our negative experiences instead of labeling ourselves in negative terms gives us the opportunity to learn from our experiences and maintain a healthy outlook (see also chapter 7).

## PREDICTING CATASTROPHE

Some people habitually focus on negative possibilities—failure, rejection, loss, pain, or catastrophe. Self-talk about imminent disasters is typically expressed in thoughts of "what if?" For instance, "What if I lose my job, and can't pay my bills?", "What if I make a fool of myself in front of all those people?", "What if I get sick and can't work any more?", "What if I don't know anyone and have no one to talk to?", "What if I can't find somewhere to park the car?" By focusing on the possibility that things might go wrong, we make ourselves anxious in the present moment and lose our ability to engage fully with the world around us.

*Brenda is a self-employed interior designer. When some of her clients are slow to pay their bills, Brenda immediately assumes that they are going to default, and starts to imagine the worst case scenario. Although nearly all of her clients pay their bills in the end, Brenda is quick to visualize scenes of conflict, litigation, and threats. This creates anxiety, wastes her energy and distracts Brenda from her current projects.*

\*

*Jan became worried after she had told one of her work colleagues about her diagnosis of breast cancer three years ago. Although her colleague had reassured her that she would not tell anyone, Jan continued to worry that other people might find out. For the next two weeks she lay awake at night, thinking, "What if she tells someone, and then everyone finds out, and then it will get back to management, and they'll decide that I'm a bad risk, and then they'll ask me to leave and I won't be able to get another job?"*

✳

*Michael was initially delighted when the government announced substantial tax cuts for self-funded retirees, a change that would directly benefit him. However, after only a few days Michael started to worry. "What if the government loses office at the next election, and the opposition reverses the tax cuts as soon as they get in?" Later, another thought occurred to him. "What if the government gets reelected, and takes back the tax cuts once it gets back into office? These things can happen." After some time, the possibility of other negative events entered his mind.*

The truth is that the world is full of uncertainty. The things that Brenda, Jan and Michael worry about could conceivably happen, although the likelihood is very small. By exaggerating the likelihood of their feared events they make themselves unnecessarily anxious. One of the great challenges in situations we cannot control (or where we have already done all we can) is to learn to live with some uncertainty. This means acknowledging that bad things can happen but they are unlikely, and recognizing that even if they should happen we will cope.

## COMPARING

Many people appraise their status, success and personal worth by comparing themselves with others. The comparisons may be limited to members of their own peer group—friends, family, people their own age or those they went to school with. Or they may be made with a broader group, including the rich and famous—media personalities, movie stars, business moguls and even politicians. Comparing ourselves can make us feel inadequate or bitter, as invariably there are people who do better than us in any given area.

*Mia felt excited when she arrived at the staff Christmas party, but soon became despondent when she saw how attractive some of the other women looked. She suddenly felt frumpy and unattractive. To add insult to injury, one of her colleagues had lost 20 pounds and looked fantastic!*

✳

*Roger can't help feeling resentful when he reads about the mounting wealth of one of the country's top entrepreneurs. It feels like someone is rubbing his nose in it, saying, "You just haven't cut it!"*

✳

*After listening to adoring speeches about members of the groom's family, Sol leaves his friend's wedding feeling utterly depressed. "This is what a family should be like," he thinks to himself. "Mine is so dysfunctional!"*

✳

*Marty was diagnosed with breast cancer four years ago, and is devastated upon hearing that a famous film star has recently died of the disease. Suddenly she is terrified about her own mortality.*

## EXERCISE 2.1

For each of the following examples:
  a) identify the faulty thinking pattern that creates distress (e.g. black-and-white thinking, personalizing, predicting catastrophe)
  b) identify any shoulds or inflexible beliefs. *Sample solutions at the back of the book.*

1.  Jo's two adult daughters have never married or settled, and Jo constantly worries about their future. She can't help thinking that if she had been a better mother, they would have been more settled by now.
2.  In the course of a social evening, Helen made a comment about refugees. As soon as the words left her mouth, Helen realized that the comment sounded narrow-minded, and she wished she had never said it. Although no one said anything, Helen's only memory of the night was her stupid remark, which spoiled the whole evening for her.
3.  Kay is a lively and interesting person, however she often feels inadequate because she never completed a college degree. Although she is highly regarded by her friends, Kay believes that she is not smart enough.
4.  Pauline works for a large corporation that is currently undergoing a restructure. This makes her feel extremely anxious because she assumes that she will be retrenched, and that she won't be able to find another job.
5.  Thomas looks back at his life and all he can see is a series of failures and rejections.

6.  Peter is a musician and in his recent performance he felt that he just couldn't engage the audience. He thinks of the concert as having been a complete disaster.

7.  Robert has had a pain in his abdomen for some time, but he is terrified to go to the doctor, as he thinks it might be cancer.

8.  Celia gets very sweaty when she is socially anxious, particularly in unfamiliar social situations. The sweating makes her even more anxious because she is sure that people notice it, and must be wondering what is wrong with her.

9.  Bill has made two attempts at starting his own business, and on both occasions, he decided not to go ahead. Bill feels disgusted at his own lack of courage and tells himself that he is gutless and a failure. He tells himself that he has never achieved anything worthwhile in his entire life.

10. Fred felt depressed after his friend told him about the investment property that he had recently purchased. Fred can barely afford to pay his rent, let alone buy an investment property.

11. Sally does not have any respect for one of her work colleagues, whom she regards as a complete jerk. As far as Sally is concerned, nothing that he says has any merit, and everything he does is completely stupid.

12. Michael notices a $15 debit for government taxes in the bank statement from his mutual savings account. To Michael this seems excessive, and he assumes that the building society must be trying to cheat him.

13. Nina and Brian went through some difficult times during their marriage. While their relationship improved substantially after they attended some counseling sessions, they still have occasional arguments. Whenever this happens, Nina immediately assumes that the marriage is not going to work, and the counseling has been a waste of time.

14. After working for four years as a financial manager in a large company, Nola has left in upsetting circumstances—a falling out with her supervisor. Now her confidence is eroded and Nola has serious doubts about her own ability to do a good job.

15. As a young artist, Rodney struggles to make a living from his work. He recently went along to a friend's exhibition, which was extremely successful. Rodney left feeling depressed.

16. Melanie feels guilty at not doing the housework, but then becomes angry when her husband starts cleaning the house. She assumes that he is trying to humiliate her.

## IN SUMMARY

➤ Upsetting emotions such as anger, frustration, guilt, anxiety and depression are very often caused and perpetuated by beliefs that are negative or irrational. These beliefs are held as rigid rules, or "shoulds," within our mind.

➤ Negative beliefs can cause us to feel bad, and to behave in ways that are self-defeating.

➤ Most people have certain patterns of thinking that contribute to unnecessary distress. These are called "faulty thinking" or "thinking errors," and include awfulizing, black-and-white thinking, overgeneralizing, personalizing, filtering, jumping to negative conclusions, mind reading, blaming, predicting catastrophe and comparing.

➤ To develop more psychologically healthy ways of thinking, we need to identify our own thinking patterns that contribute to upsetting emotions. The best way to do this is to monitor our cognitions at times when we find ourselves feeling upset and to try to identify the specific thoughts and beliefs.

## THREE

# Disputing Negative Cognitions

Personal happiness is possible, even in an unhappy world. Now, you won't
be as happy in an unhappy world as in a better one. I don't think there's
much doubt about that, but you can still choose to be pretty damned happy,
even in a poor environment. That's possible. And fighting irrationality and
trying to be happy in a nutty world has great advantages in itself. It's
challenging. It's interesting. It's rewarding. It's self-helping ... Your very
determination to work at it can keep you reasonably happy.

ALBERT ELLIS

Being aware of our negative thoughts and beliefs is an important first step in the process
of developing healthy, realistic cognitions. However, mere awareness does not
automatically change the way we think. Once we have identified some of our negative
perceptions, the next step is to dispute them. This means questioning the faulty aspects
of our thinking, and identifying more realistic and helpful ways of perceiving our
situations. Let's look at a range of disputing strategies that can be used to challenge and
ultimately change unhelpful or negative cognitions.

## LOGICAL DISPUTING

Many upsetting emotions are caused by unrealistic or irrational thinking. Therefore, a
useful way to alter these cognitions is to dispute them logically. This involves challenging
irrational assumptions that things *must* or *must not* be a certain way, and identifying
alternative, more helpful ways of perceiving our situation.

Here are some examples of logical disputing statements that can be used to challenge
the common irrational beliefs (described in chapter 2).

| BELIEF | LOGICAL STATEMENT |
|---|---|
| I must be loved and approved of by everyone. | I prefer people to like me but it's unrealistic to expect everyone to like me. Just because some people may not like me doesn't mean that I'm not OK. I can cope even if some people don't like me. |
| I must be competent, adequate and achieving in every respect. | I am competent in some things and not in other things. While I can work on improving my skills, there is no reason why I must be competent in every area. |
| The world should be a fair place and I should always be treated fairly. | The world is full of injustice. Lots of things aren't fair, and chances are that at times I'm going to experience some injustice. |
| People should have the same values and beliefs as me, and they should do things the way I would do them. | People have the right to have different values and beliefs from my own, and will sometimes say or do things that I don't like. It would be nice if people always did what I believe is right, but there is no reason why they must. |
| Certain people are bad, and they should be blamed for their actions. | People sometimes behave unfairly or inconsiderately, and so do I. I can criticize their behaviors, but I don't have to damn or condemn them as people. |
| When I do something badly, I am a bad person, a failure, an idiot. | Like everyone else, I sometimes make mistakes or do silly things, but that doesn't make me a failure or a bad person. I have done millions of things over the course of my life, and labeling myself on the basis of just a few of my behaviors is irrational and self-defeating. |
| The world should provide me with what I need. Life should be comfortable. I shouldn't have to suffer or be inconvenienced. | It's nice when things go well for me, and much of the time they do. But, there is no reason why things must always go smoothly. Hassles are a normal part of life. |
| It is awful when things don't go the way that I would like. | It is disappointing and inconvenient when things don't go the way that I would like, but it is very rarely awful or catastrophic. There is no reason why things must always go the way I would like them to. |
| It's easier to avoid problems than to confront and deal with them. | Avoiding my problems may be easier in the short term, but not in the long term. It is often helpful to move outside of my comfort zone to confront problems and try to solve them. |
| Human unhappiness is caused by life circumstances, and it's impossible to be happy when things are not going well for me. | Life presents challenges at times, but I have the ability to avoid major distress by learning to think in a rational, psychologically healthy way. I can learn to feel good even when some things are not going smoothly. |
| If there is a chance that something bad might happen, I should dwell on it now. | There is no point in dwelling on situations that I can't control. Dwelling on them doesn't change the outcome, and only makes me miserable. I can deal with problems if and when they happen. |
| There is a correct solution to every problem and it's awful if I can't find it. | Most problems do not have one correct solution, but many possible solutions. Our decisions can only be based on the information that is available to us at the time, and often there is no obvious choice. |

## WRITE IT DOWN

Throughout this book we will see lots of examples of how negative or faulty thinking can be logically disputed. Some cognitions are easier to challenge than others, and those that are less ingrained can often be challenged mentally by thinking of more helpful ways to perceive our situation. However, long-held and deeply ingrained beliefs are most effectively challenged with a pen in hand. Identifying the cognitions that make us feel bad and writing down statements that directly challenge them transforms vague notions into clear concepts. It also adds an extra level of processing and therefore reinforces those concepts within our mind. In addition, writing down rational statements creates a record that we can refer to whenever we need additional reinforcement. Rereading those statements helps to fix them within our mind, and moves them from a purely "head" level to a deeper "gut" level.

## USING THOUGHT-MONITORING FORMS

To challenge unhelpful cognitions, we need to identify the thoughts and beliefs that are making us feel bad. The best way to tune into these is to write them down on a thought-monitoring form. Although this can also be done on a blank sheet of paper or in a diary, using a form helps to organize our thoughts, and therefore makes the process easier.

Cognitive therapists have devised various types of thought-monitoring forms for this purpose. The forms have been given different names—thought journal, dysfunctional thought record, thought-monitoring form and REBT self-help form. The forms vary in design and complexity. Some provide space for recording beliefs as well as thoughts, while others focus primarily on thoughts. For instance, Beck's dysfunctional thought record provides space for scoring the strength of our emotions and the degree to which we believe our thoughts to be true before and after challenging the negative thoughts. Ellis's RET self-help form provides space for recording beliefs, Socratic questions and rational statements. While there are advantages and disadvantages in using different types of forms, there is no evidence that one type is more effective than others in helping people to change their thinking.

The thought-monitoring form that I recommend is easy to use, and provides space for identifying and disputing beliefs as well as thoughts. It also provides space for recording positive actions, and so encourages the use of problem-solving as well. (If you would like to see other thought-monitoring forms, check the books listed in the General Books section of Recommended Reading.)

## POSITIVE ACTIONS

Although it is not always possible to solve a problem, it is important to always consider possible solutions. Sometimes positive actions lead to complete resolution of the problem. At other times we are unable to change any aspect of our situation, and all that we can do to feel better is modify our cognitions. In many challenging situations we can use both strategies—that is, we can take some action to try to improve the situations and

## THOUGHT-MONITORING FORM

| | |
|---|---|
| **SITUATION** | |
| **FEELINGS** | |
| **THOUGHTS** | |
| **BELIEFS** | |
| **THINKING ERRORS** | ❑ Shoulds  ❑ Jumping to negative conclusions<br>❑ Awfulizing  ❑ Mind reading<br>❑ Black-and-white thinking  ❑ Blaming<br>❑ Overgeneralizing  ❑ Labeling<br>❑ Personalizing  ❑ Predicting catastrophe<br>❑ Filtering  ❑ Comparing |
| **DISPUTE**<br>Alternative, more balanced view?<br><br><br><br>What would I tell a friend who was in this situation? | |
| **POSITIVE ACTIONS** | |

work on changing the way we think about it as well. Solving problems where we can and using cognitive strategies to deal with the things that we cannot change is what the highly celebrated Serenity Prayer is all about:

 God give me the serenity to accept the things that I cannot change
The courage to change the things that I can
And the wisdom to know the difference.

Here are some examples of how thought-monitoring forms can be used to logically dispute unhelpful cognitions:

*Elizabeth was half-way through writing an essay for her college course, when her computer crashed. Her immediate response was to panic, and she spent most of the day fretting and crying. That evening Elizabeth decided to challenge her catastrophic thinking using a thought-monitoring form.*

| | |
|---|---|
| **SITUATION** | Computer crashed when I was in the middle of writing my essay. |
| **FEELINGS** | Felt devastated. Panicked. |
| **THOUGHTS** | This is a complete disaster! I may end up failing this essay. |
| | Where am I going to find another computer at such short notice? |
| **BELIEFS** | Things should always go smoothly. It's awful when things do go wrong. |
| | The consequences of this situation will be disastrous. |
| **THINKING ERRORS** | Awfulizing, predicting catastrophe, shoulds |
| **DISPUTE** | I prefer things always to go smoothly, and much of the time they do, but there is no reason why they must always go smoothly. Hassles are an unavoidable part of life. This is a pain in the neck, but it's not a disaster. It's going to involve a lot of extra work and running around, but I can deal with it. It's a challenge—I can cope with it. |
| **POSITIVE ACTIONS** | Call Jan (friend who knows about computers) and ask if she can come over and take a look at my computer. If she can't fix it, take it in for repairs. |
| | Call Cheryl, and ask if I can use her computer for the next week. |
| | Call college tutor, explain the situation and ask for an extension on the deadline. |

In challenging situations where possible solutions exist, problem solving is the most sensible first step. Finding solutions puts us back in control and helps to remedy the situation. However, in order to effectively explore the options, we need to be calm and rational. Challenging catastrophic cognitions in the above example helped Elizabeth to feel less panicky, and to focus her energy on positive actions.

*Sonia separated from her husband Don a year ago, after he started a relationship with another woman. Sonia feels anxious every time she thinks she might see Don at social functions or when he comes to pick up the children on weekends. Because her distress is so intense, Sonia decides to try to challenge the unhelpful cognitions that cause her to feel this way. She writes the following notes on her thought-monitoring form.*

| | |
|---|---|
| **SITUATION** **FEELINGS** | Going to Christine's party. Expect that Don will be there with his new woman. Feel nervous. |
| **THOUGHTS** **BELIEFS** | I won't be able to look relaxed. People will see how uncomfortable I am. They'll feel sorry for me, and Don will think I'm pathetic. I must show everyone that I'm coping well. People will think badly of me if they see me looking uncomfortable. Don must not see me looking vulnerable or self-conscious. |
| **THINKING ERRORS** | Predicting catastrophe, mind reading, shoulds |
| **DISPUTE** | I prefer to appear relaxed and comfortable, but it's not the end of the world if I don't. I would not think badly of someone in my position who looked uncomfortable, and it's unlikely that other people will think badly of me if I look uncomfortable. In fact, most people have been very supportive. What Don thinks doesn't matter any more. He is no longer part of my life. I don't have to impress him or prove anything to him now. |
| **POSITIVE ACTIONS** | Call Erica and ask if she and Joe can pick me up on the way, so that I don't have to go there on my own. Tell them that I might need their support at the party, just in case I'm feeling fragile. |

*Steven's aged father in England had written to him asking Steven to come for a visit. Steven has had financial problems and was unable to go. Shortly afterward his father died, and Steven feels very guilty for not having gone to see him.*

| | |
|---|---|
| **SITUATION** **FEELINGS** | Reread Dad's last letter to me. Cried. Felt extremely guilty. |
| **THOUGHTS** **BELIEFS** | Oh, God, why didn't I just go and see him? It would have made him happy. I'm such a rotten person. I should have been available when he asked me to come. I should have known that he might die soon. I'm a bad person because I didn't go to see him. |
| **THINKING ERRORS** | Shoulds, blaming, labeling |
| **DISPUTE** | I prefer to be supportive and available to my family, and I usually am. However, I can't always do what my family members ask me to do. Sometimes I need to take my own circumstances into account. I'm sorry I didn't go, but at the time it was very difficult and I didn't know how sick he was. If I had known, I would have put everything else on hold and I would have gone to see him. It's easy to see things clearly in retrospect, but it wasn't easy to see them at the time. Not having gone does not make me a bad person. |
| **POSITIVE ACTIONS** | Write down all the things that I would have liked to have said to my father before he died. Talk to Sandra about it. |

*Pete is the general manager of a successful marketing company. Recently sales have been down, and Pete is angry at the lack of commitment and poor attitude of some of the sales staff. He writes the following notes in his thought-monitoring form.*

| | |
|---|---|
| **SITUATION** | Sales were down for the third quarter in a row. |
| **FEELINGS** | Feel angry and frustrated. |
| **THOUGHTS** | That team is bone lazy—all of them. |
| | They waste a lot of time and put very little effort into their work. They just don't care. |
| **BELIEFS** | Everyone should have the same work ethic as me. |
| | They should all be as highly motivated as I am. |
| **THINKING ERRORS** | Labeling, overgeneralization, shoulds. |
| **DISPUTE** | I wish they were more diligent, but it's unrealistic to expect everyone to have the same standards that I do. Working in sales is very demanding, and it's reasonable that they ease off at times. It's up to me to develop strategies to increase their motivation and turn around our sales. |
| **POSITIVE ACTIONS** | Conduct a thorough review to identify the reasons for reduced sales, and look at ways in which we can motivate the sales team. |

## MOVING FROM THE "HEAD" TO THE "GUT" LEVEL

People who use CBT often say that logically they can see that their thinking is negative or irrational, but on a "gut" level it is difficult to change. This is not surprising. Many of the beliefs that we begin to challenge have been part of our thinking for decades, so it is unrealistic to expect them to disappear overnight. However, we can learn to assimilate (i.e., accept on a deeper level) almost any belief that makes sense to us logically, if we put in the time and effort. Disputing is most effective when we take the time to fill in a thought-monitoring form and read over our logical statements repeatedly, until they start to feel true on a deeper level. For really stubborn beliefs, it is helpful to keep a list of logical statements on a flash card in your wallet or diary. Pull out and read your flash card whenever your negative thoughts resurface (that is, whenever you find yourself feeling upset again) or any time that you have a spare moment. In addition, you can display your logical statements strategically, in places where you are likely to notice them—the fridge door, the bathroom mirror, by the telephone, the screen saver in your computer, next to the toilet. Read over them as often as you can to remind yourself of a better, psychologically healthier perspective. Whenever those upsetting emotions resurface, challenge your cognitions with a brief, rational disputing statement such as:

➤ This is inconvenient, but it's not a disaster.
➤ He has the right to accept or reject my advice.
➤ Hassles are a normal part of life.
➤ Everybody has the right to be wrong.

# EXERCISE 3.1: PRACTICE LOGICAL DISPUTING

For each of the following examples, write down some logical disputing statements that could be used to challenge the negative thoughts and beliefs, and suggest some positive actions that could be taken. *Sample solutions at the back of the book.*

## The neglected birthday

| | |
|---|---|
| **SITUATION** | Husband didn't make a fuss about me on my birthday. |
| **FEELINGS** | Felt hurt, angry. |
| **THOUGHTS** | He doesn't care about me. |
| **BELIEFS** | Birthdays are important. |
| | If he loved me, he would have made a fuss. |
| **THINKING ERRORS** | Jumping to negative conclusions, shoulds |
| **DISPUTE** | |

**POSITIVE ACTIONS**

## The frustrated public servant

| | |
|---|---|
| **SITUATION** | I was supposed to finish that report today, but wasted the entire day and achieved very little. |
| **FEELINGS** | Feel frustrated, anxious and angry with myself. |
| **THOUGHTS** | I'm so hopeless! Have wasted the entire day and achieved nothing. |
| **BELIEFS** | I should always use my time productively. |
| | Because I have achieved very little I am a hopeless person. |
| **THINKING ERRORS** | Labeling, overgeneralization, shoulds |
| **DISPUTE** | |

**POSITIVE ACTIONS**

| **The forgotten breakfast arrangement** | |
|---|---|
| SITUATION | I made an arrangement to go out for breakfast with a special friend, but forgot all about it and slept in. By the time I remembered she had left. |
| FEELINGS | Felt guilty and anxious. |
| THOUGHTS | She must be angry and disappointed with me. She probably thinks less of me now. This could ruin our friendship. |
| BELIEFS | If I say I'm going to do something I should always do it. It's terrible to let people down. The consequences of this situation are likely to be very serious. |
| THINKING ERRORS | Jumping to negative conclusions, awfulizing, shoulds, predicting catastrophe |
| DISPUTE | |
| POSITIVE ACTIONS | |

## DECATASTROPHIZE

The terms "awfulizing" and "catastrophizing" describe the human tendency to exaggerate the negative consequences of undesirable situations (see chapter 2). As a result we experience our predicament as though it were truly catastrophic, even though in most cases it is only undesirable or unpleasant. In fact, any negative situation can be experienced as a disaster, if we think about it in that way. By exaggerating the "badness" of negative events, we can make ourselves intensely anxious, frustrated, guilty, embarrassed, depressed or resentful.

This is not to say that nothing can be catastrophic or truly awful. There are some things that are extremely bad—contracting a very painful, degenerative, incurable disease; being the victim of a brutal attack; the death of a loved one; or becoming a quadriplegic as a result of an accident. On an "awfulness" scale of 0 to 100, these things could be rated as somewhere between 80 and 100.

However, most of the things that go wrong in our lives are nowhere near that bad. The vast majority of life's problems fall somewhere between 0 and 20 on the "awfulness scale." Even though events like making a stupid statement in front of people we want to impress, missing a flight or losing a contract may feel like a major catastrophe at the time, in the total scheme of things their consequences are usually not that bad. The trouble is that when we awfulize, we experience situations as though they are totally awful—around 100 on the awfulness scale.

> ❝ Is the flat tire discovered just before you have to leave for an appointment the worst thing that could have happened to you? Wouldn't two flat tires with only one spare have been worse? Wouldn't a broken leg have been worse than that? Or how about a flooded basement, a large tree crashing onto your house, a fire in the kitchen, a friend's suicide, a call from the police about your child's fatal accident on the way to school? Wouldn't each one of them have been worse than a flat tire? We don't wish to be macabre about it, but many things could certainly be worse than the flat tire that you initially evaluated as the worst thing that could have happened to you. ❞ R.M. GREIGER AND P.J. WOODS, *THE RATIONAL EMOTIVE THERAPY COMPANION*

If you are someone who tends to awfulize a lot, you inflict unnecessary suffering upon yourself in all sorts of situations. You frequently experience upsetting emotions such as anxiety, frustration, anger, hurt and depression because you perceive that things are much worse than they really are. Because awfulizing creates a great deal of unnecessary distress, it is important to catch ourselves in the act, and to consciously question our view of reality. Here are some simple questions that help to put things in perspective:

AM I AWFULIZING?
➤ Does it really matter?
➤ Will this matter in five years' time?
➤ On an awfulness scale of 0 to 100 percent, how bad is this?
➤ How would a positive person see this?
➤ What can I be grateful for?
➤ Is this within my control? What can I do about it?
➤ What is most likely to happen?
➤ Is there anything good about this situation?
➤ What can I learn from this experience?

## SOCRATIC QUESTIONING

Some negative thoughts are reasonably easy to challenge, and simply recognizing that our thinking is irrational and looking for a more balanced perspective helps us to feel better. However, many cognitions are more resistant to change, and this is where **Socratic questioning** can be helpful. This technique is based on a method developed by Socrates, the ancient Greek philosopher who used a series of provocative questions to challenge people's underlying assumptions. The aim of Socratic questioning is to hold our cognitions up to logical scrutiny, identify any evidence that discredits them, and come up with a more reasonable perspective.

Many different types of Socratic questions can be used to challenge irrational cognitions. Let's take a look at some that can be applied in most situations:

**Examples of Socratic questions**
1.  What are facts and what are my subjective perceptions?
2.  What evidence supports my perceptions?
3.  What evidence contradicts my perceptions?
4.  Am I making any thinking errors?
5.  How else can I perceive this situation?

> *Rodney experienced an upsetting incident over a lunch-time celebration at work. Having heard that one of his colleagues was leaving, Rodney volunteered to go out and buy some doughnuts for the occasion. Unfortunately, by the time that Rodney had returned with the doughnuts the celebration was almost over. Apparently no one had bothered to wait for him, even though he had gone out of his way to contribute. Rodney feels hurt and humiliated.*

Most of us can sympathize with Rodney's situation and would probably feel peeved if it happened to us. However, the amount of hurt that we experience and the length of time for which we remain upset will depend on our cognitions. The more rigid and negative our thoughts, the more distress we will experience.

Rodney decides to subject his thinking to Socratic questioning.

**1. What are facts and what are my subjective perceptions?**
**The facts:** Work colleagues didn't wait for me to start lunch when I went out to buy the doughnuts.
**My perceptions:** They don't like me. They are treating me with contempt. If they respected me, they would have waited for me. I have been humiliated.
**2. What evidence supports my perceptions?**
They started the celebrations without me.
**3. What evidence contradicts my perceptions?**
The staff are usually pretty friendly to me and I get on quite well with most of them. When I walked in with the doughnuts, a few people said that they should have waited for me.
**4. Am I making any thinking errors?**
I am jumping to negative conclusions, personalizing and awfulizing. I'm presuming that if people don't behave considerately towards me, it must mean that they don't like me. I'm interpreting this in a negative way—that it's deliberate and personal.
**5. How else can I perceive this situation?**
Most people at work are busy with their own stuff, and they don't always think about other people. They didn't wait for me because they didn't think about me—not because they don't like me. People do take my needs into account much of the time, but not always. I don't always take other people's needs into account either.

*Jill has had a longstanding disagreement with her neighbors over the removal of a large tree that affects both properties. This evening when Jill came home from work she noticed that her dog Jessie had not eaten his dinner—an unusual event, as Jessie normally has a healthy appetite. Jill immediately went into a panic. She thought that the neighbors had poisoned Jessie and that they were trying to get back at her for not cooperating with them over the tree. After a lot of distress, Jill decided to use Socratic questioning to challenge her perceptions.*

## 1. What are facts and what are my subjective perceptions?

**The facts:** Jessie did not eat his dinner this evening.

**My perceptions:** Jessie has been poisoned by the neighbors.

## 2. What evidence supports my perceptions?

Jessie did not eat his dinner—he normally has a good appetite.

## 3. What evidence contradicts my perceptions?

Jessie is not showing any other signs of being seriously ill, which would probably be the case if he had been poisoned. I have had some disagreements with the neighbors in the past, and they have never been malicious or vindictive towards me.

## 4. Am I making any thinking errors?

I am jumping to negative conclusions.

## 5. How else can I perceive this situation?

There are hundreds of possible reasons why Jessie did not eat his dinner—I have absolutely no evidence that he has been poisoned or that this has anything to do with the neighbors.

*Elsa's husband has been working long hours, and when he comes home he is often tired and uncommunicative. Elsa feels hurt and rejected. "He doesn't love me any more," she thinks to herself. "If he cared he'd want to spend more time with me, and he'd want to talk to me when he arrived home." Elsa decides to challenge her cognitions by using Socratic questioning.*

## 1. What are facts and what are my subjective perceptions?

**The facts:** Bill is working long hours, and he is often quiet when he comes home from work.

**My perceptions:** Bill doesn't love me.

## 2. What evidence supports my perceptions?

Bill is not very communicative when he comes home, and he has not shown any desire to cut down his work hours.

**3. What evidence contradicts my perceptions?**

Bill is still affectionate to me at times. When something upsets me, he shows his concern and says things to try to make me feel better. On weekends when he's relaxed he's more communicative.

**4. Am I making any thinking errors?**

I am personalizing and jumping to negative conclusions.

**5. How else can I perceive this situation?**

Bill works long hours because his work is very important to him, and he is trying to create a successful business. He is often quiet when he comes home because he is exhausted. I have no evidence that his feelings towards me have changed. However, I can communicate more, and tell him how I feel. Perhaps we can negotiate a more balanced arrangement with his work hours.

# BEHAVIORAL DISPUTING

The way we behave often serves to reinforce our existing cognitions, including those that are unrealistic or self-defeating (see chapter 1). For instance, when we behave coldly or rudely towards someone we dislike, we reinforce the belief that they are a bad person and deserve our contempt. When we avoid confronting an unpleasant task, we reinforce the belief that it is a loathsome task. When we behave unassertively with our friends we reinforce the belief that we must always try to please others. When we avoid doing things that involve the possibility of failure, we reinforce the belief that failure would be catastrophic. By behaving in these ways, our cognitions remain unchallenged and are often strengthened over time.

While our behaviors can serve to reinforce unhelpful cognitions, they can also be used to dispute them. Behaving in a way that is inconsistent with certain cognitions can help us to discover that those cognitions are incorrect. This process is called **behavioral disputing** because we challenge our cognitions using behaviors rather than thoughts. It is also often referred to as doing a **behavioral experiment** because we deliberately change our normal behavior, and observe the consequences, like a scientist doing an experiment. The aim is to discover whether or not our cognitions were valid. If the negative outcomes that we had expected turn out to be correct, we can use logical disputing to decatastrophize, look at the reasons for the outcome and, if appropriate, plan further behavioral experiments using different strategies. If, on the other hand, the negative outcomes we had expected do not eventuate, we come to realize on a deeper level that our perceptions are wrong. Behavioral disputing is the most powerful way of challenging negative beliefs because we learn directly through our experiences. It enables us to release strongly held fears and stubborn cognitions that have refused to budge with other types of disputing.

> 66 Words may help you to understand something
> Experience allows you to know. 99 NEALE DONALD WALSH

*Fred works as a supervisor in a government department, and stays back for hours each evening to complete his outstanding work. Fred is reluctant to delegate tasks to members of his team because he believes that they might not do a good job. Consequently, he is often overloaded with work, and arrives home late each evening. Fred recognizes that his beliefs include, "If I delegate tasks to other people they may not do a good job, and the consequences might be serious."*

Fred can challenge his beliefs logically, by disputing the perception that only he is capable of doing the tasks to an acceptable standard. He may use Socratic questioning to objectively examine the evidence for and against his thinking. In addition, Fred can use a behavioral experiment. This will involve delegating some of the work to his team members, and observing whether or not his beliefs are correct. If Fred discovers that most of the delegated work is done to an acceptable standard, he will have powerful evidence to invalidate his belief that only he can do the job properly. If, on the other hand, the work is not done adequately, Fred will need to spend more time training members of his team, and communicating more clearly what he expects from them. Delegating again after his team have been properly trained will help Fred discover that many of the jobs he is currently doing can be effectively done by other members of his team.

*On two occasions over the last year, Ruth's car was hit from behind while she was stationary at traffic lights. On one of those occasions she suffered severe whiplash. Now Ruth is afraid to drive, as she believes that if she does, she will have another accident.*

Ruth can challenge her beliefs logically, by realistically rating the probability of having another accident, and acknowledging that it is extremely low. She can also remind herself that she had been driving for nearly twenty years, and until last year has only had a couple of minor accidents. However, the most powerful and effective challenge to Ruth's catastrophic cognitions will come from behavioral disputing. Ruth's behavioral experiment will involve getting into her car (initially taking a supportive friend with her) and driving around for short distances. As she discovers through her experience that no negative consequences arise, her next experiment will be to drive alone and gradually increase the distance that she drives. As her confidence increases, she chooses to drive on more busy roads. The discovery that nothing terrible happens provides a direct challenge to Ruth's catastrophic thinking, and enables her to regain her confidence over time.

Behavioral disputing is a particularly useful tool for challenging irrational fears, as directly confronting the things we fear helps us to perceive, on a deeper level, that they are not dangerous after all (see chapter 6).

> *Neil never communicates his true feelings because he wants to be perceived as masculine and strong. He believes that talking about feelings is "girls' stuff." Recently Neil went through a personal crisis that culminated in the break-up of his marriage. Although he feels depressed and lonely, Neil is reluctant to seek counseling as he believes that talking about his problems would be a sign of weakness. He also believes that he is a bad person, and that if he was to be totally honest, a counselor would judge him harshly.*

Neil can challenge his beliefs logically, by reminding himself that being depressed is a good reason to see a counselor, and that this does not mean that he is weak or defective. He can also use Socratic questioning to examine the evidence that supports and contradicts the idea that he is a bad person, and to help him recognize that he is irrationally labeling himself. In addition, Neil could challenge his beliefs through *behavioral disputing*. Neil's behavioral experiment involves arranging to see a counselor, and in spite of his anxiety, talking honestly about his feelings and experiences. This experiment helps Neil to discover that revealing his history and problems to an appropriate person does not lead to negative consequences, and that it actually helps him to feel better.

> *Jerry hates socializing. The strain of trying to make conversation with people he doesn't know makes him feel anxious, and Jerry fears that he may end up standing alone all night. As a result Jerry deliberately avoids parties and most other social functions. By staying at home, Jerry escapes the discomfort of feeling self-conscious and awkward. However, avoiding these situations also reinforces Jerry's perception that going to parties is a frightening thing to do.*

Jerry can use logical disputing to challenge his belief that it would be awful if he ended up standing by himself at social functions. He may also use Socratic questioning to examine the evidence for his perception that he never enjoys himself at parties, and he may reframe his thoughts to acknowledge that although it may be somewhat boring, no catastrophic consequences are likely to occur. In addition, Jerry can challenge his beliefs via a behavioral experiment. This will involve actively seeking out and going to social functions at every opportunity. Exposing himself to his feared situations enables Jerry to discover that he hardly ever stands by himself the entire evening, and that even on those rare occasions where it happens, the consequences are not disastrous.

### EXERCISE 3.2: PRACTICE BEHAVIORAL DISPUTING

Suggest behavioral experiments that can be used to test the unhelpful cognitions in each of the following situations. *Sample solutions at the back of the book.*

1. If I speak up in front of the class I will make a fool of myself—they will laugh at me.
2. I just can't take that flight—I'll have a panic attack and collapse or go mad.
3. I should always say what people want to hear because otherwise they won't like me.
4. There is a wrong and right decision, and I have to be a hundred percent sure of the right decision before I make a move.
5. If I try to talk to people at that conference, they might not respond, and it would be absolutely awful!
6. That essay needs to be perfect. I can't submit work that is less than perfect.
7. Exercise is important, but I'd need to get up an hour earlier to fit it in. It's too difficult to get up early.
8. It's awful to be alone. It's better to be with anyone than to be by myself.

## GOAL-DIRECTED THINKING

So far we have looked at disputing our cognitions logically, by directly challenging the unhelpful aspects of our thinking, and behaviorally, by taking actions that challenge unrealistic cognitions. Another method of disputing is called **goal-directed thinking**. This involves focusing on the self-defeating nature of our cognitions—recognizing that our current perceptions prevent us from achieving the things we want. In goal-directed thinking we remind ourselves to stay focused on our goals.

In its most simple form, it means asking ourselves, **"Does thinking the way I do help me to feel good or to achieve my goals?"** When we challenge our cognitions using goal-directed thinking we can either ask this question or, alternatively, we can tailor our question to address our particular situation:

➤ Does telling myself that my work has to be perfect help me to get things finished on time?

➤ Does staying angry with my partner help us to be happy together and to have a good relationship?

➤ Does focusing on the injustice of this situation enable me to feel good and get on with my life?

➤ Does demanding that others should have the same values that I do help me to get on with people?

➤ Does telling myself that I am a bad person for making that mistake help me to have good self-esteem?

> ➤ Does worrying about the way I look tonight help me to relax and enjoy the evening?

Goal-directed thinking can be used in almost any situation, but it is particularly useful when we feel angry, resentful or frustrated.

> *Cynthia and her husband have gone away for a holiday to a beach resort with their friends, John and Nancy. After two days, Cynthia starts to feel annoyed by some of the things that John and Nancy are doing. For a start, they are not making an equal contribution to buying the daily provisions. Secondly, Nancy takes ages in the bathroom every morning, and John appears to be a lot more selfish than Cynthia had realized. As time goes on, John and Nancy seem to become more and more irritating. By day six, even the way they breathe is annoying!*

The problem for Cynthia is that thinking in this way is making her feel bad, and is ruining her holiday. Cynthia decides to challenge her response using goal-directed thinking, by focusing on the self-defeating nature of her cognitions, **"Does thinking the way I am help me to feel good or to achieve my goals?"**

> *I've come here to have a good time, but I'm feeling resentful and annoyed much of the time. Getting irritated by their behavior is only punishing me—I'm ruining my own holiday! I can choose to let go of these feelings by accepting our differences, and not worrying about petty things.*

In addition Cynthia can challenge her beliefs using logical disputing.

> *They don't contribute as much as we do, but the amount of money involved is trifling, and they're not doing it on purpose. Most of the things that annoy me about them are trivial. They are basically well-meaning, although they do things differently to us. It's really not such a big deal.*

✳

> *Karen has had a falling out with a fitness instructor at her gym. Now she can't stand him. Every time she sees him, the word "jerk" comes instantly to her mind. Whenever she hears him talking to others, she mutters "idiot" under her breath. The problem for Karen is that thinking this way makes her own life more difficult. Her resentment actually diminishes her ability to enjoy being at the gym.*

As Karen comes to realize that her attitude is self-defeating, she uses goal-directed thinking to motivate herself to change her response—**"Does thinking the way I do help me to feel good or to achieve my goals?"**

> *Focusing on his faults makes me bitter and wastes my energy. It also makes coming to the gym less enjoyable. As I'm here almost every day, I want to feel comfortable, and not worry about him. It's in my own best interests to stop criticizing him and just focus on getting fit!*

In addition, Karen challenges her beliefs using logical disputing:

> *He's not someone I would choose to spend time with, but on the other hand he's not a terrible person. He behaves in accordance with his own values and beliefs, and he has the right to be who he is. I don't have to like him, but I also don't have to focus on his flaws.*

✳

> *Linda has agreed to go out to a restaurant with a group of friends. The woman who organized it has extravagant tastes, and one look at the menu reveals that Linda is in for an expensive evening. Linda feels angry that whenever her friend selects a restaurant, it is always expensive.*

Now Linda can spend the rest of her evening fretting about the prices and her friend's thoughtlessness. Alternatively, she can choose to use goal-directed thinking, **"Does thinking the way I do help me to feel good or to achieve my goals?"**

> *I'm here now. Focusing on the prices is not going to make the meal any cheaper— it's only going to ruin the evening for me. I choose to let this go now, and just have a good time.*

Linda can also use logical disputing to remind herself that even though it will be an expensive meal, in the end it will not make a significant difference to her overall budget. In addition, she can tell herself that next time her friend wants to arrange a meal, she is going to suggest the restaurant herself or at least reserve veto rights for any that are too expensive.

## EXERCISE 3.3: PRACTICE GOAL-DIRECTED THINKING

Suggest goal-directed thinking for the people in each of the following situations. *Sample solutions at the back of the book.*

1. Kim is celebrating her fortieth birthday, and her mom has turned up uninvited to the party. Kim doesn't want her mother to be there, and believes that her presence will spoil the whole evening. She feels angry and resentful.
2. Sandra is angry with her partner because he made so little effort to converse with her parents when they went there for lunch. To pay him back, he is in for some cold-shoulder treatment over the next few days.
3. Richard agreed to go to the movies with his girlfriend, even though he had a lot of studying to do before his approaching exam. Throughout the film Richard feels anxious and irritable as he thinks to himself that he should not have come. He has so much work to do—he should have been more assertive.
4. Cindy has noticed that one of her work colleagues has a poor work ethic and spends much of her time on personal telephone calls. Although she chooses not to say anything to her, Cindy feels infuriated by her colleague's behavior.

# IN SUMMARY

➤ **Logical disputing** is the most commonly used technique for challenging unhelpful cognitions. This involves identifying the negative aspects of our thinking, challenging those cognitions and coming up with more realistic and balanced ways of perceiving our situations.

➤ It is usually helpful to write down our negative cognitions and disputing statements, as this assists us to clarify and reinforce more helpful ways of thinking. A thought-monitoring form is a useful aid.

➤ Cognitions that are difficult to dispute can also be challenged via **Socratic questioning**. This involves putting our thoughts under logical scrutiny by asking some specific challenging questions.

➤ A powerful way of challenging irrational cognitions is **behavioral disputing**. This involves setting up a behavioral experiment that gives us the opportunity to test whether our cognitions are correct, and discovering through experience that our thinking is frequently faulty.

➤ **Goal-directed thinking** can help to **motivate** us to change our cognitions. It involves focusing on the self-defeating nature of our thoughts—recognizing that our current cognitions do not help us to feel good or achieve the things we want.

## FOUR

# Overcoming Frustration

*Our life is composed, like the harmony of the world, of discords as well as of different tones, sweet and harsh, sharp and flat, soft and loud. If a musician liked only some of them, what could he sing?*

MONTAIGNE

Frustration is a feeling that we experience when we do not get our needs met or when some obstacle impedes our ability to get what we want. We often feel frustrated when we are confronted with hassles that cannot be easily resolved. No one enjoys frustration, but some people can handle it better than others. Many people have **low frustration tolerance**—LFT for short—which means they get frustrated easily. Albert Ellis first described the notion of LFT in the 1960s. Ellis sometimes referred to it as **can't standitis** because people with LFT frequently complain that they cannot stand this or that. Consequently, they upset themselves excessively in all sorts of situations.

As a general rule, the fewer frustrating situations we have had to endure, the lower our tolerance for frustration. Babies and young children have particularly low tolerance for frustration because they have not yet learned to experience and deal with situations where they do not get their needs met. As we get older, we gradually come to accept that hassles are a normal part of life, and our tolerance for frustration grows—however, many of us still don't cope well with not getting what we want. In fact, people who live in modern Western countries frequently suffer from LFT, precisely because we are so used to getting our needs met much of the time.

Advances in modern technology and increased affluence over the last half-century have had a huge effect on our lives. Modern medicine has enabled us to avoid or control many of the deadly diseases that afflicted our ancestors and still affect people living in poorer countries today. Many unpleasant conditions—from headaches to indigestion, constipation, nausea, anxiety, itching, insomnia and even impotence—can be relieved by swallowing a pill. Internal plumbing in our homes has enabled us to maintain good hygiene with a minimum of effort, and avoid facing the elements when we go to the toilet at night. Modern appliances enable us to stay warm in winter and cool in summer. Boredom can be assuaged with the press of a button, and hunger can be alleviated by going to the fridge. Detailed information about any subject can be accessed in a matter of seconds. There are even devices that enable us to communicate with people on the other side of the world instantly. All of these developments are for the good—they have made our lives easier and more comfortable than they ever were for our parents or grandparents. However, there is a downside.

We expect our lives to be easy, and we have not learned to accept and deal with the difficult and painful situations that are an unavoidable part of life. We become overly upset when things go wrong or when we are confronted with pain, hassles or discomfort. We grumble and complain. We awfulize. We demand that it must not be so. We insist that unless things are as they should be, the situation is intolerable. Consequently we experience a range of upsetting emotions, including anger, depression, panic and feelings of hopelessness.

> *Harry is having a bad day. He left home at 6 am to go to the gym, only to find that the doors were still locked. Apparently there was a mix-up with the keys, and one of the fitness instructors has had to go home to get a spare set. Harry is fuming. "What a waste of my time! I could have slept in," he thinks to himself. After his somewhat abridged workout, Harry battles the rush hour traffic, which is particularly bad this morning, and by the time he gets to work he is feeling angry and irritable. To add to his frustration, Harry is told that his secretary has called in sick. "Great!" Just when he thought that things couldn't get any worse, Harry is informed that the computer network is down as a result of a virus, and it will take several hours before it is fully operational. "That's all I need!" he thinks to himself, as his blood pressure rises and his agitation grows. Life is just one big hassle!*

Harry's business partner, Ian, is dealing with similar problems, but unlike Harry, Ian keeps his cool. When things go wrong, Ian stays calm and focuses on finding solutions. Although he does not enjoy hassles, Ian does not awfulize when they happen or demand that they should not arise. Ian thinks differently to Harry, and is therefore able to deal with problems without making himself overly upset about them.

While Harry blames his troubles on other people, the traffic, technology and bad luck, his biggest problem is his thinking. No one enjoys it when things go wrong, especially when several things go wrong at once. The reality is, however, that hassles are an unavoidable part of life. The challenge is to accept this simple truth, while trying to find solutions whenever possible. Whether we are dealing with a computer virus, a car that won't start, a child who won't cooperate, employees who call in sick or people who think differently from ourselves, it is important to problem-solve whenever we can. This means exploring our options and doing what we can to fix the problem. However, in situations where there is nothing that we can do, our best strategy is to practice acceptance, instead of demanding that problems should not exist. Ironically, the expectation that we should not experience pain and that things should go smoothly actually makes those situations more upsetting than they would otherwise be.

*When hassles arise, demanding that they must not exist*
*and refusing to accept them only makes things worse.*

## PATTERNS OF THINKING THAT GENERATE LFT

Low frustration tolerance stems largely from shoulds, black-and-white thinking and awfulizing. We demand that things must go our way (shoulds) and we believe that unless they do, the situation is intolerable (black-and-white thinking). We add to our suffering by exaggerating the negative consequences of those situations (awfulizing).

> 66 Conditions absolutely must be the way I want them to be and not unduly block me from my pleasures and goals or my life is horrible … whine whine whine … 99 ALBERT ELLIS

- *Patricia is depressed at having to stay home to work on her thesis while her friends are going out and having a good time.*
- *Hugh believes that only one political party can solve the country's problems and he becomes angry and despondent when it fails to win the election.*
- *Miriam is depressed because the renovations on her house are taking much longer than expected and the chaos is unbearable.*
- *In his job Nick has to deal with members of the public, whom he considers demanding, difficult and stupid. Consequently he hates going to work each day.*
- *Bob walks out of the bank after having stood in line for 20 minutes. He is furious at the lack of service, and at the fact that he will need to go back there on a second occasion.*
- *Lee feels depressed because she believes that she must be in a committed relationship in order to be happy.*

For each of the people in the above examples, LFT plays a role in their unhappiness. While the situations themselves are not desirable, ultimately it is their low tolerance for frustration that makes each person particularly upset.

COMMON BELIEFS THAT CAUSE LFT
- ➤ My life should be easy and comfortable. I should get what I want.
- ➤ I shouldn't have to endure hassles.
- ➤ I can't stand doing things I don't enjoy.
- ➤ It's awful when things go wrong or when people don't do the right thing.
- ➤ I shouldn't have to experience stupidity, incompetence or poor service from others.
- ➤ Things should never go wrong in my life.
- ➤ Because I don't like certain things, I shouldn't have to put up with them.

*Stan is setting off to work on Monday morning. As he opens the garage door he discovers that someone has parked their car over his driveway. "Damn it!" he thinks to himself. "Just what I needed! What am I going to do now?" Stan feels frustrated and angry.*

Although many of us might feel the same way, the question is, given the circumstances is it possible to feel any other way? Let's see what Stan is thinking at the moment:

THOUGHTS
- ➤ This is such a pain in the neck!
- ➤ How am I going to get to work?
- ➤ Why can't people just do the right thing?

Stan's beliefs include:

BELIEFS
- ➤ People should always act responsibly and do the right thing.
- ➤ My life should always proceed smoothly.
- ➤ It's awful when things go wrong or when I am inconvenienced.
- ➤ The consequences will be disastrous.

As Stan is aware that he is responsible for his own feelings, he tries to think of some helpful statements to calm himself down:

DISPUTING STATEMENTS
- ➤ I wish people always did the right thing, but the reality is sometimes they don't.

➤ Things go wrong for everybody at times. Frustration is a normal part of life.

➤ This is a nuisance, but it's not a disaster. On the awfulness scale it only rates five percent. It's not going to matter in five years' time.

➤ What's the worst thing that can happen?—I'll have to catch public transport to work today. What's the best action that I can take right now?

Disputing the belief that things must always go smoothly and recognizing that hassles are an unavoidable part of life makes it a little easier for Stan to cope with the situation. Decatastrophizing the magnitude of the problem by reminding himself that it is not important (five percent on the awfulness scale) also helps him to keep things in perspective. Although his frustration has not completely disappeared, Stan feels a lot calmer and is therefore better able to focus on finding solutions. Stan now considers his options:

POSITIVE ACTIONS

➤ Sit in the car and honk the horn for ten minutes.

➤ Knock on the doors of neighbors to ask if they know who owns the car.

➤ Leave a note on the windshield of the car, asking the owner to move it.

➤ Call the police and ask for their assistance.

➤ Call the supervisor at work to tell him what happened. Let him know that I will be a bit late for work this morning. Take the train and bus to work.

The police contacted the owner of the car in the late afternoon, and it was finally shifted that evening. While the whole episode was a nuisance, Stan realizes that it was not a disaster. However, he could have experienced it as a disaster if he had continued to awfulize and demand that it should not have happened. Stan actually felt proud of his ability to take control over his feelings and keep things in perspective. He was then motivated to paint a big "No Parking" sign on the door of his garage. Although the sign does not guarantee that no one else will ever park in front of his garage again, it reduces the likelihood that it will happen. Knowing that he has done all that he can to prevent the problem from happening again also makes Stan feel good.

*Robert bought tickets for himself and his girlfriend, Alicia, to see one of his favorite entertainers in concert. The time printed on the ticket was 7 pm. Although this seemed early, Robert assumed that it must be an early show. However, when they arrived at the venue at 6:45, the door was locked and there was a sign outside stating that some tickets had been printed with an incorrect starting time. In fact, the supporting act was due to commence at 8 pm, while the main act was due to start at 9:15. As it began to dawn on him that they had arrived two-and-a-half hours early, Robert became increasingly frustrated and angry. He would have liked to demand his money back, but there was no one to speak to—the box office was closed. Alicia was in the same situation as Robert but she was not the slightest bit perturbed. In fact, her only concern was Robert's reaction.*

So here we have two people in exactly the same situation—one highly agitated, the other totally unruffled. Why do they respond so differently? That's right, it's all about cognitions. As Robert has rigid, inflexible beliefs about how things should be, he makes himself extremely frustrated and upset, not only in this situation but also at many other times. Let's take a look at the cognitions that cause Robert to feel this way:

THOUGHTS
➤ They've screwed up! How outrageous!
➤ Over two hours until the main act—what a waste of time! I could have done lots of other things instead of hanging around here!

BELIEFS
➤ People should be efficient and reliable. It's terrible when they're not. Mistakes like this shouldn't happen.
➤ All my time should be spent productively. I should never waste time.
➤ It's bad to have time on my hands with nothing planned.

As Robert noticed that Alicia had remained totally unphased, he started to question his own response. "Perhaps I am overreacting," he thought to himself. "Alicia must think I'm a jerk." Robert decided to challenge some of the cognitions that were making him feel so bad:

DISPUTING STATEMENTS
➤ This is inconvenient but it's not a disaster. It's really not that important.
➤ I don't have to use all of my time productively—it's OK to have time on my hands sometimes.
➤ We can find other things to do until the main act comes on.

Decatastrophizing the situation helped Robert to calm down and relax. After regaining his composure, Robert talked to Alicia about how they could use the time that was now available to them. They decided to do the following things:

POSITIVE ACTIONS
- Walk down to the movie theater to see if there are any films that we would like to see.
- If there are no suitable movies, go down to a cafe for a focaccia and coffee.
- If we still have time left over, go and watch the opening act.

When he looked back on the situation, Robert realized that he could have spoiled a perfectly good evening by whining, complaining and generally making a fuss. While he could have demanded a refund when the box office opened, this would have been like cutting off his nose to spite his face, as both he and Alicia wanted to see the show. By catching himself in the process of awfulizing, and making a conscious decision to stop, Robert prevented himself from ruining the evening. As it turned out, both Robert and Alicia had a good time, and Robert learned a useful lesson on the benefits of being flexible.

SIMPLE DISPUTING STATEMENTS TO MANAGE FRUSTRATION
- This is a hassle, and that's OK.
- It's not life-threatening, it's not important.
- Don't sweat the small stuff!
- Frustration is a normal part of life.
- If I miss out on something that I want, I *can* stand it.
- This is a hassle. TOUGH! Where is it written that it should always be easy?
- Things invariably go wrong at times. I don't like it but I can handle it.
- Stop whining and complaining!

## USING A THOUGHT-MONITORING FORM

Although a thought-monitoring form is an effective tool for disputing, it is not always convenient to use one. In the last two examples, for instance, it would not have been feasible for Stan or Robert to have pulled out a thought-monitoring form at the time they needed it most. When it isn't practical to use a form, our next best solution is to dispute our unhelpful cognitions mentally. Simple statements, such as "Don't sweat the small stuff," "It's not life threatening" or "It's only a 5 on the awfulness scale," can be handy in these situations, as they give us an instant and uncomplicated reminder to cool it. However, if the upsetting emotions persist beyond a day or so, completing a thought-monitoring form is likely to produce the best results. The process of writing down our thoughts and beliefs helps us to see the irrational nature of our cognitions and enables us to identify more logical ways of thinking about our situation. Writing our disputing statements also gives us useful material to refer to for reinforcement, if our upsetting emotions should resurface.

*Leanne agreed to her boss's request to stay back at work to finish a project. When she returned home that evening Leanne discovered that her dog, Fred, had escaped through a broken plank in the backyard fence. After calling around anxiously, Leanne discovered that Fred had been picked up by the pound, and it would cost her $200 to retrieve him. Anxiety turned into frustration and anger. It seemed so unfair—she was doing them a favor at work, and now she found herself inconvenienced and out of pocket.*

| | |
|---|---|
| **SITUATION** | After agreeing to work late, I came home to discover that Fred had escaped and had been picked up by the pound. It will cost me $200 to get him back. |
| **FEELINGS** | Feel angry and frustrated. |
| **THOUGHTS** | How unfair! I was doing them a favor at work, and now this happens! If I'd said no, it wouldn't have happened. |
| **BELIEFS** | The world should be fair—generous actions should be rewarded. I was being obliging to my employer, therefore I shouldn't be penalized. The consequences of my agreeing to work late have turned out to be disastrous. |
| **THINKING ERRORS** | Shoulds, awfulizing |
| **DISPUTE** | It was my choice to agree to stay back and work. It's also my responsibility to get the fence repaired. There is no law stating that if I do a good deed, I won't experience any negative consequences. Bad things can happen, even when you're doing something good. This is frustrating, but frustrations are a part of life. Things go wrong at times for everybody. Although it seems like a lot of money, my dog is safe and that is worth more than $200. In the end, it is not going to make a big difference to my financial position. It's not the end of the world. |
| **POSITIVE ACTIONS** | Call handyman and arrange to get the fence repaired as soon as possible. Pay the $200 and collect Fred from the pound. |

In some situations, it is not enough to simply challenge our cognitions—we need to do something to fix the problem as well. In fact, some situations cry out for action.

*Nina frequently feels frustrated because her two young sons often make a mess in various rooms of the house, and take no responsibility for tidying up after themselves. As a result, Nina is constantly walking around cleaning up after them. Her husband, Tim, does little to help her. Nina fills out her thought-monitoring form as follows:*

| SITUATION | The boys are constantly making a mess, and I walk around cleaning up after them all the time. Tim doesn't help me. I came home late yesterday and the place was a pigsty. |
| --- | --- |
| FEELINGS | Felt extremely frustrated. |
| THOUGHTS | I can't stand this mess! They are such pigs! Why can't they take some responsibility for cleaning up after themselves? Why does it always fall to me to clean up after them? |
| BELIEFS | They should be more responsible. They should take an interest in keeping the house clean. They should have the same priorities and concerns that I do. They should be more supportive and helpful to me. |
| THINKING ERRORS | Shoulds, labeling, awfulizing |
| DISPUTE | I wish that they were more responsible and helpful, but there is no reason why they must be. They are behaving like normal kids of their age. If I want them to help, I'll have to work out some strategies to motivate them. Tim does a lot of other things around the house that I don't do. He's also very good with the kids. I'd like him to help more with the housework, so I'll have to talk to him about it. |
| POSITIVE ACTIONS | Have a long talk to Tim—tell him how I'm feeling, and what I'd like from him and the kids. Have a family meeting. Talk to the boys about what I expect from them. Implement an incentive scheme—make their allowance conditional on their cleaning up their rooms, and not leaving their things around the house. Deduct from their allowance for each time they leave a mess. |

In this example, taking action is an important part of the solution. While Nina can reduce her frustration by reminding herself that her children's behavior is normal, and that her husband helps her in other ways, it is also important for her to communicate with her husband and children. Good communication can help us to solve many problems and reduce the likelihood of others arising in the future.

## EXERCISE 4.1

1. Check any of the following situations where you have experienced LFT:
   - ❑ being stuck in traffic
   - ❑ the behavior of your children
   - ❑ wanting something that you can't have
   - ❑ having to do a boring or difficult task
   - ❑ dealing with someone who thinks differently to yourself
   - ❑ dealing with someone who does things slowly
   - ❑ physical limitations brought on by aging or a health problem
   - ❑ mistakes you have made
   - ❑ your partner not wanting the same things you do
   - ❑ poor service
   - ❑ waiting in a slow-moving line
   - ❑ errors in bills that have been sent to you.

2. What were the consequences of your LFT on:
   - the way you felt?
   - the way you behaved?
3. Would you prefer to respond differently when similar situations arise in the future?
4. For each situation, write down rational statements to help you avoid excessive frustration in the future.

## LFT AND PROCRASTINATION

Low frustration tolerance (LFT) creates or adds to unnecessary distress in various situations. Because we expect things to proceed smoothly, we become overly upset when they do not or when we are confronted with situations that are difficult, painful or unpleasant. LFT also has another disadvantage—it gives rise to procrastination and self-defeating behaviors. If we find it difficult to endure situations that we do not enjoy, we put things off and sometimes avoid doing them altogether. This can be a problem because achieving many of the things that are important and worthwhile requires us to take actions that involve some discomfort. Confronting someone about an unresolved issue, leaving an unsatisfactory job, doing regular exercise, making a potentially unpleasant telephone call, completing a course, improving our diet or initiating contact with a new acquaintance—situations like these often require a willingness to step outside our comfort zone. This explains why so many people remain stuck in abusive relationships, unhealthy lifestyles, lonely lives and soul-destroying jobs.

The path of least resistance is seductive because it is easy. All we need to do is keep on doing what we've always done. However, we miss out on opportunities to improve our circumstances or to feel in control. We remain victims.

> 66 LFT then becomes short-range hedonism: indulging in immediate self-gratifying, in spite of its future consequences. 99 ALBERT ELLIS

*Susan has been in an unhappy marriage for the last six years. She frequently complains that her husband is mean-spirited, miserly, controlling and hard to live with. Although she would love to leave, Susan has never seriously contemplated doing so or even standing up to her husband. So why does an intelligent, vivacious and attractive woman like Susan remain married to someone she detests? The answer is LFT. To Susan, the inconvenience and upheaval that would be involved in leaving her husband seems greater than the unhappiness of living in a loveless marriage. Susan has chosen familiar suffering in preference to the uncertainty of change.*

Initiating any change, even moving out of a miserable marriage, involves the possibility of pain and unhappiness—fear of the unknown, inconvenience and loneliness. People with LFT often remain in unsatisfactory situations for years because, in spite of their unhappiness, it seems easier and safer to stay where they are.

> 66 A full life is a life full of pain. But the only alternative is not to live fully or not to live at all. 99 M. Scott Peck, *The Road Less Traveled*

Of course this does not mean that people who are in unhappy relationships should always leave their partner. Sometimes there are good reasons for staying in a less than perfect relationship. However, whatever we choose to do, we increase our chances of being happy when our choices are based on rational considered judgments rather than inertia or LFT.

---

**EXERCISE 4.2**

1. Describe a situation where you have been putting off doing something that you need to do.
2. To what degree does LFT contribute to your procrastination in this situation? _____%
3. What would you need to believe to feel motivated to act? (For example, "It's not really so difficult; it will get easier once I get started; sometimes it's good to do things that I don't enjoy; the rewards are worth it," and so on. See also chapter 9.)

---

## BEHAVIORAL DISPUTING FOR LFT

In addition to logical disputing, we can modify our cognitions by using behavioral disputing—taking actions that enable us to discover that our assumptions are incorrect (see chapter 3). A good behavioral experiment for challenging LFT is to choose to do things that move us outside our comfort zone. Exposing ourselves to situations that are difficult or unpleasant enables us to realize that they are not really so awful and that we can stand it after all. Ironically, once we stop trying to run away from discomfort, life becomes easier. As we increase our tolerance for frustration, we get more things done, and situations that would normally upset us no longer matter.

*Doing things we don't enjoy ultimately makes them more enjoyable.*

*Betty used to get frustrated every time she had to attend dinners and functions with certain members of her extended family. She considered them to be ignorant and stupid, and hated having to spend time with them. Consequently, every family get-together was a major ordeal. Sometimes she made up excuses to get out of attending, much to the annoyance of her husband and mother. Sometimes she came along begrudgingly but made no effort to converse. Finally, Betty decided to try to change her attitude. Her first decision was to stop making excuses and attend all the family dinners she was invited to. When she attended, she deliberately chose to sit next to and talk with the very people she found most objectionable. Instead of ignoring or judging them, Betty listened to what they had to say, and tried to see things from their point of view. Although her own views were quite different, Betty came to accept that they are entitled to think the way they do. By making herself attend family functions and talk to people that she had previously ignored, Betty gradually realized that they were not so terrible after all. What used to be a major chore gradually became painless, and occasionally almost pleasurable.*

66 Look for the fun and enjoyment—not merely the pain and problems—of doing difficult things that are in your best interest. Try to focus on the joyous challenge of doing them, and not only on the trouble and effort. 99 ALBERT ELLIS

*Ken gets frustrated whenever he perceives that he is wasting time. The belief that he should always use his time productively and that it's bad to waste time causes him to become frustrated whenever he is stuck in traffic, when he has to wait in a line or when the service is slow. Sometimes he becomes so agitated that he makes a scene and behaves obnoxiously. Under threat of divorce from his wife, Ken decides to challenge the beliefs that create his frustration by deliberately seeking out the slow lane. He starts by driving his car at a slower speed and avoiding lane changes and pushing in on other drivers. In the supermarket he chooses to stand in the longest line and often allows people who have just a few items to get in front of him. When dining out he reassures the waiter that he is in no hurry. By deliberately exposing himself to situations in which he is made to wait, Ken gradually learns that even when things take extra time, the consequences are never really a problem. They simply take longer—that's all.*

✳

*Greg has been steadily putting on weight since he stopped playing football ten years ago. Now in his mid-forties, Greg recognizes that he needs to lose weight. His doctor has advised him to modify his diet and do some exercise every day, but this doesn't sound easy. Greg enjoys his junk food and has little time during the day for exercise. He'd like to make those changes, but why does it have to be so hard?*

To get himself started Greg recognizes that his problem is LFT, and makes it a personal quest to confront and overcome it. As an initial step Greg makes a commitment to get out of bed at 6 a.m. each morning from now on (even those cold winter mornings when he'd much prefer to stay in bed) and do a brisk one-hour walk. In addition, he commits to saying no to junk food. This will mean buying a sandwich or roll for lunch each day, avoiding chips and deep-fried foods, and no more grazing on ice cream and rich desserts after the evening meal. There is no doubt that sticking to his commitment is going to be difficult. Whether Greg ultimately succeeds will depend on his ability to overcome his LFT. Allowing himself to experience the discomfort of rising early each day for his morning walk, and the pain of denying himself some of his favorite food will help to challenge the beliefs "I must have what I want" and "It's awful to do things that I don't enjoy." Accepting pain without demanding that it should not exist will help Greg to increase his tolerance for frustration and, ultimately, make it easier for him to stick with his new lifestyle.

> 66 When people ask me how to do something, I remind them that they already know how. They are really asking, "What's the easy way?" On planet Earth, "easy" is hard to find. Any accomplishment requires effort, courage, and will. . . . Nothing changes until we find the will to follow through. Our inner adversaries won't go away until we've faced them—until we do what feels right and necessary, in spite of the fear or insecurity that may lurk within. 99 DAN MILLMAN, *NO ORDINARY MOMENTS*

## IT SHOULD NOT HAVE HAPPENED!

One pattern of thinking that frequently causes frustration and self-downing is the belief that something that happened should not have happened. Sometimes we make this assumption about other people's behaviors ("He shouldn't have done that"), but more often we think it in relation to our own ("I shouldn't have done that.") The more rigidly we believe that we should or should not have done what we did, the more upset we become. Although it is useful to learn from our actions and try to avoid making the same mistakes again, telling ourselves that we should not have done what we did is both pointless and illogical.

*I should be able to envisage all possible problems*
*and prevent them from happening.*

All events are causally determined—this is a basic scientific principle that applies to human behavior as well as to the laws of nature. Everything that happens in the universe occurs because the circumstances that prevail at the time cause it to happen. Whether a volcano erupts or a leaf falls from a tree or your computer crashes, it is because all the factors that were necessary for those events to occur were present at that time. This same principle also applies to human behavior. Everything we say and do, including those things that turn out to have negative consequences, happen because all of the factors that were necessary for them to occur were present at that time. We could not have behaved differently, given all of the factors that prevailed, including our limited knowledge and awareness at that point in time, and if all of those circumstances recurred, we would do the very same thing. In retrospect, we can see the consequences of our actions and recognize that it would have been better to have done some things differently. After the event, we can learn from the experience (new knowledge and awareness) and try not to repeat our mistakes. However, as we did not have that knowledge and awareness at the time, blaming ourselves for our past actions is both irrational and self-defeating.

> *This is a personal example: After severe hailstorms in Sydney some years ago, the roof of our house was badly damaged. As many houses in the area had also experienced hail damage, roofers were scarce, and it took several weeks before I finally found a company that agreed to do the work within the next month. The company insisted that I pay a deposit of ten percent before they started the job. As our insurance company had provided us with a check for the full amount quoted, I simply passed this on to the roofing company. In the three months that followed, no work was done, and our roof continued to leak. My telephone inquiries were often ignored or rebuffed, and sometimes I couldn't get through to anyone at all. Finally, the news came—the company was in receivership with debts of over $2 million. The money would not be refunded, and no, the work would not be done. "Sorry . . . bad luck."*

In looking back on what happened, it's easy to see that paying the full amount upfront was a mistake. Once the money had been paid, the company had no incentive to make our job a priority. If I had paid ten percent rather than the full amount, perhaps the job would have been done or at worst, I would have lost only ten percent.

In retrospect, it is easy to be self-damning, frustrated, angry and perhaps even depressed. I can blame the company for being so unethical and blame myself for being so stupid. I can tell myself over and over again that I was an idiot, and that I should never have done what I did. But is it logical to say that I shouldn't have done what I did?

When I handed over payment for the full amount, I was acting with the awareness that was available to me at that time. (Actually, it did momentarily occur to me that paying upfront might be risky, but I chose to go ahead because my overriding assumption was that things would be OK.) If I had had greater awareness that something might go wrong, I obviously would not have paid the full amount upfront. So it is totally illogical for me to now tell myself that I should not have done what I did. Given my awareness and thought processes at the time, I could not have done things differently—that's causally determined reality.

*Demanding that things that have happened should not have happened*
*is as irrational as shouting at the sky on a rainy day,*
*demanding that the sun should shine.*

## GOAL-DIRECTED THINKING

If it sounds like I am letting myself off the hook too easily, let's look at it from another angle. Will it serve my interests to blame myself for my "stupidity," rage at the roofing company and make myself frustrated, angry or depressed? Will doing so help me get my roof repaired? Will it enable me to feel good or to achieve my goals? Will it serve any purpose at all? It is easy to become upset in situations like this. The challenge, however, is to learn from the experience without whipping ourselves for making mistakes. The best way to do this is to accept that we cannot foresee the future or prevent bad things from happening, and to decide what we will do next time if a similar situation arises.

*Paul has recently injured his back after lifting the monitor of his computer from the storeroom floor. Paul feels particularly frustrated because he had declined his colleague's offer to lend a hand. "Why didn't I get him to help me?" he thinks to himself. "What an idiot I am!" Now Paul has two problems—the first is his bad back, the second is his frustration and self-downing. After a couple of days of chewing away at himself, Paul decides to challenge his upsetting cognitions by using a thought-monitoring form.*

| | |
|---|---|
| **SITUATION**<br>**FEELINGS** | Injured my back when I lifted the new computer monitor from the storeroom floor.<br>Feel frustrated and annoyed with myself. |
| **THOUGHTS**<br><br>**BELIEFS** | I should have accepted Bert's offer for help. I should have been more careful. What an idiot I am! Now I have really stuffed things up. This could be a permanent injury.<br>I should be aware of all possible problems and prevent them from happening.<br>I should never make mistakes. |
| **THINKING ERRORS** | Shoulds, labeling, blaming, predicting catastrophe. |
| **DISPUTE** | It's easy to be wise in retrospect—not always so easy at the time. Everyone makes mistakes at times, and so do I. Now I can see that lifting the computer was risky, but I didn't see it at the time. It's happened now—blaming myself won't change things and will only make me feel bad. All I can do is learn from this experience so that I don't do it again. |
| **POSITIVE ACTIONS** | From now on, ask for help if I need to lift anything heavy.<br>Make an appointment to see a physical therapist. |

REMEMBER

➤ We all make mistakes at times.

➤ Bad things happen at times to every person.

➤ Beating ourselves up does not solve our problem or help us in any way.

➤ When there is nothing we can do, our best strategy is to learn from the experience and resolve to do better next time.

---

**EXERCISE 4.3**

1. Describe a situation where you condemned yourself for something that you did.
2. Was your self-condemnation: irrational? self-defeating? (Hint: think about causally determined reality, and things that make you feel bad, but don't solve your problem.)
3. Describe a more healthy and realistic way to view similar situations in the future.

# IN SUMMARY

➤ Frustration is a feeling that we experience when we do not get what we want.

➤ People living in Western countries often have low frustration tolerance (LFT) because we have come to expect our lives to be easy and comfortable. This expectation causes us to become overly upset in situations where we do not get our needs met.

➤ LFT also contributes to procrastination and self-defeating behaviors. For instance, we choose to satisfy our immediate needs rather than looking after our long-term best interests.

➤ In situations where we find ourselves feeling frustrated, it is always helpful to look at problem solving first.

➤ To increase our tolerance for frustration, we need to challenge the beliefs that create LFT. This can be done by using logical or behavioral disputing.

# FIVE

# Managing Anger

Anger stuns. It frightens. It makes people feel bad about
themselves ... The more anger you express, the less effective
your anger becomes, the less you are listened to, and the more
cut off you may begin to feel from genuine closeness.

M. McKAY, P.D. ROGERS, J. McKAY *WHEN ANGER HURTS*

Anger is an emotion that we experience when we perceive that something is bad or unfair. It is fueled by the belief that things must not be this way. In most situations anger is directed at other people over some perceived injustice, however, sometimes we feel angry at ourselves, or at an entity such as an organization, a government, a system or the world at large. Anger is often accompanied by the perception of threat. Even though we may feel outraged, part of us feels unsafe or threatened. This is particularly the case when the perceived injustice affects us personally.

> *Emma was not in her office when her colleague Katie came in looking for her. Katie stopped and took a peek at Emma's pay check, which was lying on the desk. Looking at the statement filled her with rage. Although Emma and Katie did similar work, it turned out that Emma got paid almost $10,000 more. Katie was furious. Without thinking about the consequences she marched straight into her boss's office and demanded a pay raise.*

Katie's anger is fueled by the perception that she is missing out on a fair deal.

Anger often affects the way we behave. When we feel angry we may lose our patience, act on impulse, become aggressive or say things that we later regret. Intense or prolonged anger drains our energy, impairs our concentration and interferes with our ability to be happy and to have good relationships.

## APPROPRIATE VERSUS INAPPROPRIATE ANGER

An occasional burst of anger is not usually a problem. Sometimes it is appropriate to feel angry, as long as our response is in proportion to the situation. So for instance, it may be reasonable to feel angry when you discover that your fellow employee is getting more money for doing the same job as you or when someone has unfairly accused you of something you did not do or when you discover that someone has lied to you. However, it is the intensity and duration of our anger and the way that we behave that determines whether or not our response is reasonable.

> *Nicki's husband, Bill, criticized her in front of their dinner guests, so it was reasonable for Nicki to feel angry. It was also appropriate for her to talk to Bill about his behavior after the guests had gone, and to explain to him why it had upset her. However, if Nicki got so mad that she hurled abuse, smashed the dishes and sent her dinner guests packing, the intensity of her anger would be inappropriate and self-defeating. Apart from upsetting herself, regular bursts of intense anger are likely to destroy Nicki's marriage and reduce the number of friends who are willing to risk future dinner invitations.*

## THE FIGHT-OR-FLIGHT RESPONSE

Think back to a time where you were involved in a hostile confrontation with another person. If you were tuned into what was happening to your body, you may have noticed that your heart was beating harder and faster than usual, your face had become flushed and you were feeling hot and sweaty. You may also have noticed that your breathing was faster than normal and that your muscles had tensed up. These and other changes are part of a primal response to situations that are triggered by a perception of threat. It is called the **fight-or-flight response** because during the millions of years over which we evolved the response provided our ancestors with the extra reserves of energy they needed to either fight with a predator or to run away.

During the fight-or-flight response, a number of physical changes happen. Most of these are geared towards increasing our intake and consumption of oxygen, and producing a rapid source of available energy. When we perceive that something is bad or unfair, our brain sends an electrical impulse to the adrenal glands, at the top of our kidneys. In response to this impulse our adrenal glands release the hormone adrenaline, which in turn triggers a series of other changes in our body. When we perceive a threat or injustice, the body responds in the same primitive way that it did millions of years ago.

➤ Our breathing becomes more rapid.

➤ Our nostrils and air passages in the lungs expand to enable us to take in more air quickly.

➤ Our heart beats harder and faster and our blood pressure rises. This enables the oxygen that has entered through our lungs and into the bloodstream to be rapidly delivered to the muscles where it is needed for energy.

➤ Our liver releases glucose to provide an additional quick source of fuel.

➤ Digestion and other bodily processes that are not immediately essential slow down or stop.

➤ Blood is diverted to the muscles, which tense up in preparation for action.

➤ Our mind becomes focused on the source of threat.

# BENEFITS OF ANGER

Although our body is gearing up for a "battle," in most of the stressful situations that we find ourselves in today this readiness for action is not really useful. However, sometimes anger can have its benefits.

## ENERGY AND MOTIVATION

The high level of arousal generated by the fight-or-flight response can put steel in our spine and give us the courage to confront someone or do something positive to solve a problem. For instance, anger might spur you to confront an inconsiderate neighbor, challenge someone who has spread a nasty rumor, talk to your partner about an unresolved issue, write a letter to a newspaper about some injustice, arrange an appointment with your local congressman, donate some money for a just cause or complain to the manager about poor service. Anger can be a particularly useful motivator for people who are not normally particularly assertive. Spurring us to action can help us to solve a problem and therefore get our needs met.

## POWER

Getting angry can also give us power, as once we get mad, we can be pretty scary. Most people hate being on the receiving end of someone else's wrath and will go out of their way to avoid it. This means that we can sometimes intimidate people into giving us what we want. In hospitals, restaurants, hotels and on planes, angry, demanding people tend to get more immediate attention and better service than those who are passive and patient. In families and in workplaces, people who are prone to anger often have others walking on eggshells, doing what they can to avoid conflict. While this might make them feel powerful, there are of course lots of disadvantages in using anger in this way.

# DISADVANTAGES OF ANGER

A short period of anger is not usually a problem, as long as it is in proportion to the circumstances, and does not cause us to behave in an aggressive or self-defeating way. On the other hand, long-term, intense or frequent episodes of anger can have detrimental effects on many aspects of our lives, including our ability to feel good, to stay focused on the tasks that we need to perform, to enjoy good relationships, to function effectively and to achieve the things that we want. Anger affects our thoughts, physiology and behaviors.

## THOUGHTS

Feeling angry interferes with our ability to think clearly and rationally. It steals our attention away from other issues and turns our focus to perceived violations, injustices and people's badness. This can in turn cause our anger to grow. Anger is sustained and escalated through **rumination**—reprocessing of negative thoughts over and over again. "And then he said . . . and I said . . . and he said . . . How dare he! I should have said . . ." Angry thoughts cause our anger to intensify, which in turn leads to more angry thoughts and more anger. This vicious cycle can keep us stuck in an angry state for long periods of time.

## PHYSICAL RESPONSES

Anger is one of the most physically arousing emotions. If we are experiencing only a brief episode of anger, our level of arousal returns to normal within a short period of time. However, frequent or persistent anger keeps us in a chronic state of tension and arousal, which puts additional stress on the adrenal glands and other organs of the body. These changes can cause sustained elevation in blood pressure, resulting in increased risk of hypertension and heart disease.

## BEHAVIORS

Anger often spurs people to behave aggressively. We may argue, attack, abuse, hit, blame or withdraw. Unless we are in a situation that involves genuine physical danger (in which case being prepared to attack could be useful), this type of behavior is inappropriate and unhelpful, and invariably creates more problems than it solves. Anger may also provoke impulsive behaviors and cause us to exercise poor judgment. In some cases it can lead to physical violence, destruction of property and abuse of alcohol or drugs.

Although an occasional burst of anger may enable us to intimidate others, this is not usually a good way of getting our needs met. Because aggressive behavior alienates people, we are less likely to win their goodwill and support in the longer term. At best, angry outbursts will make people wary of us; at worst, they will make us enemies.

Angry responses create tensions within our existing relationships and may cause us to hurt the very people we care about. Sometimes we say or do things that we later regret. Within families, the power imbalance created by frequent angry outbursts often leads to alienation, poor communication and the breakdown of relationships. Individuals who are easily moved to anger are often friendless—people do not want the aggravation, so they keep away.

While anger is often expressed in hostile or aggressive behaviors, sometimes it is expressed through passive behaviors—called **passive aggression**. The aim is to punish or hurt the other person through subtle strategies such as silence or withdrawal. So we may choose to ignore them, to physically distance ourselves or to respond to their attempts at conversation coldly with monosyllabic statements. While passive-aggressive behaviors can make people feel bad (including ourselves at times), they are not good strategies for maintaining healthy relationships.

Anger also limits our opportunities for negotiation and problem solving when we need to resolve issues with other people. Angry exchanges put people on the defensive and create an atmosphere that is not conducive to good communication. Once people feel threatened, it becomes virtually impossible to negotiate in a spirit of goodwill. We are far more likely to get our needs met and maintain healthy relationships when we communicate assertively rather than aggressively. Assertive communication enables us to convey what we think, feel and want, while respecting the rights and feelings of others (see chapter 10).

## BRIEF VERSUS LONG-TERM ANGER

People experience anger in different ways. Some people are prone to brief episodes of acute anger, where a particular situation will trigger an angry explosion. These people may fly into a rage and experience rapid physical arousal in seconds, however, the storm passes quickly and their anger dissipates. The main problem with this type of angry outburst is the damage that can be done in the heat of the moment. It is during times like these that people abuse their spouses, bosses alienate their staff, drivers deliberately plow into other cars, parents hit their children and friendships are destroyed. So even though the angry outburst may be brief, the harm done may be extensive.

Other people experience long-term anger or resentment. This type of anger is the result of faulty thinking and rumination—demanding that things should not be as they are, blaming, ruminating and repeatedly revisiting unhelpful cognitions. Some people harbor a grudge or feel resentful for years. Unlike a brief episode of anger, long-term anger eats away at us, stealing our attention, impairing our ability to focus on other things and draining our energy over long periods of time.

# STRESS IS A FACTOR

Being under stress from other areas in our lives can shorten our fuse, and make us more prone to angry outbursts. Physical tension and arousal reduce our tolerance for hassles, so that even a minor annoyance can feel like a catastrophe. For instance, if you are under a lot of pressure at work, you are more likely to get mad over some minor issue that might not normally upset you. People who are in long-term stressful situations (e.g., unemployment, financial hardship or unhappy relationships) are particularly likely to experience episodes of anger, as constant stress substantially reduces tolerance for things that go wrong.

Even our physical environment can influence our responses. Spending time in a noisy, overcrowded or hot environment can create a pressure cooker effect, which leads to angry outbursts. Statistics on homicides and acts of physical violence show that these events occur twice as often in the summer months as during cooler times of the year.

# THE VULNERABILITY FACTOR

As we saw earlier, anger is often associated with a sense of vulnerability. Although on a conscious level we are concerned about some perceived injustice, our anger may also help us to diffuse feelings such as fear or hurt. By becoming angry, we override emotions that make us feel vulnerable with emotions that make us feel strong.

> *Tony felt threatened when his girlfriend told him that their relationship was over, and asked him to move out of their apartment. He responded with an angry, abusive tirade against her. Tony's anger displaced his initial feelings of hurt and rejection.*

✳

> *Bert felt intense anger towards his wife's medical specialist after he informed the couple that her cancer had spread. Bert's anger helped to displace the fear that gripped him as he contemplated a new, frightening reality.*

✳

> *Sophie feels hurt and rejected by a work colleague who has shown no interest in her, in spite of her regular attempts to flirt with him. Her initial feelings of hurt subsequently transformed to anger. This helped to override the pain of rejection that she initially experienced, and made her feel a little less vulnerable.*

✳

*Don responds angrily whenever his wife questions some of his parenting strategies. Don perceives his wife's comments as criticisms, and this makes him feel threatened. On a deeper level Don wonders whether he is doing a good job with the children, and whether he is a good father. His anger overrides his feelings of insecurity and self-doubt in relation to his parenting skills.*

## EXERCISE 5.1

1. Think of a situation in which you have felt very angry.
2. What aspects of the situation did you consider to be bad or unfair?
3. Can you identify any fear, hurt or vulnerability that contributed to your anger?

## DISPLACED ANGER

Sometimes we may find ourselves venting our spleen at an innocent person. Displaced anger happens when we have no one to blame or when we are unable to express our anger at the appropriate person. For instance, Fred cannot vent his anger at his demanding boss, so he shouts abuse at other drivers on his way home, snaps at his wife, yells at his children and kicks the dog. A child who feels angry and helpless about the domestic violence at home may pick fights with weaker students at school or abuse his teachers. Bert felt angry with his wife's medical specialist, even though he knew he was not to blame for his wife's cancer—there was just no one else to blame. Displaced anger is irrational and unfair because we direct it at people who are not responsible for our pain.

## TOO MUCH ANGER

Some people are easily moved to anger. We tend to walk on eggshells in their presence, as we know that it does not take much to upset them. These people often have high expectations of themselves and the rest of the world and are frequently enraged when things fail to live up to them. Many of the unhelpful beliefs that create upsetting emotions stem from the messages we received from our parents and significant others during our early childhood. So for example, if your parents conveyed a black-and-white view of the world or demonstrated unhelpful ways of responding to perceived injustice, you might find yourself thinking and acting in a similar ways.

# THE ANGER-PRONE PERSONALITY

Researchers have found that anger and aggressive behavior can sometimes be influenced by physiology—brain chemistry or defects within the brain. Evidence from scientific studies suggests that in some individuals, biological factors create a predisposition towards aggressive behavior. For instance, people who have abnormally high levels of certain hormones (prolactin in women, testosterone in men) show higher than normal levels of hostility and aggression. Other studies that examined the brains of violent men have found that impulsive aggression and violent behaviors may be influenced by faulty regulation of neurotransmitters—the chemical messengers in the brain. In particular, the disruption of serotonin has been linked to aggressive behaviors in some cases. Other studies have found that abnormalities in certain parts of the brain (the amygdala and prefrontal cortex) can increase the predisposition towards aggressive behaviors. Although these biological factors occasionally play a role in anger and aggression, they are not the primary cause of anger for most people. Further, even people who have a biological disposition towards aggression can learn strategies to help them manage their anger when they are motivated to do so.

Negative childhood experiences can also create a lifelong disposition towards anger. For instance, past experiences of emotional abuse or trauma can make people highly vigilant to perceived threats, even as adults, and therefore prone to angry responses. These experiences put people on guard against further hurt later in life, so that even perfectly innocent gestures or comments might be perceived as threatening, and may therefore provoke an angry or defensive reaction. For this reason some people flare up in response to minor provocation or to what appears to be no reason at all. Events that are in some way associated with the original traumatic experience are especially likely to provoke intense, inappropriate anger. So for example, a woman who has experienced sexual abuse as a child may feel inappropriately angry at the sexual attention she receives in her adult relationships. A man who had experienced violent abuse from his domineering father may later respond with extreme hostility towards his supervisor, police or any person in a position of authority.

# TOO LITTLE ANGER?

Some people rarely express anger. This may reflect a genuine lack of anger or it may be due to the suppression of anger. When we suppress anger we put on a brave face, while below the surface we are seething with resentment. Suppressed anger often leads to passive-aggressive behaviors—we make subtle carping, negative comments or try to undermine the other person. People suppress their anger because they do not know how to express it appropriately or because they believe that it is wrong to feel angry. The problem with suppressed anger is that we continue to stew. Instead of spending our energy on repressing the emotion, we would actually be far better off using anger management strategies to help us release our anger or reduce its intensity.

In contrast, there are some people who rarely experience anger. For these people, it takes a lot of provocation to make them mad. Usually, this reflects good psychological adjustment—they have flexible expectations and do not demand that things should be different from the way they are. This ability to be flexible makes them likeable and easy to live with, although occasionally it can have a downside. As anger helps to motivate us to confront or stand up for ourselves, people who rarely experience anger sometimes behave unassertively in their interpersonal relationships. If we have no expectations of a fair deal from others, we may sometimes be willing to endure poor treatment without complaint. I have occasionally seen people tolerate unreasonable demands as well as physical or emotional abuse, often from a spouse or family member. The absence of anger means that they are not sufficiently motivated to stand up for themselves or set limits for what they are willing to tolerate. In these situations, some degree of anger could actually be helpful.

## HOLD IT IN OR LET IT OUT?

There is a commonly held theory that it is better to let your anger out than to hold it in. The theory presupposes that an explosive response—yelling and screaming for instance—is a healthy way of releasing anger. Some of the psychotherapies that have been popular in past decades (e.g., Janov's "Primal Scream" therapy) were designed to encourage people to release their anger through screaming. Even today, some therapists encourage angry clients to pound a pillow, hit a punching bag or just sit in the car with the windows rolled up and scream.

It is true that physical activities such as hitting a punching bag, digging in the garden or going for a run can help to release pent-up anger or frustration. If we are experiencing just a brief episode of anger then physical activity is an ideal way of releasing the pressure. However, physical activity does not resolve sustained anger or resentment.

While exercise can help us to let off steam, yelling at another person is rarely an effective way of resolving anger. In fact, yelling often provokes others to yell back at us, and this may just stoke the fire. Evidence from many studies shows that people often feel more angry after an explosive response, not less, because aggression causes anger to escalate. In addition, yelling is often hurtful to the people we care about, and this can leave us feeling guilty and remorseful afterwards.

> 66 Some people think that if they shout loud enough then other people will do what they want ... This might produce compliance, but it does not produce cooperation or problem-solving ... Dealing effectively with difficult situations requires composure. 99 RAYMOND W. NOVACO

## EXERCISE 5.2

1. Think of a time when you shouted at someone because you felt angry.
2. Did shouting make you feel better or worse? Did you feel guilty or regretful later?
3. How did shouting affect your relationship with the other person? Would it have been better to have communicated assertively rather than aggressively?

## STRATEGIES FOR MANAGING AND LETTING GO OF ANGER

Although it may not always be possible to avoid getting angry in the first place, we can learn strategies to keep our anger in check and prevent it from escalating out of control. Strategies that are useful for overcoming the habit of sudden angry outbursts are different to those that help us to deal with more sustained anger. So first of all, let's look at strategies for dealing with explosive anger.

### EXTINGUISHING THE FUSE—PREVENTING AN ANGRY EXPLOSION

People who are prone to angry outbursts know only too well the downside of uncontrolled anger—lost friendships, problems at work, broken marriages and social alienation, to name but a few. It is therefore important to have a strategy in place, ready to go as soon as the "fuse" has been lit.

An essential skill for preventing the escalation of anger is to learn to recognize the physical sensations that signal its onset. Become vigilant to the internal signs of arousal that accompany an angry flare-up and use them as your cue to take control. Sensations that you may notice when your anger starts to erupt may be a hot, flushed feeling, pounding heart, trembling hands, sweaty palms or clenching of your jaw. Become acutely aware of those physical responses as soon as they arise—they are your cues to take control, using the **Stop–Breathe–Leave** technique.

#### The Stop–Breathe–Leave technique

"Stop!" Say the word "stop" inside your mind or out loud, and visualize a stop sign or flashing lights at the same time. This will short-circuit your automatic response, and remind you that you can choose to respond differently.

**"Breathe."** Take in a few deep breaths to lower your arousal and distract yourself from the perceived injustice.

**"Leave."** Physically remove yourself from the situation—don't hang around. Depending on the circumstances, it may be appropriate to go outside, go for a walk or do some other form of exercise. In a work environment or situations where leaving may not be possible, walk away for just a few minutes by going to the bathroom or to another room and take some long deep breaths. Doing so will keep you out of harm's way during the most testing period, when the urge to lash out is at its peak. If possible, work off some of the extra energy that your anger has mobilized with physical exercise—even running up and down the fire escape stairs can reduce your arousal and agitation.

### Stay goal-focused

Once you have removed yourself from the situation, use goal-focused thinking (see chapter 3) to put things into perspective. Ask yourself, "What is my goal here?" To get along with people? To have happy, well-adjusted children? To have a good relationship with my partner? To be successful in my career? To avoid unnecessary stress? To enjoy the evening? To look after my health? Whatever goal is relevant to your current circumstances, always focus on what really matters, and recognize how getting angry stops you from achieving the things that matter.

### More time out

For most people, leaving the scene for even a few minutes will deactivate a potentially explosive response. However, for those who experience more prolonged explosive anger, it may be necessary to take some additional time out. Depending on the circumstances, you might go for a walk, listen to music, do some gardening or make some unrelated telephone calls. Taking additional time out gives you the opportunity to calm down, focus on your main goals and if necessary, plan some possible solutions. It also reduces the likelihood of saying or doing things that you may later regret.

If you are prone to angry outbursts, it is a good idea to plan your time-out activity. Once you recognize your anger surfacing, tell yourself "I need time out," and move to the activity that you have prepared. This increases your ability to stay in control.

> *Rena goes into the bedroom and closes the door after failing to reason with her screaming two-year-old. Although Rena doesn't like to leave her daughter for long, taking some time out prevents Rena from losing her temper and smacking or yelling at her child.*

✳

*Elizabeth goes into the garden for a little while when her mother, who suffers from dementia, becomes too demanding and unreasonable. This gives Elizabeth a chance to calm down and remind herself that her mother can't help being the way she is.*

✳

*Following an unpleasant confrontation with his boss, Rick calls his accountant, picks up the dry cleaning and pays his gas bill. Although Rick needs to go back and speak to his boss, taking time out to focus on mundane issues gives him the space to regain his composure and put things back in perspective.*

✳

*When Roy becomes angry at his teenage son's unreasonable behavior, he goes into the lounge room and listens to his favorite opera. The time out gives him the chance to calm down and prevents him from yelling at his son and therefore inflaming the situation.*

## REDUCE YOUR PHYSICAL AROUSAL

Anger is one of the most physically arousing emotions. Anger triggers the fight-or-flight response—a state of heightened arousal that prepares our body for action. When we reduce our level of arousal, our anger also recedes. For this reason, strategies that lower our arousal, such as physical exercise, slow breathing and deep relaxation, can also reduce feelings of anger.

Physical arousal can in itself make us more susceptible to anger. For this reason, people who become aroused easily are advised to avoid consuming large amounts of coffee and other drinks containing caffeine, and to try to get adequate sleep each night (sleep deprivation makes us irritable). Drinking excessive amounts of alcohol can also increase the likelihood of an aggressive outburst because of its disinhibiting effects.

### Exercise

Physical exercise enables us to use up the extra reserves of energy that we generate via the fight-or-flight response. Although our level of arousal increases during the process of exercise, it drops substantially after we have finished, and helps our body to relax. Vigorous exercise also stimulates the secretion of endorphins—our body's natural opiates—which increase our sense of well-being. For this reason, exercise is an excellent anger management tool. While the most frequently recommended types of exercise are aerobic (brisk walking, jogging, cycling or working out in the gym), any sort of vigorous activity, including pumping iron, hitting a punching bag or even sexual activity can help to reduce anger levels. Perhaps less enjoyable but equally effective is vigorous housework—mopping the floor, washing the windows, vacuuming the house or digging in the garden.

### Diaphragmatic breathing

For thousands of years, the breath has been used in practices such as yoga and meditation for reducing physical arousal and inducing a state of inner calm. Slow, deep breathing into the lower lungs is a useful strategy for lowering physical arousal at times when we feel angry or anxious. Repeating calming words, such as "relax" or "letting go" each time we breathe out can help to deepen our level of relaxation (see Diaphragmatic Breathing, chapter 6).

### Deep relaxation

Deep relaxation is a physical state in which all of our major muscle groups are extremely relaxed. The level of relaxation is far deeper than in our normal everyday experience. As it is difficult to practice deep relaxation while we are highly aroused, the technique is not really suitable during the acute stage of anger (exercise or rhythmic breathing is more appropriate at that stage). Deep relaxation is a maintenance tool which, when practiced daily, lowers our overall arousal and so reduces our predisposition toward becoming angry in the first place. The practice is particularly useful for hot reactors—people who become angry very easily.

## DEALING WITH SUSTAINED ANGER

Unlike explosive anger, which is usually over within a few minutes, more sustained anger requires a longer-term approach. The remainder of this chapter deals with strategies for managing anger that does not fade within a few hours or after a good night's sleep.

### Problem-solve

Whenever we perceive that some injustice has been done, it is sensible to think about actions we can take to redress it. Sometimes there is nothing we can do, and our only option is to accept the situation, using the various cognitive strategies described in this chapter. At other times we can resolve the situation—partially or completely, through problem solving. Whether or not we succeed, knowing that we gave it our best shot provides some consolation. If, in spite of our best efforts, we do not manage to change things, it helps to know that we tried and that there is nothing more we can do.

Whenever you find yourself feeling angry about a particular situation, look for aspects that might be within your control. Remember the key question: **What is the best action I can take to resolve this problem?**

*Rochelle feels angry because she received a fine after parking in a spot that was poorly marked. She really couldn't tell that it was a no parking zone.*

✳

*Eva lent her friend a book that was precious to her. Upon enquiring about the book six months later, her friend denied ever having borrowed it. Eva feels angry at her friend's attitude.*

✳

*Karen feels angry at her partner, Tony, because he doesn't contribute to the housework.*

✳

*Rowan has paid a substantial sum of money to have his bathroom renovated and is angry at the shoddy workmanship.*

In each of the above examples, the people feel angry because someone has done something that they regard to be bad or unfair. In each case, there are actions that they could take in an effort to resolve the injustice. Rochelle might write to the City to explain that the parking area was poorly marked, and send a photograph of the spot to support her case. Eva might communicate assertively with her friend, tell her that the book was precious to her and ask her to make a special effort to look for it. Karen might talk to Tony about their current domestic situation, to let him know that she is unhappy about doing all of the housework herself, and to ask him to contribute his fair share. Rowan needs to call the tradesman and politely but assertively explain the specific problems that need to be remedied. He might also consider taking further steps if he fails to get a reasonable response, such as lodging a complaint with the appropriate consumer body or consulting a lawyer. In many cases, taking some sort of constructive action enables the problem to be resolved, either partially or completely.

## Sometimes it is better to let it go

Sometimes we find ourselves in situations that are plain unfair, and there is nothing we can do to change them. Or, we may recognize that our chances of achieving a just solution are small, while the cost of pursuing it is likely to be high. Fighting an unwinnable battle may not be worth the time, effort, energy, stress or financial cost involved. Sometimes when we weigh up our chances of success against the likely cost of failure, we might make a perfectly rational decision to let it go. In situations like these, it may be best to practice acceptance. The acceptance affirmation below can be particularly helpful when we find ourselves in situations that we do not like, but cannot change.

> 66 ACCEPTANCE
> THIS IS HOW IT IS.
> NOT HOW IT
> – Was
> – Might have been
> – Should have been.
> NOT HOW
> – I wanted it to be
> – Hoped it would be
> – Planned it would be.
> I ACCEPT THAT THIS IS HOW IT IS.
> Now I get on with my life
> in a positive way. 99
> AUTHOR UNKNOWN

## EXERCISE 5.3

1. Think of a situation that you currently feel angry about.
2. Is there anything that you can do to remedy the situation?
3. What do you need to accept in relation to this situation?

*Antonio works as a carpenter on building sites for a large building company. He is an excellent tradesman—conscientious, hardworking and ethical. He takes pride in his work and always puts in one hundred percent whenever he is sent out on a job. Unfortunately, few of his fellow workers share his attitude. The majority are laid back, and some are indifferent, sloppy and careless in their approach to their work. Antonio finds their attitude infuriating. Although he has complained to the boss on a few occasions, no one has bothered to address the problem. Antonio's anger and resentment towards his fellow employees causes him to hate the job and makes him irritable and hard to live with. In addition, he has recently started getting headaches and stomach problems that seem to be stress-related. Although Antonio is looking out for another job, he knows that this won't necessarily solve the problem, as he has encountered similar attitudes in nearly every place that he has worked. For this reason, Antonio decides to use some anger management strategies. He begins by identifying the cognitions that contribute to his anger.*

| | |
|---|---|
| **SITUATION** | Tradesmen on the job are hopeless. They work slowly, talk a lot, take lots of cigarette breaks and do sloppy work. They don't seem to care about the quality of their work. I told the boss, but he has not done anything about it. |
| **FEELINGS** | I feel angry and frustrated. |
| **THOUGHTS** **BELIEFS** | Those bastards! They really don't give a damn. People should have the same work ethic as I do. Everyone should do a decent day's work; it's absolutely terrible when they don't. |
| **THINKING ERRORS** | Labeling, shoulds, black-and-white thinking |
| **DISPUTE** | I wish they had a better attitude to their work, but there's no reason why they must. Not everyone has to have the same attitude as I do. I've seen this behavior in almost every place I've worked. It seems to come with the territory. I can't change it, so it's not worth fretting about. Things still get done, even if they happen less efficiently than they otherwise would. I've done what I can to try to fix it, and there's not much more I can do. The boss doesn't seem to be too perturbed, so why should I be? In the end, it's not my problem. |
| **POSITIVE ACTIONS** | Stay focused on my own work and don't worry about what the others are doing. If problems arise, let the boss know, but don't take responsibility for it. |

In addition to challenging his cognitions, Antonio reminds himself to stay goal-focused whenever he finds his anger resurfacing—his goal is to do a good job and to enjoy his work. He also repeats a coping statement that makes sense to him—"Keep your cool, it's not your problem!" Sometimes he takes time out from his angry thoughts by putting on his headphones and listening to some music while he works. Antonio has also stuck the "Acceptance" affirmation on his fridge at home and pauses to read it whenever he passes the fridge. He has finally come to recognize that although his work situation is far from ideal, he can cope with it. Antonio works on accepting those aspects of the job that are beyond his control and taking responsibility only for the things that he can change. Modifying his attitude has helped Antonio to feel calmer and more relaxed in his work.

### Give yourself some stewing time

When dealing with a significant injustice, we initially need some time to process our thoughts. At the onset of anger, when our sense of outrage is at its peak, give yourself permission to stew for a while. During this period it is helpful to exercise, talk about it or even write a letter. As long as you don't say or do things that you will later regret, it is OK to experience anger for a few hours or days.

### Talk about it

The very process of talking about something that we feel angry or upset about can help us to feel better. This is particularly the case if our listener is understanding and sympathetic. Sometimes all we need to diffuse the situation is to be heard and validated by a caring individual. Psychologists call this process **ventilation**, in recognition that talking to people helps us to air problems and therefore to feel better.

While talking to a third party can be helpful, sometimes it is best to speak directly to the person we feel angry at. Describing how we feel can help us to release accumulated anger and resentment, and consequently to feel better. However, it is usually not helpful to have things out with the other person during the acute stage of anger, when the likelihood of a hostile confrontation is high (see chapter 10).

### Write a letter

Sometimes it is difficult to directly confront the person we feel angry with because the issue is too upsetting and because we do not trust ourselves to remain calm or to say all that we want to say without backing down. High levels of threat and physical arousal can make it difficult to express ourselves coherently and can lead us to prattle or sound aggressive. For this reason, expressing our thoughts on paper is sometimes a better option. Writing down our concerns gives us time to compose our thoughts and express ourselves calmly and clearly. While sending the letter helps the other person to understand our position, sometimes it is the process of writing that matters and the letter can be discarded after it has been written.

### Thought stopping

Thought stopping can be helpful for dealing with recurring **ruminations** that just won't go away ("That pain in the ass . . . that's not fair . . . I hope he gets what he deserves . . ."). Before you begin, you need to prepare a pleasant fantasy that you will use to replace the unwanted thoughts. This might involve memories of an enjoyable holiday, a moment of past glory, a beautiful place that you have been to, a sexual fantasy, a person who inspires you or a hobby that you enjoy. If you have difficulty creating the fantasy, it may be helpful to write about it first, and then read over it a few times.

To practice thought stopping, you need to catch yourself in the act of rumination and immediately shout out, "Stop!", either aloud or inside your mind. To strengthen the effect, it can be helpful to wear an elastic band around your wrist and snap it as you shout "Stop!" Finally, turn your mind to the pleasant fantasy that you have prepared and focus on it for thirty to sixty seconds. If the unwanted thoughts return during that time, shout "Stop!" once again and repeat the fantasy. To be effective, thought stopping needs to be practiced consistently for as long as the ruminations continue. Initially this will happen dozens of times per day, however, with practice, the unwanted thoughts will become less frequent and will eventually disappear.

## CHOOSE TO LET GO OF YOUR ANGER

Anger comes from the perception that important rules are being violated. When we feel angry, we tend to blame other people or external events. How often have you thought in terms of "He makes me mad" or "That made me so angry!"? The truth is other people do not actually make us angry—they merely provide a stimulus. We make ourselves angry through our belief that things should not be this way.

Like all emotions, anger is generated by cognitions. Other people's actions can be antecedents for our anger, but whether or not we get mad, and how mad we become, depends on how we perceive what is happening in our world. For this reason, events that fill some people with complete rage (e.g. a friend who is chronically late, sloppy service or inconsiderate drivers) do not raise even a whisker of irritation for others.

Anger is different to most other unpleasant emotions in one important way—**we instinctively want to hold on to it**. Only rarely do we want to hold onto feelings of anxiety or depression or humiliation, but with anger it's different. When we are angry we feel so indignant about the perceived injustice that very often we don't want to let it go.

One of the first questions I ask angry clients is, "Do you want to hold onto your anger?" There is often a long pause, followed by some equivocation. Many people actually admit, "A part of me wants to stay angry." Choosing to let go of our anger may feel like we are letting the culprit off too lightly. Our sense of indignation at the perceived injustice can be a major obstacle to moving on.

> *Since her boyfriend, Jim, broke off their relationship three months ago, Cindy has been seething with rage. From Cindy's point of view, Jim's callous behavior is not worthy of forgiveness. "Why should I be the one who has to work on releasing my anger? He's been such a bastard ... I should be angry!"*

The question is, Cindy, who is suffering?

While it is totally reasonable for Cindy to feel angry in the initial period after the break-up, staying angry for months after the event is painful and self-defeating. Anger does not hurt the other person—it hurts us! Even if we are able to make the other person uncomfortable by snubbing them, bitching about them or being overtly hostile, chances are we are suffering with them. Why do it to ourselves?

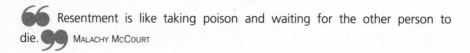

Resentment is like taking poison and waiting for the other person to die. MALACHY MCCOURT

## The cost-benefit analysis

Wanting to stay angry is one of the biggest obstacles to releasing anger. If part of you wants to stay mad, you will sabotage your own efforts to release it. For this reason, if you are not totally convinced that you want to let go of your anger, it is a good idea to do a cost-benefit analysis of staying angry. This involves drawing up two columns, and writing down the benefits in one column and the costs in the other. Let's take a look at Cindy's cost-benefit analysis of staying angry at Jim:

| BENEFITS | COSTS |
|---|---|
| • It feels right—I think I should be angry.<br><br>• It gives me and my friends something to discuss. | • It's on my mind—it distracts me from thinking about other more worthwhile things.<br>• It upsets me—I get all churned up in the stomach when I think about it.<br>• It stops me from getting a good night's sleep—I lie awake thinking about it.<br>• It makes me feel bad whenever I have to see him or any of his friends.<br>• It makes me hard to live with. I'm irritable and cranky all the time with Mom.<br>• It's such a waste of my time and energy. It stops me finding a new boyfriend. |

After weighing up the costs and benefits, Cindy recognizes that the costs of staying angry far outweigh the benefits. This makes her feel more committed to doing whatever it takes to release her anger.

### Goal-directed thinking

Anger is often self-defeating because it prevents us from getting the things we want. These things might include having a good relationship with our partner, being respected by our colleagues, getting on with our parents, enjoying a night out or simply feeling happy and relaxed. Because getting angry makes us feel bad and can impair the quality of our relationships, it is usually not in our interests to feel this way.

Goal-directed thinking (see chapter 3) can be a useful motivational technique to give up our anger. Like the cost-benefit analysis, this type of disputing helps us to recognize the self-defeating nature of our cognitions by focusing on our main goals. Remember the vital question, **Does thinking this way help me to feel good or to achieve my goals?**

> *Derrick frequently gets angry at his two teenage sons because he believes they don't study enough, and that they spend too much of their time playing computer games and watching TV. He finds himself feeling irritable with them a lot of the time, and he frequently loses his temper and yells at them. As a result there is a lot of tension in the house, and the boys often avoid or ignore him. Derrick recognizes that part of the problem is his own rigid mindset about how they should behave, and he would like to change the way that he responds towards his sons.*

Derrick decides to use goal-directed thinking to motivate himself to change his own responses:

*Does thinking this way help me to feel good or to achieve my goals?*
*My goals are to have a close family—to have good relationships with Val and the boys. Getting angry at the boys when I think they're wasting time doesn't change their behavior—it only makes them feel bad and causes them to withdraw from me. Demanding that they should think the same way I do doesn't work, and it creates distance between us. I've told them what I think several times—now I need to let it go and accept that they have the right to do things their way.*

✳

*Jenny feels angry because her partner wants to see his children from a previous marriage once a week, while Jenny would prefer him to spend the time with her. She decides to use goal-directed thinking to change her attitude.*
*Does thinking this way help me to feel good or to achieve my goals?*
*My goal is to have a happy, loving relationship with Steven, yet I get angry and give him a hard time whenever he's going to see his children. We often fight about it, and he gets upset and then I withdraw. My anger is making it difficult for us to communicate or to negotiate compromise solutions. It leads to fights and jeopardizes our relationship. It's in my own best interests to stop thinking this way.*

✳

*While Sam and Sally were preparing to go out for the evening with their friends, Sam made a comment that caused Sally to see red. "That's it!" Sally thinks to herself, "I'm really pissed off now!"*

Although Sally is tempted to stay angry and withdrawn for the rest of the evening, she recognizes that this is going to spoil her evening. Sally asks herself:

*Does thinking this way help me to feel good or to achieve my goals?*
*We're going to a nice restaurant with people I like—I want to have a good time! Why spoil it by getting angry over that comment? It's not worth it! Sally decides to stop focusing on the comment and have a good time instead.*

✳

*Danielle's mother-in-law frequently makes nasty comments about people, and is often negative and mean-spirited. (Her life philosophy seems to be, "If you can't say something bad about a person, then don't say anything at all.") Danielle can't stand her and feels resentful whenever the family have to go and see her. Danielle feels totally justified in feeling this way because she finds her mother-in-law so obnoxious.*

Danielle decides to use goal-directed thinking to motivate herself to respond differently.

*Does thinking this way help me to feel good or to achieve my goals?*
*My goal is to be happy and not get hassled. Feeling angry and resentful every time we have to see her only makes me feel bad, and it also upsets Larry. I don't want to waste my energy getting upset over this issue. I'd rather work on accepting her.*

66 Watch the cost-benefit ratio of dealing with difficult people and situations. Hating them, running away from them, refusing to cope with them may be easier in the short-run—but not in the long-run. 99 ALBERT ELLIS

## IDENTIFY AND CHALLENGE ANGER-PRODUCING COGNITIONS

66 Anger is rooted in negative thinking. It is fueled by being preoccupied with what has gone wrong or with assumptions about the bad intentions of others. One way to combat this negative syndrome is to maintain a constructive outlook about yourself and other people. 99 RAYMOND W. NOVACO

Once we are motivated to work on releasing our anger, we are ready to take the next step—to identify and challenge the patterns of thinking that make us feel angry in the first place.

### The shoulds

Of all the thinking patterns that contribute to human unhappiness, it is the shoulds that are the most pervasive and unhelpful. Shoulds play a major role in feelings such as anger, resentment and bitterness. They reflect our expectations of how people ought to behave and how the world ought to be.

*My friends should be supportive.*
*My son should study hard for his exams.*
*My husband should be able to communicate well.*
*My wife should want the same things that I do.*
*My work colleagues should be conscientious.*
*My boss should be fair.*

*The trains should run on time.*
*Shoppers should return their carts to the supermarket.*
*Pet owners should clean up after their pets.*
*Neighbors should keep their music down.*

Any of these beliefs can cause us to feel angry if we hold them as absolute truths rather than preferences. This is because the world does not conform to anyone's rules, let alone our rules. Rigid, inflexible expectations simply make us anger-prone.

Of course, this is not to say that we should have no expectations of others or that we should accept unreasonable behavior without challenging it. At times it is important to take a stand and to do what we can to resolve an injustice. However, it is also important to be flexible and accept that in the real world, people will not always do what we think they should.

> *In his work as a builder, Jim encounters problems almost on a daily basis. Materials are not delivered on time; tradesmen fail to turn up, and others go home before the job is done; rain delays construction for a week; and bills arrive for services that haven't been performed. Jim is constantly fuming. "If only people did what they're supposed to do! These people can't get anything right! They want to get paid; they just don't want to work!"*

It is totally reasonable for Jim to want his tradesmen and suppliers to be reliable, and to do whatever he can to address their inadequacies. This will involve contacting the relevant people, using his negotiation skills and exerting whatever influence he can to resolve his current problems. He may also be able to implement certain strategies to prevent similar problems from arising in the future. However, Jim's belief that people in the building trade should always be reliable, and his tendency to awfulize when they are not, does not resolve his problems in any way. In fact, it only adds to his problems by causing his rage to escalate and his blood pressure to rise.

COMMON BELIEFS THAT CREATE ANGER
➤ People should always do the right thing (or what I believe is right).
➤ The world should be fair, and people should always behave ethically and decently.
➤ I should always be treated fairly.
➤ I shouldn't be inconvenienced or put out as a result of other people's actions.
➤ If people do the wrong thing, they are horrible and deserve to suffer for their deeds.

### The "just world fallacy"

Notice that a common theme in all of these beliefs is the expectation of justice and fair play. We expect the world to be fair or at least that we should always be treated fairly. This expectation has sometimes been referred to as the "just world fallacy" and develops from an early age. Children are quick to point out injustices they perceive in their own lives— "She's getting more juice than me!" "That's not fair!" "How come he's allowed to stay up till 8:00 and I'm not?"

The problem with this expectation is that it does not match what happens in the real world. Throughout history, tyrants and despots have thrived and prospered. Even today, people live in countries governed by oppressive and corrupt regimes and suffer the injustices, deprivation and hardships meted out by their governments. Others live in affluent democratic countries and enjoy personal freedom and a comfortable existence. Within our own society, children born to poor families have fewer opportunities in life than those born to wealthy families, and people on low incomes have poorer health and higher death rates from all causes than those who are well off. Look in any large workplace and you will find talented, hardworking employees who are poorly rewarded (and sometimes discarded), while others in senior, well-paid positions lack competence and dedication. Callous bosses are often not held to account for bullying and intimidation of workers. Individuals blessed with good looks or the ability to make people laugh receive special treatment and privileges in many areas of life that are not available to the rest of us. Injustices exist within every society, every family and every workplace. Even the very system created to uphold justice in our country is inherently unfair (try taking someone to court or fighting a case without a sack of money to pay your legal bills). Perhaps we should be taught from kindergarten that many things in life are simply not fair.

*The truth is lots of things are not fair.*
*And often there's nothing that we can do about it.*

Of course, that does not mean that we should passively accept unfair, unethical or stupid behavior from others without taking a stand. If there is something that we can do to resolve an injustice, it is important to do what we can. This is why a willingness to problem-solve is crucial. However, sometimes there is absolutely nothing that we can do. A psychologically healthy approach is to take action to try to fix the things that we can while, at the same time, accepting that there are many things we cannot change.

*We can waste our energy shaking our fist at the sky*
*and demanding that things should not be this way.*
*Or we can accept that we live in an imperfect world*
*and focus on the things that are within our control.*

LOGICAL DISPUTING STATEMENTS FOR RELEASING ANGER

➤ People are motivated by their own values and beliefs. They will do what they want and not necessarily what I want.

➤ I wish the world was always fair, but unfortunately, it's not. There is no reason why I must always be treated fairly.

➤ Life is full of injustice, and from time to time, I may get my share.

➤ I have been on the privileged end of global injustice all of my life.

➤ Justice is highly subjective—what is fair to one person may not be fair to another.

➤ People behave badly at times, and so do I. I don't like it but I can live with it.

*Matt recently had a car accident that was clearly the other driver's fault. Because the driver acknowledged responsibility at the time, Matt didn't bother to get a witness—he assumed that there would be no problem. Two weeks later, a statement came from the other driver's insurance company, claiming that Matt had caused the accident. The other driver had blatantly lied about the circumstances of the accident. Matt is furious; now he will have to claim on his own insurance, and that will mean paying the excess and losing his no-claim bonus. After feeling angry for several days, Matt finally decides to challenge his unhelpful cognitions using a thought-monitoring form.*

| | |
|---|---|
| **SITUATION** | Had a car accident that was the other driver's fault. He lied about the circumstances, so now I have to claim on my own insurance. This will put me out of pocket. |
| **FEELINGS** | I feel very angry. |
| **THOUGHTS BELIEFS** | What a rotten, disgusting thing to do! How can people be so dishonest? People should always be honest and behave ethically. I should always be treated justly and fairly. It's awful if people do bad things and get away with it. |
| **THINKING ERRORS** | Shoulds, just world fallacy, awfulizing |
| **DISPUTE** | Unfortunately, the world isn't fair. Sometimes people behave dishonestly and unethically, and there's nothing I can do about it. That's reality. People like that exist. I rarely come across them, but occasionally our paths will cross. Thankfully, it doesn't happen very often. There's nothing I can do about this. I don't like it but I can live with it. |
| **POSITIVE ACTIONS** | Write a letter to the insurance company explaining what happened. Learn from the experience—if it ever happens again, get a witness, even if the other person acknowledges liability. |

## Black-and-white thinking

Anger often arises from black-and-white thinking; this is the tendency to see people and situations as either good or bad, right or wrong, black or white (see chapter 2). It is the inability to see shades of gray that makes us particularly prone to anger.

*Siobhan hates her ex-husband with a passion. "He's such a jerk," she tells anyone who will listen. Siobhan feels outraged whenever she hears that any of her friends continue to see him socially. "Either they are with me or against me," she thinks to herself, "and those who continue to see him are against me—I don't want anything to do with them." Siobhan's black-and-white thinking in relation to both her ex-husband, and the people who continue to socialize with him, simply fuels her anger and alienates her friends. It also causes her to behave in an irrational, self-defeating way (because she loses friends who continue to see him) and ultimately adds to her unhappiness. Although Siobhan blames others for her unhappiness, the key to releasing her anger lies in challenging the black-and-white nature of her thinking.*

✳

*Fiona has been put on notice by the school principal following complaints about her teaching that were made by some of her students. The principal has asked her to address a number of concerns, including lateness, lack of preparation and a failure to hand back essays. Fiona is outraged. "They are carrying out a vendetta against me," she tells her friends. "Just because a couple of hopeless students have complained, I'm being victimized!" Fiona sees the situation in black-and-white terms ("I'm right, they're wrong," "I'm good, they're bad"), and does not consider that the issues they have raised might have some validity. This is self-defeating not only because it creates unnecessary anger, but also because it prevents her from reflecting on the substance of their complaints. Fiona is therefore not motivated to look at possible weaknesses in her teaching or to take the necessary steps to improve it.*

## Injustice may be subjective

In the above example, Fiona's students thought her teaching left a lot to be desired, while from Fiona's point of view, her teaching is completely adequate, and the complaints are unjustified. This example demonstrates how the concepts of right or wrong can be highly subjective. While there are undoubtedly some situations that are unfair by any reasonable measure, many others fall into that vast area of gray. In spite of our own beliefs about good and bad, right and wrong, fair and unfair, there is no universal standard of justice that applies to every situation. Injustice is often in the eye of the beholder:

*When Leon was passed over for a promotion to a new position at work, he was furious. "That's not fair," he thought to himself. "I have worked hard for twelve years—I deserve a promotion!" From management's point of view, Leon is a "plodder"—his work is reasonable but not outstanding. They decided to give the position to a newer employee because he showed greater ability and promise. What is fair from management's point of view appears blatantly unfair from Leon's perspective.*

✳

*Ryan is outraged because, in his parents' will, they are leaving a greater proportion of their estate to his younger brother, Tom. "That's not fair," Ryan thinks to himself, "we should get an even 50/50 split." From his parents' point of view, Ryan has an excellent career and is well off while Tom is financially insecure. They chose to leave extra money to Tom because they see his needs as greater. From Ryan's point of view, the fact that he has a good job and financial security is testament to his many years of hard work—why should he be disadvantaged for that? Once again, what seems fair to one person is not necessarily fair to another.*

**Justice is often subjective. What is perceived as fair by one person is not necessarily fair to another.**

The lesson to be learned here is that although we may be strongly attached to our point of view, it is not necessarily the correct or definitive point of view. It is merely one of many possible ways of looking at our situation.

## Blaming

Blaming goes hand in hand with anger and resentment. Some people spend their entire lives blaming others for their own unhappiness. They think in terms of "It's all their fault," "If it wasn't for her, I'd be happy," "He's such a moron!" The tendency to hold certain people responsible for our own pain simply fuels our anger and makes it hard for us to let it go.

The blaming habit is strongly tied to our shoulds—beliefs about how other people should think, feel and behave. Our underlying assumption is that people who break our rules are bad and deserve condemnation or punishment. Blaming is often accompanied by labeling—creep, jerk, fool, idiot. As we can rarely punish other people or control their behaviors, labeling them and demanding that they should not be the way they are is a waste of our energy and only makes us bitter.

Of course, choosing not to blame someone does not mean that we condone their behavior. We may very well abhor their behavior, and we may take all sorts of action to try to resolve the perceived injustice. However, we may also need to accept that we live in an imperfect world, full of imperfect human beings. Each individual has their own unique set of perceptions and behaves in accordance with their own cognitions, and not necessarily in accordance with ours. When we can truly accept this, we make life easier for ourselves.

*Maxeen received a phone call from Vera—an old acquaintance who moved away many years ago. Vera asked if it would be OK for her to stay with Maxeen for six weeks, while she did a summer school French program. Without really thinking about it Maxeen agreed. Vera offered to pay some rent, but Maxeen said that wouldn't be necessary. While she stayed with Maxeen, Vera took several liberties. She would listen to her music at a loud volume, and frequently helped herself to food in the fridge and pantry. Her clothes and possessions were often lying around the house, and she frequently left the bathroom in a mess. Vera also used the telephone on a regular basis without offering to pay for her calls. While Maxeen found herself becoming more and more irritated with Vera's behavior, the final insult was when Vera did not leave a token of appreciation at the end of her stay. Maxeen stewed for days. Finally, she decided to fill out a thought-monitoring form.*

| | |
|---|---|
| **SITUATION** | Vera stayed at my place for six weeks. She took various liberties, showed little appreciation for my hospitality, and didn't even bother to buy a gift when she left. |
| **FEELINGS** | I feel furious. |
| **THOUGHTS** | What a user! She took, took, took, but gave nothing. Her stay was at some inconvenience to me, and yet she did not show even a token of appreciation. If I were staying at someone's house for six weeks, I would never have behaved like she did. I would have been very considerate and shown my appreciation. |
| **BELIEFS** | She should have shown a lot more gratitude. She should have behaved in the same way that I would have behaved in similar circumstances. It's absolutely awful that she behaved in this way. |
| **THINKING ERRORS** | Shoulds, blaming, awfulizing |
| **DISPUTE** | She behaved pretty poorly, but then again, it did not result in great cost to me. I would have been much more considerate if I had been in her situation, but she is not me. There is no reason why she should behave the same way that I would. It's really not such a big deal. I'm glad she's gone now, but the whole thing is not important. It's not worth wasting my energy on this issue. I've learned a lesson—don't let people stay over for more than a few days, unless I know them well. |
| **POSITIVE ACTIONS** | Just get on with things. If she ever asks to stay again, say no. |

## Personalizing

Whenever someone acts unfairly, rudely or aggressively towards us, we frequently take offense because we perceive their behavior as a personal attack. However, other people's behavior reflects their own particular personality, life events, cognitions and communication style—often it is not about us at all. It is for this reason that we may feel relieved to discover that others feel the same way about them. For instance, when we discover that others also dislike that unpleasant supervisor at work or that crabby neighbor or the difficult sister-in-law, it reassures us that the disagreeable behavior is about *them*, and not necessarily about us.

> *Nathan's buttons are pressed whenever people treat him in an offhand way. When he is driving and another driver fails to give way to him, Nathan feels violated and gets angry. When waiters speak to him in a haughty tone, Nathan feels put down and wants to kill them. When the taxi he tries to hail fails to stop for him, Nathan takes it as a personal rejection and sees red. When his friend does not return his telephone call, Nathan feels snubbed. When the intransigent bureaucrat is unwilling to bend the rules, Nathan feels that he is being personally slighted. And when his boss, who is consistently unpleasant to everyone, makes a curt remark, Nathan wants to pick him up by the collar and throttle him.*

At times people will behave rudely, badly, selfishly or in ways that we do not like, but we don't have to take it personally. It is not always about us. When someone lets you down or behaves badly, ask yourself, "What does their behavior tell me about this person?"

> *Bev's mother has a bad habit of criticizing her driving whenever Bev takes her to do the shopping, to visit a friend or to a doctor's appointment. Bev feels furious. She writes the following notes on her thought-monitoring form.*

| | |
|---|---|
| **SITUATION** | Took Mom to visit Grandma at the nursing home today. She complained about my driving the whole way. |
| **FEELINGS** | I felt like strangling her. |
| **THOUGHTS** | How ungrateful! Why can't she just sit there and appreciate the fact that I'm doing her a favor? She's so neurotic—I can't stand her when she's like this! |
| **BELIEFS** | People should be grateful for generous acts. She should be calm and reasonable. It's awful that she behaves that way. |
| **THINKING ERRORS** | Shoulds, personalizing, labeling, awfulizing |
| **DISPUTE** | I wish that she was more calm and easy going, but that is not her nature. She's always been anxious, and now that she's older she's even more anxious. That's why she behaves that way. Her behavior reflects who she is—I don't have to take it personally. I don't like the way she behaves, but I can understand and accept it. |
| **POSITIVE ACTIONS** | Talk to Mom calmly when we get home. Try to explain to her that it annoys me when she criticizes my driving. Ask her to try to relax—remind her that we always get there and back in one piece. (Don't expect miracles—accept that she's not likely to change much.) |

## Empathy—we are all just trying to live

> 66 Forgiveness is not an occasional act
> It is a permanent attitude 99 Martin Luther King, Jr.

It's easy to feel anger and resentment towards people who say or do things that we do not like. It is much harder to understand them—their thoughts, their motives, their insecurities, their pain. Our anger often disappears when we can see a situation from the other person's viewpoint. Perhaps you have already experienced a situation in the past where you developed some understanding for someone you initially disliked? Once you could understand how it is for them, you stopped judging them. Anger turned to compassion. We can develop empathy towards almost any person when we can see their vulnerabilities and understand how things are for them.

We are all trying to live, using the resources that are available to us. Our resources are things like our cognitions, our problem-solving skills, our social support, our innate sense of security and self-worth and our ability to communicate and get on with people. The resources available to each of us are determined by two factors:

➤ our life experiences
➤ our biology (including thousands of chemicals and structures that
   determine our psychological predispositions, reactivity to stress,
   intelligence, energy levels, physical strength, memory and many other
   processes).

Some people have been dealt a great hand, both biologically and in their life experiences. As a result they are well equipped to deal with life's challenges—they think adaptively and have effective communication skills, a sense of humor, good self-esteem and lots of friends. They are generous and good-natured because they feel secure and have a positive view of themselves and the world. Other people have been dealt a meager hand—for them life is a struggle. They have few resources to call on and they respond to situations in whatever way they can. They may be arrogant or rude, and lack the self-awareness to even realize it. Behaviors that appear to be unreasonable, selfish, stupid, neurotic, boorish or obnoxious often reflect the person's limited resources with which to respond to life's challenges. Some people don't know how to respond any differently. It is of course possible for people to change the way they think by consciously reflecting on their own responses, listening to feedback from others, learning from life experiences, writing down disputing statements to their negative thoughts and even reading self-help books. However, before getting to this point they need to be aware that their own thoughts and behaviors are the problem, and they need to feel motivated to work on changing them.

*The hateful, the intolerant, the rude, the obnoxious.*
*You do not need to wish them to go to hell.*
*They are already there.*

Understanding how it is for other people, and why they behave as they do, does not mean that we must like their behavior—in fact, we may loathe it. However, it releases us from blaming and labeling them, and enables us to stop taking it personally.

    66 The reason to forgive is for your own sake. For our own health. Because beyond that point needed for healing, if we hold on to our anger, we stop growing and our souls begin to shrivel. 99 M. Scott Peck

## Behavioral disputing

Behavioral disputing can be one of the most powerful techniques for releasing anger or resentment towards someone we deal with, such as a work colleague, a neighbor or a family member. Here is a behavioral experiment that you can conduct to dispute your belief that "this person is despicable and deserves my contempt"—choose to treat them in a friendly and reasonable manner, as you would treat a friend. Note that you do not need to be obsequious—just friendly. (An alternative approach for a person that you do not see on a regular basis is to send them a card, letter or friendly email.) This is one of the most difficult things to do because it goes against our instinctive desire to punish the other person and make their life miserable, yet that is our challenge. Changing our behavior toward our perceived adversary changes the dynamics between us, and so, changes the way we feel. When the other person senses our laying down of arms, the release of tension is nearly always a source of relief. In most cases they respond in kind, and the feelings of mutual animosity diminish—we feel more comfortable in their presence and they in ours.

"But what if the experiment goes horribly wrong?" you ask. "What if I am nice to them, and they are nasty back to me? Doesn't that give them a victory?" While in most cases, people respond positively to a peace offering, even if this does not happen, the consequences are never catastrophic. We have lost nothing and can enjoy the moral high ground, knowing that we have behaved in a conciliatory and decent way. After all, we do not need to let other people set the agenda on how we should behave.

Most people who do this exercise express surprise at its effects—it can bring an end to bitterness that has lasted for years, and free us to focus on the things that really matter. If you are struggling to do this exercise, it may be useful to start with a cost-benefit analysis of holding onto hostilities. Does feeling angry and resentful towards this person really serve your best interests? Remember to stay focused on the big picture!

## Coping statements

We have already seen how the process of thought-monitoring and disputing helps us to challenge anger-producing thoughts. In addition, we can select specific disputing statements to focus on whenever our anger resurfaces. These coping statements can be written down and displayed in a prominent place to serve as a visual reminder, and can be mentally repeated any time that our anger resurfaces. Here are some examples of coping statements:

> ➤ Everyone behaves according to their own values and rules.
> ➤ People don't have to do what I think is right.
> ➤ The world is not fair.
> ➤ If it's beyond my control, let it go.
> ➤ Stay goal-focused—remember the big picture!
> ➤ Keep your cool and you're in control.
> ➤ He/she is not perfect, and neither am I.
> ➤ People are just people. They are neither good nor bad.
> ➤ Justice is in the eye of the beholder.

## Communication

The actions that we can take to resolve a problem vary, depending on the particular situation we are faced with. Sometimes it is helpful to write a letter; at other times it may help to speak to the manager, lodge a complaint, make some phone calls or rally people for support. Whatever action we choose to take, one process is always involved— communication. Good communication skills are our most valuable tool for solving problems, redressing injustices and getting on with people.

Communicating with others when we feel angry can help us in two ways.

Firstly, when we tell someone that they have done (or are currently doing) something that is a problem to us, they may choose to change their behavior. Sometimes people are simply not aware of how their actions affect us, and telling them how we feel may encourage them to do things differently. For instance, if you feel angry because a friend is frequently late, telling her how this affects you may encourage her to be more punctual in the future.

If you feel angry because a work colleague does not carry out some of his responsibilities and this impacts on your job, then talking to him about this in an open, nonthreatening way may motivate him to lift his game. If you feel angry because your partner put you down in front of other people, telling her how her behavior upset you may encourage her to be more sensitive and tactful in the future.

Secondly, the very process of communicating can sometimes make us feel better. Telling someone that we feel angry or upset over something that has happened can allow us to release a lot of anger. This is particularly the case if we speak directly to the person we feel angry with. If we are able to communicate in a calm, nonthreatening manner, people sometimes validate what we say. This means that they express understanding for how we feel or acknowledge that we have the right to feel the way we do. Occasionally, they may even acknowledge that they did the wrong thing or apologize for their behavior. Granted, this does not always happen, but in situations where it does, it is like salve to our wound. We can forgive and recover from almost any transgression when people are willing to acknowledge they were wrong or say that they are sorry.

> *Helen has finally plucked up the courage to tell her friend Emily that she feels hurt and angry that Emily failed to support her during her hour of need, when her marriage was falling apart. Emily feels sorry and ashamed, and acknowledges to Helen that she had behaved poorly. While her past action cannot be undone, her expression of remorse enables Helen to let go of her anger, and consequently, their friendship endures.*

Although it is usually appropriate to speak to the person who is directly involved, sometimes we may need to approach a third party who has the power to intervene. This is particularly the case when our initial approach gets us nowhere. So for instance, you might end up speaking to the school principal about the unsatisfactory behavior of one of your child's teachers or to the bank manager about the lack of service at your branch or to the foreman about the poor attitude of some of your fellow tradesmen.

Sometimes we may need to communicate in writing. This is usually necessary when we wish to make a formal complaint. We might also communicate in writing if there needs to be a record of our complaint or when we find face-to-face communication too difficult. Taking time to compose our thoughts on paper often results in clearer and more constructive messages. Whatever the circumstances, our case is strengthened with calm, rational communication, whether spoken or written. We are far more likely to get a favorable response when we are perceived as reasonable and conciliatory, as opposed to hostile, accusing or unreasonable.

Of course, even excellent communication skills do not guarantee that we will always get our needs met. Unfortunately, no system of communication in the world can ensure that other people will always do what we want; but constructive communication increases the likelihood of resolving problems and it helps us to keep people on side, enjoying healthy relationships that are based on mutual respect.

Given that communication is such an invaluable resource, it is surprising how often we shy away from using it ("It won't work ... what's the use?"). Often it is because we feel uncomfortable bringing up an issue that involves a perceived injustice. The situation is already upsetting to us, and the possibility of an unpleasant confrontation may be extremely anxiety-provoking. It might seem easier to rationalize that talking about it will not work anyway. However, it's important to keep in mind that communication does not necessarily result in conflict. Good communication involves sound judgment, negotiation and diplomacy, and very often leads to a reduction in tension and improved relationships (see chapter 10).

## EXERCISE 5.4

For each of the following situations describe:
- actions that you could take that might help to resolve your anger
- the beliefs that contribute to your anger
- disputing statements that you could use to reduce your anger.

*Sample solutions at the back of the book.*

1. Someone you considered to be a friend was not available to help you when you needed them.
2. Your partner has behaved rudely in a social situation.
3. A friend is constantly late. You have made a lunch date with her and have been kept waiting for over an hour.
4. Someone keeps putting their garbage in your paper recycling bin when you leave it out for collection.
5. You have told someone something in confidence, and now you have discovered that they have told others about it.
6. You are extremely inconvenienced by some ridiculous bureaucratic procedure imposed by a particular government organization.
7. Due to staff cutbacks at a telecommunications company, you are kept waiting on hold for half an hour each time you try to call them.
8. You have been substantially overcharged by a tradesman.
9. The company you work for has a ruthlessly exploitative policy towards its employees.
10. Someone is rude to you for no reason.

## IN SUMMARY

➤ Anger is created by the perception that something is unfair, and is usually accompanied by feelings of threat or vulnerability. While it can sometimes motivate us to behave assertively or to solve a problem, anger has many negative consequences.

➤ Acute, explosive anger is potentially harmful because it generates destructive behaviors and alienates other people. Less intense but more sustained anger is also self-defeating because it drains our energy, impairs our relationships, makes us unhappy and can adversely affect our health. Different strategies are appropriate for dealing with the different types of anger.

➤ Unlike other upsetting emotions, people often want to remain angry because they believe it is justified. However, anger hurts us more than the other person. An important first step in releasing anger is to recognize the cost of holding onto it, and to make a decision to let it go.

➤ A number of cognitive strategies can help to release anger, including a cost-benefit analysis, goal-directed thinking, thought monitoring and disputing, empathy and coping statements. Accepting that injustice is unavoidable at times, and that justice is sometimes subjective, can also help to release anger.

➤ Behavioral strategies that are useful in the management of anger include problem solving and arousal reduction techniques, such as physical exercise and deep relaxation. In addition, behavioral disputing—choosing to behave in a friendly manner towards someone we resent—can be a powerful strategy for releasing anger. Utilizing effective communication can also resolve anger by lowering interpersonal tension.

# Coping with Anxiety

The mind is in its own place, and in itself
Can make a heaven of hell, a hell of heaven

JOHN MILTON

Anxiety is that feeling of apprehension and dread that comes with the perception that something bad might happen. It is often accompanied by unpleasant physical symptoms, such as an increase in our heartbeat and breathing rate, tightness in the chest, increased muscle tension and sweating. While everyone feels anxious from time to time, intense or chronic anxiety can be an acutely crippling condition that severely impairs our ability to do things, enjoy life or feel safe in our world. Problems related to anxiety are the most common reasons for people to seek the help of a psychiatrist or psychologist. Both men and women suffer from anxiety, however, women are more than twice as likely to be affected by anxiety and its disorders.

Anxiety is created by a perception of threat—a sense that something bad is going to happen. We call this **state anxiety** because it is a temporary state that passes once the threat has disappeared. Running late for an appointment, having to confront someone about an unpleasant issue or having to give a speech are situations that often trigger state anxiety. The feeling may last for a few minutes, a few days, several weeks or, in some cases, for months. For instance, when you see the flashing light of a police car in your rear-view mirror, you might experience a short burst of anxiety; once the car passes, you relax and feel immediate relief. Anxiety about needing to confront someone may last several days or weeks (the longer you put it off the longer it lasts), and anxiety about your finances or your child's illness may last for many months. Usually however, once our perceived threat passes, so too does the anxiety.

## COMMON THREATS

We tend to become anxious when we perceive that something we value is threatened. The most common threats are to our:

> ➤ physical safety—such as when we are walking alone at night or when awaiting the results of a pathology report
> ➤ material well-being—such as when we are faced with a large debt, risk of redundancy or when starting up a new business
> ➤ self-esteem—such as when we are going to a job interview or to make a speech
> ➤ social safety—such as when we have to confront someone or when we think that someone disapproves of us.

## ANXIETY VERSUS FEAR

Many experts have tried to distinguish between anxiety and fear, however, their opinions differ. Some say that fear is a response to specific events (such as failing an exam or not meeting a deadline) while anxiety is a response to vague, less-defined notions of threat. Others say that fear is a response to an immediate threat (e.g., facing your audience), while anxiety is a response to a more distant threat (e.g., having to give a speech). Some define fear as a cognitive process (an appraisal of danger), while anxiety is the emotional state, including the physical symptoms that accompany those cognitions. Many experts use the two words interchangeably, suggesting that they are essentially the same thing. As there is no universal agreement on the difference between anxiety and fear, within this book the two terms refer to essentially the same thing.

## EVOLUTIONARY BENEFITS

Evolution favors anxiety—historically, anxious individuals had a survival advantage. Over the millions of years in which we evolved, anxiety heightened our ability to detect threats in the environment and provided us with a rapid surge of energy to help us escape from those threats. The mobilization of energy reserves that occurs in response to threatening situations is called the fight-or-flight response (see chapter 5). The response produces a series of physical changes, and our mind becomes intensely focused on the source of threat. This increase in tension keeps us alert and enables us to move quickly if we need to protect ourselves.

For our Stone-Age ancestors, the fight-or-flight response optimized their chances of survival by producing the extra reserves of energy needed to either run away quickly or to stay and fight it out. Even today, there are some situations where the fight-or-flight response can still be useful. For instance, if you find yourself in a physically threatening situation such as being chased by a vicious dog or caught up in a drunken brawl, the increase in energy triggered by the fight-or-flight response will enable you to run harder and faster than usual or to protect yourself if you are attacked. However, the world we live in has changed dramatically since the time of our early ancestors, and the nature of situations that we find threatening has also changed. In the vast majority of situations today, the perceived threat is to our emotional rather than physical safety: deadlines, unpleasant phone calls, demanding customers, growing credit card debt, exam stress, demands at work, hostile confrontations. Although none of these situations presents an immediate threat to our survival, we still respond as though our life is at stake. However, getting highly aroused and ready for action in these situations is no longer helpful. In fact, the physical changes caused by ongoing anxiety can lead to problems such as tension headaches, muscle cramps, stomach trouble, jitters, irritability, exhaustion and even panic attacks.

*Stephen is a talented young design consultant who has been running his own business for nearly ten years. Although the business is thriving, Stephen feels anxious much of the time. When he is busy, he worries that he may not be able to keep up with the demand for work. When he is not so busy, he worries that he may not be able to continue generating work. Stephen also worries about his ability to meet deadlines, satisfy client expectations, compete with new large design companies and retain the current premises. While Stephen is regarded as one of the top designers in the field, his anxiety makes it difficult for him to enjoy his success or feel optimistic about the future.*

## PREDISPOSITION TO ANXIETY

Like Stephen, many people are predisposed towards becoming anxious. We call this **trait anxiety** because the predisposition is part of the individual's inherent personality. People who tend to be anxious perceive the world as unsafe and often assume that bad things are likely to happen. Accordingly, they are more likely to notice and focus on possible dangers in everyday situations ("My child might have an accident," "I might miss the plane," "They might think badly of me"). They also typically overestimate the likelihood that bad things will happen. This can be a major obstacle to feeling good, as it can stop us from being able to relax, focus on the things happening around us and "smell the roses."

Studies that compared anxiety levels between identical versus nonidentical twins have found that a predisposition towards anxiety is partly determined by our genes. Our early childhood experiences also influence this trait. For instance, parents who set excessively high standards, who are extremely critical or who communicate an overly dangerous view of the world are more likely to have anxious children who grow into anxious adults. Stressful experiences in adult life (such as assault or trauma) can also cause us to perceive the world as less safe than before, and therefore increase our disposition towards becoming anxious. Of course, disposition does not mean we are destined to suffer from high levels of anxiety for the rest of our lives, but it means we need to work harder than other people to keep our anxiety in check.

## WE GET ANXIOUS ABOUT DIFFERENT THINGS

While most people perceive certain situations as threatening, we often differ in the specific things that worry us. Some people get particularly anxious when there is a chance that someone may disapprove of them, but they are far less concerned about threats to their physical safety. Other people get anxious about threats to their financial security, but do not get overly concerned about disapproval from others. Some people get particularly anxious about threats to their physical health, but do not worry too much about their performance at work.

## ANXIETY DISORDERS

While state anxiety is a normal response to threatening situations, some people also suffer from anxiety disorders. Studies estimate that ten to twelve percent of the population suffers from an anxiety disorder at some time in their lives. These include generalized anxiety disorder (see below), panic disorder, agoraphobia, social phobia, obsessive compulsive-disorder, post-traumatic stress disorder and specific phobias, such as fear of flying, heights and spiders. The symptoms of anxiety disorders and their effects on our behavior are more pervasive and debilitating than normal state anxiety. Anxiety disorders can interfere with our ability to do things like keep a job, catch a plane, drive a car, leave the house, have friends, enjoy normal relationships or feel safe in the world. Many people who have anxiety disorders also suffer from depression.

Because anxiety disorders are more disabling than state anxiety they are difficult to control through self-help alone. If you suffer from an anxiety disorder, it is highly advisable to seek treatment from a mental-health professional with expertise in this area. CBT treatment for anxiety disorders involves more specific methods than the strategies outlined in this book, and in some, more resistant cases, medication may also be recommended. The information provided in this chapter focuses mainly on the management of state anxiety, although some of the information will also be useful for dealing with anxiety disorders. If you would like more information about the management of specific anxiety disorders, see Recommended reading at the end of this book.

**Generalized anxiety disorder** (GAD for short) is one of the more common anxiety disorders, and affects about five percent of the population. It is sometimes referred to as "the worrying disorder" because people with GAD worry excessively. As a result they also frequently experience symptoms such as restlessness, irritability, difficulty in concentrating, problems with sleeping, fatigue and depression. Because they feel anxious most of the time, they find it difficult to relax or enjoy life.

*Gina has GAD and is anxious about her health. While standing outside at a party one evening, Gina noticed some blood on her finger and, assuming it to be her own, instinctively licked it. This was not a problem until she discovered that the blood actually belonged to a young man who was standing on the veranda above her, who had cut himself with a bottle opener. The realization that she had licked someone else's blood sent Gina into a tailspin, as she immediately thought that it might be HIV-contaminated, and that she would therefore get AIDS. Although there was no evidence that the blood was contaminated (or that licking someone's blood is a significant risk for AIDS), Gina's natural tendency to focus on threats, and to grossly overestimate the likelihood that bad things will happen, caused her to panic.*

## THOUGHTS, BODY AND BEHAVIOR

Like most emotions, anxiety affects the way we think, the way our body responds, and the way that we behave.

### THOUGHTS

While certain patterns of thinking cause us to feel anxious (see later in this chapter), the reverse is also true—anxiety influences the way we think. Feeling anxious narrows our attention to the things we fear, and this can limit our ability to think clearly or to process other information in a normal way. So for instance, if you feel anxious about talking to people at a dinner party, you might find it more difficult than usual to converse with fellow guests and hear what they have to say. If you are anxious about having to give a speech, you might experience a mental blank just as you are about to start, as focusing on your fear reduces your ability to think about other things. (For this reason, people are often encouraged to count to ten or imagine the audience in their underwear—turning your mind to other things helps you to relax and restore your focus.)

### BODY

As we saw earlier, anxiety triggers the fight-or-flight response. The perception of threat sets off a surge of adrenaline, which in turn causes an increase in heart rate, blood pressure, breathing rate, oxygen consumption and muscle tension. Ongoing anxiety may produce other physical symptoms, such as heart palpitations, diarrhea, dizziness, digestive problems, loss of appetite, sleep difficulties and fatigue. In some cases, anxiety can cause panic attacks (see page 134).

## BEHAVIOR

A moderate degree of anxiety is not usually a problem, and can sometimes be helpful. In sport for instance, the anxiety that comes prior to competition can actually increase motivation and push players to excel. Preexam anxiety can motivate students to study hard and perform well on the day, and public speaking anxiety can motivate the speaker to prepare thoroughly and give a brilliant performance. Moderate levels of anxiety in response to a demanding job can keep us motivated and productive. While some anxiety is not necessarily a bad thing, the issue here is one of degree. Severe anxiety impairs our performance and makes us feel bad. High levels of anxiety in response to demands at work lead to errors, reduced productivity and burnout; intense anxiety during the big football game impedes performance; the stage actor who is terrified on opening night may stutter and forget his lines; and intense anxiety before the exam can lead to mental blanks and errors.

When we are anxious, people often notice that something is wrong, even if we do not say a thing. Our manner often becomes strained and serious, and we tend to get agitated more easily. Because our senses (particularly hearing, smell and sight) become acutely focused on our surrounding environment, a small noise or sudden movement might cause us to jump. Feeling anxious may also increase our desire for short-term comfort, like eating, smoking or drinking.

### Escape responses

The unpleasant feelings associated with anxiety often drive us to seek out some sort of escape. Many people try to numb the unpleasant feelings by drinking alcohol, binge eating, smoking or using drugs. Because these things often do provide us with temporary relief, we are inclined to use them again and again. The problem with using escape responses is that they do not provide a long-term solution, and often create more problems than they solve. In fact, anxiety is a common precursor to addictive habits and self-defeating behaviors.

Some people try to minimize their anxiety by choosing to keep away from the situations in which they feel anxious. Accordingly they might avoid attending social situations, applying for a job, driving a car, standing up for their rights, spending time alone or going to work. Running away from scary situations enables us to avoid some short-term discomfort but it keeps us feeling frightened and vulnerable; these escape responses can also impose major limits on our lives. Not confronting our fears means that we never learn to overcome them or to live with them. In fact some people become crippled by a cycle of anxiety and avoidance, which makes it difficult to lead a normal life.

 Life shrinks or expands in proportion to one's courage. 〝 ANAÏS NIN

# PATTERNS OF THINKING THAT CONTRIBUTE TO ANXIETY

While we experience anxiety as physical and emotional discomfort, the feeling stems largely from our cognitions—the perception that our world is unsafe. Recognizing the patterns of thinking that create anxiety and learning to modify them helps us to release or substantially reduce our fear.

## WORRY

Worry is the apprehensive thinking that accompanies anxiety. Worrying thoughts focus on the possibility that bad things might happen, such as the possibility of loss, injury, rejection, failure or shame. Everyone worries at times, but people who are predisposed towards anxiety worry a lot, and some people worry constantly about one issue or another.

For some people, worrying can be relentless and uncontrollable. In spite of attempts to stop, troubling thoughts can keep resurfacing, impairing their ability to concentrate, relax or enjoy the good things in their lives. This has sometimes been called the "what if?" syndrome because we typically focus on the possibility of negative events—"What if I lose my job?," "What if they've had an accident?," "What if I fail?", "What if I make a fool of myself?," "What if I get sick and can't work any more?," "What if we lose all our money?"

### Feeling compelled to worry

As strange as it may seem, people sometimes feel compelled to worry because they unconsciously assume that worrying is protective. This is called "magical thinking" because there is the irrational assumption that if we expect the worst, it won't eventuate. It is easy to see how this belief can develop. If in the past you have worried thousands of times about potential disasters that never came to pass, you may have developed an unconscious association between worrying and positive outcomes. Thus, you subsequently feel compelled to worry because it feels like this will protect you from possible harm.

Some people feel compelled to worry for another reason—it prepares them for the worst. As one woman put it, "If I expect some disaster and it doesn't happen, then I will feel relieved. If it does happen, then at least I'll have prepared myself." While this type of thinking might appear to be logical, it is actually irrational and self-defeating. Because the majority of things that we worry about never actually happen, we create a lot of unnecessary suffering and deprive ourselves of the opportunity to feel good in the here and now by focusing on events that are unlikely to arise. In effect, our worrying creates much more real and immediate suffering than the situations that we fear.

> ❝ Why destroy your present happiness by a distant misery,
> which may never come at all?
> For every substantial grief has twenty shadows,
> and most of the shadows are of your own making. ❞ SYDNEY SMITH

*The pain of anxiety is invariably greater than*
*the pain of the situations we fear.*

*Greg hates going to the dentist and consequently he has avoided dentists for the last fifteen years. Finally, under threat of divorce from his wife, Greg reluctantly agrees to go. Although his appointment was not for another four weeks, Greg's anxiety began as soon as the appointment was made and continued, on and off, for most of that period. On the dreaded day as he sat in the waiting room contemplating his fate, Greg's anxiety was intense—his heart was pounding and his chest was tight. Finally, the dental examination confirmed his worst fears—two cavities that needed filling. Now, while Greg did experience some discomfort during the procedure, the worst of it lasted for only a few minutes—sixty seconds for the injections and five minutes of drilling. Ironically, the anxiety that Greg experienced beforehand lasted for weeks, and was actually more distressing than the dental work itself.*

✻

*My own recent experience of planning a trip to Melbourne during winter illustrates the same principle. A mid-year break seemed like a good opportunity to visit my family, so I booked a flight to Melbourne for a short stay. The weather in Melbourne can be miserable at the best of times but in the middle of winter it is invariably cold and windy. As I feel the cold more than most people, I spent the entire two weeks prior to the trip dreading the winter chill. As it turned out, Melbourne's weather was no problem at all—I was either bundled up or indoors for the whole five days—and I enjoyed the opportunity to catch up with family and friends. The trip itself was enjoyable, while the previous two weeks of negative anticipation were a pain! I put this experience down to another timely reminder that the bulk of our misery comes from negative anticipation rather than the event itself.*

## PREDICTING CATASTROPHE

People who are anxious frequently engage in catastrophic thinking. We overestimate the likelihood that negative events will happen and we mentally exaggerate their consequences if they should occur.

- *They'll find out that I made a mistake, and then they'll think I'm hopeless and they'll want to get rid of me.*
- *If they can see how nervous I am, I'll be the laughing stock of the whole place and I will never be able to face them again.*
- *I will probably lose that contract, and then everyone else will stop coming to me, and then my whole business will be ruined.*

Because we overestimate the likelihood of harm, our situations appear to be potentially disastrous and we respond with high levels of anxiety.

*Barbara made a career move to a new company six months ago, and has been doing very well. However, recently she made a mistake while transferring money, which ended up in the wrong account. Although the error was found and corrected, Barbara feels anxious that people in management will find out and will therefore think badly of her.*

Barbara decides to dispute the cognitions that cause her to feel anxious.

| | |
|---|---|
| **SITUATION** | Realized that I'd transferred that $5000 into the wrong account. I fixed the error, but people might still find out. |
| **FEELINGS** | Feel very anxious. |
| **THOUGHTS** | Everyone will know that I've made a mistake.<br>I'll look like a complete fool.<br>People in management will think that I'm hopeless.<br>This will seriously undermine my credibility in the company. |
| **BELIEFS** | I should never make mistakes.<br>People will think badly of me if they find out that I've made a mistake.<br>Making this mistake means that I'm incompetent. |
| **THINKING ERRORS** | Predicting catastrophe, jumping to negative conclusions, labeling |
| **DISPUTE** | All people make mistakes. That is part of being human.<br>It's OK to make mistakes at times, especially as I am new in the job.<br>People are rarely as judgmental or damning as I am of myself. I would not think badly of a new employee who made a similar mistake. People are not likely to think that I'm hopeless—just inexperienced.<br>It is unlikely to have any long-term effects on my career. |
| **POSITIVE ACTIONS** | Speak to my supervisor and explain how the mistake was made, and that it won't happen again. |

## EXCESSIVE NEED FOR APPROVAL

Everyone wants to be liked and approved of, however, for some people the need for approval is excessive and self-defeating. Being overly concerned with approval often stems from a deep-seated belief that we are not good enough and are therefore prone to rejection. We look for validation from others as a means of reassuring ourselves that this will not occur. An excessive need for approval can create considerable anxiety, as there is always a risk that some people may not like us. The fear of disapproval makes us reluctant to take social risks or to respond assertively when dealing with people. In particular, we dread situations that involve a possibility of conflict and will sometimes go to great lengths to avoid them.

> *While having his house renovated, Rick noticed some faults with the workmanship in the kitchen and bathroom. When he spoke to his builder, Rick received reassurance that his concerns would be addressed, however, the job has now been completed and most of the faults remain. Rick knows that he should talk to his builder again and insist that the problems be addressed, however, the thought of a possible confrontation makes Rick feel anxious. As he hates to cause trouble or get people pissed off, Rick chooses to say nothing and rationalizes that the faults are not really such a big deal. Rick's behavior is typical of people who have an excessive need for approval. The anxiety generated by the possibility of conflict causes us to behave unassertively and to ignore our own interests for the sake of keeping the peace.*

An excessive need for approval also causes us to become overly sensitive to the messages that we receive from others—both verbal and nonverbal. Therefore we feel hurt or anxious if someone seems a little more distant than usual, and we are more likely to misinterpret neutral comments or gestures as signs of disapproval or rejection. As we are highly concerned about scrutiny from others, we might also be self-conscious about how we perform. Thus we tend to worry about things that we say or do, and about how others might perceive them.

## Behavioral disputing

Like most of our beliefs, the excessive need for approval and fear of rejection is reflected in the way we behave. For instance, we might typically try to please or impress people by agreeing with them, not clearly stating what we think or want, being excessively generous or trying too hard to be likeable. In the above example, Rick avoided telling his builder what he really thought of his workmanship because he feared the possibility of disapproval. While logical disputing can help to challenge the beliefs associated with fear of disapproval, the most powerful shift in thinking happens when we directly confront our fears via our behaviors.

For those of us who worry too much about what others might think of us, behavioral experiments are a great way to test the validity of our assumption that catastrophic consequences will follow if we step out of line. One way to do this is through shame attacking exercises originally recommended by Albert Ellis, largely based on his own experiences as a young man:

> 66 I decided to attack my fear and shame with an exercise in the park. I vowed that whenever I saw a reasonably attractive woman up to the age of 35, rather than sitting a bench away as I normally would, I would sit next to her with the specific goal of opening a conversation within one minute. I sat next to 130 consecutive women who fit my criteria. Thirty of the women got up and walked away, but about 100 spoke to me—about their knitting, the birds, a book, whatever . . . I realized that throughout this exercise no one vomited, no one called a cop and I didn't die. The process of trying new behaviors and understanding what happened in the real world instead of in my imagination led me to overcome my fear of speaking to women. 99 ALBERT ELLIS

Any behavior that we believe will increase our risk of negative appraisal by others can be used for shame attacking. More conventional exercises include using assertive communication in situations where we would normally be submissive or being honest and open about things that we feel ashamed of. Not wearing makeup for a week can be a good shame attacking exercise if your confidence rides on your appearance. In addition, Ellis recommended some more challenging exercises that help to overcome excessive fear of disapproval. Although they might sound a little bizarre, the goal is to learn through experience that disapproval by others does not result in serious negative consequences. The following examples will give you some ideas:

- ➤ Get into an elevator and stand facing your fellow travelers instead of the door.
- ➤ Sing to yourself while standing at a crowded bus stop.
- ➤ Wear attention-grabbing clothes, such as a t-shirt with an outrageous logo, a loud tie or a funny hat.
- ➤ Go into a DVD rental store and loudly ask where you can find their pornographic section.
- ➤ Walk up to someone in the street and tell (rather than ask) them the time.
- ➤ Skip for two blocks on the sidewalk of a busy street.
- ➤ Start a conversation with fellow passengers each time you catch the train or bus.

Exercises such as these enable us to learn that even when we look silly or draw attention to ourselves, most people don't pay us much attention, and even if some people do think that we are strange, the consequences are invariably trivial. While many of the above examples are directed towards strangers, we can devise similar exercises for confronting fear of disapproval by people we know.

In addition, always look for spontaneous opportunities to move out of your comfort zone and risk disapproval. Whenever you find yourself thinking, "I can't do that—it might look bad," use this as your cue to rise to the challenge. Create exercises that specifically target your own particular fears. For instance, if you frequently avoid expressing your opinion for fear of disapproval, then challenge yourself by being honest when the opportunity arises. Say what you think rather than what you believe others want to hear, and observe whether there are any real negative consequences. If you frequently agree in order to win people's goodwill, then practice expressing your disagreement at times when you do not agree. If you use excessive generosity to win other people's affection, then consciously curb this behavior—or better still, ask *them* to do *you* a favor, and observe the consequences.

Behavioral disputing is anxiety-provoking—initially these exercises increase our anxiety because we are acting in direct conflict with deeply held beliefs. However, by repeatedly confronting our fears via behavioral experiments, our beliefs start to change. For instance, we come to realize that assertive communication rarely results in negative consequences, and often has positive consequences. Further, even if some people do not approve of us, we learn that we can handle it. This shift in our thinking enables us to avoid substantially more anxiety in the longer term.

---

### EXERCISE 6.1

If you have an excessive need for approval, write down some things that you sometimes do to win goodwill from others. Design some behavioral experiments to evaluate your assumption that you need to behave this way in order to be liked, and put them into practice for the next few weeks. What are the consequences of modifying your behaviors? Does it result in the rejection or disapproval that you expect? Are there any positive consequences?

---

## PERFECTIONISM

The belief that we must do things perfectly often results from the parental messages we received in childhood. Parents who are overly critical and demanding, who have very high expectations of their children, whose love and approval appears to be contingent on their child's performance or who model perfectionism through their own behavior frequently engender perfectionism in their offspring. In addition, those of us who are anxious by nature are drawn to perfectionism because it creates the illusion of being in control. We strive to do things perfectly because that makes our world seem manageable and less scary. It may also sustain our desire for approval, as we believe that our achievements will help us to gain the respect and admiration that we so keenly want.

While some people may think that being a perfectionist is a good thing, the belief that things must be done perfectly is both self-defeating and anxiety-producing. Perfectionism generates a lot of anxiety, as in spite of our need to do things perfectly, there is always a chance that we may not. Consequently, we become anxious over the possibility of not living up to our own high standards. Perfectionist attitudes also cause procrastination, as the fear that we may not do a perfect job makes it hard to get started. In addition it makes us inefficient, as our inability to say, "That's good enough; what's next?" causes us to spend too much time on particular tasks. In most situations the advantages of putting in many extra hours of work are marginal, while the costs are often substantial. So wanting to do a brilliant job can lead to a frustrating impasse at either end—not being able to get started or not being able to stop.

Perfectionism also causes us to become overly concerned with small flaws and mistakes, and to downgrade our achievements and successes. We fail to acknowledge the things that we do well but we self-flagellate when our performance falls short of expectations. Because we are highly critical of our performance we often feel frustrated and dissatisfied. As a consequence, perfectionism limits our ability to enjoy life and to feel good about ourselves, and increases our risk of becoming depressed. Many people with perfectionist traits also set very high standards for other people—partner, friends, family or work colleagues. Accordingly, they tend to be especially critical and hard to live with, and consequently their relationships suffer.

Now this is not to say that a perfectionist attitude is always inappropriate. Certain situations do require extremely high standards. Surgeons, for instance, need to be perfectionists when they are conducting surgery because people's lives are at risk. Bomb disposal experts and military people working in combat zones also need to be perfectionists, as small errors can have dire consequences. There are other critical or dangerous situations where it is absolutely necessary to be meticulous. For most of us however, perfectionism is neither helpful nor effective.

*Cassie works as a research assistant to a respected radio presenter who conducts regular interviews with interesting, high-profile guests. In addition to finding speakers for the program and researching their backgrounds, Cassie also does a preinterview telephone chat with each guest in order to find out more about them. The chat enables her to brief the presenter on key issues to discuss on air. Being a perfectionist by nature, Cassie believes that she has to read through all of her researched material about each guest before she calls them, as she would hate them to think that she was unprepared. Because of time limitations, she is not always able to do this, and consequently Cassie becomes extremely anxious when making preinterview calls without having first read all of her notes. Her high levels of anxiety cause Cassie to have doubts about her ability to do the job. While she believes that the job itself is very stressful, the truth is that Cassie's anxiety is caused by her perfectionism, as her belief that she has to have read all the material is both unrealistic and impractical. Ironically, trying to do her job too well makes Cassie less efficient, as the additional gains of reading all the background notes are marginal at best. Interestingly, the quality of the final product—the interview—is always high, regardless of whether Cassie has spent hours reading her research notes or no time at all.*

Although perfectionism is often manifested in our attitude to our work, we can also have perfectionist attitudes in other areas, such as in the way that we dress and groom ourselves, the things we buy, the expectations we have of our partner, friends and children, the way we play sport or partake in leisure activities, and even the way we maintain our house.

*Raylene has a perfectionist attitude to house-keeping. While having a clean and tidy house gives her a sense of pride, Raylene's perfectionist attitude has a downside. On the rare occasions when the house is not looking its best, Raylene feels bad. When a friend drops by unexpectedly, Raylene feels anxious and uncomfortable. She worries that her friend might notice the mess and think badly of her. The problem is not the fact that Raylene likes to keep a beautiful house. Aiming for excellence in any area that interests us can be rewarding. The problem is Raylene's belief that her house must always look fantastic and her inability to say, "That's OK," at times when it doesn't. Instead of adding to her pleasure, Raylene's perfectionist attitude makes her edgy and lessens her ability to enjoy her lovely house, as well as the company of her visitors.*

**Behavioral disputing**

Perfectionism lends itself well to behavioral disputing because it has such a strong effect on the way we behave. For those of us, like Cassie, who have perfectionist attitudes in relation to our work, a good behavioral experiment is to set time limits on the tasks that we do and observe the consequences. Cassie decided to limit the time that she spends on reading about a guest speaker's background to one hour. By discovering that this had no negative effect on program preparation or the quality of the radio interview, Cassie's assumptions changed, and consequently she became more efficient and relaxed in doing her job. Raylene chose to leave the beds unmade for a week. While initially this made her more anxious, over time she discovered that lowering her standards did not result in negative consequences, and so her anxiety subsided. In addition, she resisted the urge to take three days off work to clean the house before her brother arrived from France, and once again discovered that this made no difference to the enjoyment of his stay.

*Tarne's perfectionism creates problems in his work as a journalist, as his need to do a perfect job causes him to procrastinate. He has learned to overcome this problem by commencing with the aim of writing a poorly worded draft. Once the draft has been written, his anxiety drops, and he is then able to work on refining it. Lucinda is also a perfectionist, and has a similar problem in her work as a ceramic artist. She has learned to overcome her procrastination by giving herself permission to do mediocre work. When her expectations are reduced, her anxiety drops, and she is then able to start working creatively. While both Tarne and Lucinda manage their anxiety by keeping their expectations modest, this does not impair the final quality of their work.*

✳

*Mario challenges perfectionist attitudes in relation to his writing by checking his emails only once before sending them.*

✳

*Todd chooses to deliberately make errors in his weekly tennis game, to help him challenge perfectionist attitudes about the standard of his game.*

✳

*Nicky commits to spending no more than ten minutes on doing her makeup, and bans her usual habit of changing her clothes repeatedly before going out, in order to challenge perfectionist attitudes in relation to her appearance.*

✳

*Adrian deliberately leaves his office in a slightly messy state each day, to challenge his obsessional attitudes about tidiness.*

✳

*Freya starts cooking dinner at 5 PM when entertaining friends. Choosing to cook a simple pasta and salad instead of an elaborate gourmet meal, and allowing herself only a couple of hours to cook before her friends arrive helps Freya to challenge perfectionist beliefs about the standard she needs to achieve when having friends for dinner.*

### EXERCISE 6.2

If you are a perfectionist, write down some examples of situations where your perfectionist attitudes have negative consequences. Design some behavioral experiments that you can undertake to test the validity of your assumptions regarding the need for perfection, and put them to the test over the next few weeks. What are the consequences of modifying your perfectionist expectations?

## EXCESSIVE NEED FOR CONTROL

Taking control over challenging situations (through things like problem solving or disputing negative thoughts) can help us to feel good. It enables us to reduce unpleasant feelings such as anxiety and helplessness, and creates a sense of mastery. However, having an excessive need for control has the opposite effect—it contributes to increased anxiety, frustration, self-defeating behaviors and very often, unhappy relationships.

People who are anxious by nature often have an excessive need for control. We try to make our world safe and predictable by minimizing the chances that things will go wrong. Consequently we anticipate, search out, prepare, initiate, preempt, fix, warn, arrange, check, adjust, plan, explain and organize. The problem is that there are many things that we cannot control, and trying to do so only makes us anxious and hard to live with. Sometimes we need to accept that we cannot fix certain things and that it is best to just let events take their own course. Sometimes we need to let go and trust that things will be OK or at least that we will cope even if things do not go our way.

*Do what you can,*
*But don't expect to be omnipotent.*
*Accept that some things are beyond your control.*

*Valerie's seventeen-year-old daughter, Cheryl, has recently announced that she is going to live with her boyfriend, Mark. Valerie is beside herself. Although Mark is always polite, Valerie finds him to be rather simple. He is not particularly well educated or well spoken and he lacks ambition. Valerie can't understand what Cheryl sees in him. She also thinks that Cheryl is too young to live with her boyfriend and that she will only end up getting hurt.*

Now, it is perfectly normal for Valerie to be concerned about Cheryl's welfare. Like any parent, Valerie wants to minimize the chances that her daughter will be hurt or unhappy. It is therefore important for her to talk to Cheryl, explain her concerns, point out some possible downsides of her plan, and perhaps suggest some alternatives ("Why don't you just continue to go out for the next six months, and he can stay over on weekends? Then, if you still feel the same way after six months, you can find somewhere to live together."). Depending on Cheryl's personality and her relationship with her mother, she may or may not take Valerie's advice on board. The point is that once she has talked to her daughter, there may be little else that Valerie can do. Like many parents of teenage children, Valerie may need to accept that she can no longer control her daughter's actions, and that Cheryl has the right to do what she believes is the best for her. Relinquishing control is often difficult, but trying to hold onto it when there is nothing that we can do is even harder. For the sake of our sanity we need to learn when to let go.

Valerie works on challenging her unhelpful thoughts and beliefs by disputing some of her cognitions.

| | |
|---|---|
| **SITUATION** | Cheryl came home last night and announced that she intends to leave home, and to live with Mark. |
| **FEELINGS** | I felt anxious and angry. |
| **THOUGHTS** | Where does she get these ideas? She is much too young to live with Mark. Her decision is bad, and she is likely to get hurt. |
| **BELIEFS** | I should be able to protect Cheryl from all possible pain. If she does get hurt through this experience, it will be terrible. She should do what I believe is right. |
| **THINKING ERRORS** | Catastrophizing, jumping to negative conclusions, shoulds |
| **DISPUTE** | She may end up hurt, but then again, she may end up very happy with Mark. If she is not happy with Mark, she can always come home. Even if it doesn't work out, she may learn from this experience. I wish she would do what I believe is right, but there is no law that says she must. She has the right to do what she thinks is best for her. If she is hurt through this experience, she'll probably recover. Lots of things in life are painful, and I can't protect her from all possible pain. |
| **POSITIVE ACTIONS** | Talk to her. Explain the reasons for my concern. Suggest a compromise solution but accept that she is not obliged to agree to it. |

## Behavioral disputing

The excessive need to control events in our lives can be challenged by using behavioral experiments—daring ourselves to relinquish control. For instance, if you normally feel the urge to try to fix things for other people, make a decision to take a backseat for a change. If you often try to control your partner or your children, consciously choose to surrender control, and observe whether catastrophic consequences follow. In the above example, Valerie initially disputed her unhelpful cognitions, and then chose to relinquish control over her daughter's decision. When Cheryl finally moved in with Mark, Valerie discovered that the consequences were not so terrible after all.

Lucia has an excessive need for control over her children. She frequently admonishes them for not studying enough, hanging out with the wrong friends, dressing badly and listening to the wrong type of music. When her teenage daughter comes home with pierced ears, Lucia is furious—she would never have allowed this! Lucia decides to challenge her need to control her children's lives by choosing to be less interfering. While she continues to provide normal parental guidance, Lucia gives her children greater freedom in the decisions they make, the way they spend their time and the things they like to do. By taking a more passive stance Lucia discovers that there are no catastrophic consequences, that her children are happier and that they can make reasonable decisions for themselves.

✳

Pip likes to have things his way. Whenever he goes out with his friends to see a movie or to have a meal, it must always be to a place that he chooses or approves. If he does not get his way, Pip is in a bad mood for the entire evening. Pip can challenge his excessive need for control by letting others make these decisions, and choosing to go along with them. In opting to go with the flow, Pip learns that he does not always have to be in control. Letting others lead has no major adverse consequences and often has some positive spin-offs, like not feeling responsible if the movie or the meal turns out to be unenjoyable.

✳

Glen insists that his colleagues should use a work system that he has devised, even though they prefer an alternative system. He is also reluctant to delegate jobs because he likes to have full control over every stage of projects. This causes Glen to become inefficient and sometimes creates tension with his staff. Glen decides to challenge his lack of flexibility by adopting the system devised by his colleagues and objectively evaluating its pros and cons. In addition, choosing to delegate certain tasks enables Glen to learn that relinquishing some control has lots of advantages, and ultimately makes his job easier.

✳

Jana has a strong need for control over her weight and is consequently extremely inflexible in her eating habits. In order to challenge her obsession with weight, Jana commits to eating more spontaneously, having some nondiet snack food every day, and ordering dessert when eating out. Breaking her rigid food rules helps Jana to *realize that no catastrophic consequences arise, and the massive weight gain that she had feared does not eventuate.*

✳

*Peter gets anxious whenever his girlfriend Claudia talks to other guys. When they go out to social functions, he keeps a constant eye on her and if he sees Claudia speaking to a young male, he makes angry or sarcastic comments to her on the way home. He gives Claudia a hard time when she wants to go out with her friends because he is concerned that she might meet someone else in his absence. Peter's attempts to control Claudia's behavior actually reinforce his insecurities and do not help him to overcome his fear. A good behavioral experiment for Peter is to relinquish all efforts to control Claudia's behavior and to stop monitoring her activities. While initially this will increase his anxiety, with time Peter will discover that his relationship is safe, and that he does not need to control Claudia in order to keep her. On the contrary, Claudia will feel more happy and committed to the relationship when Peter's controlling behavior ceases.*

✳

*Felix feels a strong need for control over his life and seeks to have a regular, predictable routine each day. When unplanned events crop up, such as when friends drop in or call with suggestions for things to do, he feels put out and usually resists. Felix recognizes that his lack of flexibility is caused by anxiety and decides to challenge his instinctive response. He makes it his policy to take up opportunities whenever unplanned events arise, and to allow himself to deviate from his plans. At times, he even makes his own suggestions for spontaneous activities, like a walk in the park or going out for a meal. Being less structured enables Felix to discover that he doesn't need to have a planned and predictable routine every day and that spontaneity often adds to his enjoyment of life.*

## EXERCISE 6.3

Write down any areas where you have an excessive need for control. Design some behavioral experiments that you can do to test the effects of relinquishing control and put them into practice over the next few weeks. What are the consequences of giving up control in these areas—does it result in the negative outcomes you fear? Are there any positive outcomes?

# PROBLEM-SOLVE

Whenever we find ourselves in a stressful situation, the most appropriate first step is to look for solutions. Problem solving increases our sense of control, and so the very decision to do something makes us feel better. In situations where possible solutions exist it is usually helpful to act sooner rather than later, as procrastination only prolongs the agony.

*Power is knowing what needs to be done*
*and having the courage to go out and do it.*

The amount of control that we can exert in any situation varies, depending on our circumstances. Sometimes there is nothing that we can do to change the situation, in which case we need to use other strategies, such as disputing catastrophic thoughts, Socratic questioning or relaxation techniques to manage our anxiety. However, possible solutions frequently do exist, and brainstorming our options is a good place to start—**What actions can I take to resolve this problem?**

> *Jeanette works as an editor in a large publishing company. The demands of the job have grown over the last twelve months, and over that time she has done her best to manage her workload. Recently Jeanette was given some additional jobs with tight deadlines, and this sent her anxiety levels soaring. Being extremely conscientious, Jeanette felt obliged to deliver on time but she didn't know how she was going to do this. She felt a constant tightness in her chest and sometimes found it hard to breathe.*

Jeanette recognized that she had to *do something*, as the stress of unrealistic deadlines was overwhelming, and impaired her ability to do her job. While she thought about resigning, this seemed like a drastic step, so she decided to explore other options. She wrote down the following list of possible solutions:

- ➤ Prioritize my jobs and focus on the most urgent ones.
- ➤ Talk to Louise (work colleague) to see if she'd be willing to help out with some of my projects.
- ➤ Come in early and stay late every night this week.
- ➤ Come in on the weekend and finish off the more urgent jobs.
- ➤ Talk to Beth (team manager), explain my situation to her and ask for help.

As Jeanette worked through these strategies, she found that prioritizing her jobs and staying until late each evening helped her to feel more in control. Her decision to come into work on the weekend, while not something she relished, gave her additional breathing space and lowered her anxiety. She also talked to her colleague, Louise, who was sympathetic but unable to take on any additional work. Louise strongly encouraged Jeanette to talk to Beth, as she was the person who could lighten her load.

> *Jeanette became aware of her strong resistance to the idea of talking to Beth, and realized that this stemmed from her beliefs about asking for help ("I should always do it all myself," "Asking for help means I'm incompetent," "She will judge me harshly.") In order to be effective in her job, Jeanette needed to challenge some of the faulty thinking that impeded her ability to solve her current problems. ("I prefer to complete all tasks by myself, but that isn't always possible," "Asking for help when my workload is excessive is a sign of competence," "Experience has taught me that people rarely judge me as harshly as I judge myself.") Once Jeanette challenged the limiting beliefs that made her so reluctant to talk to Beth, she was able to approach her and have a useful discussion. This resulted in the extension of some of her deadlines, and a more realistic workload.*

When we find ourselves becoming anxious or burdened, looking for solutions is the best place to start. Partial or total solutions are often available, if we think creatively. On some occasions, we will also need to challenge the faulty thinking that weakens our resolve and keeps us stalling. Fear of negative appraisal by others is one of the common psychological obstacles to problem solving. Recognizing and challenging the obstacles that get in the way is sometimes critical for getting things done (see chapter 9).

*There are some things that we can change, and others that we can't.*
*Our job is to work out which is which,*
*and to focus our energy on things that we can control.*

## EXERCISE 6.4

For each of the following situations suggest:

a. the thoughts and underlying beliefs that contribute to their anxiety
b. disputing statements that could be used to reduce their anxiety
c. some positive actions (problem solving) that could be used to reduce their anxiety.

*Sample solutions at the back of the book.*

1. Eve is anxious about going to a social function where she won't know anyone.
2. Beatrice feels anxious about running late for a doctor's appointment.
3. Kim is anxious about having to give a speech to a large audience of professional people.
4. Rick is anxious about having to make a potentially unpleasant phone call.
5. Fay feels anxious about having to confront her neighbors about their dog, which is constantly barking.
6. Jeremy is anxious about an approaching job interview.
7. Clive feels anxious about having to return some goods to the shop.
8. Olivia feels anxious because her daughter has slept in and may miss her flight for the vacation that she has planned.

# CHALLENGE CATASTROPHIC THINKING

We have already seen examples of how to dispute anxiety-provoking thoughts, using a thought-monitoring form. In the next section, we will look at other cognitive strategies that can be used to challenge catastrophic thinking.

## DECATASTROPHIZE

Decatastrophizing means mentally bringing the problem back to its proper perspective. We may end up recognizing that a situation rates only a 5 or a 10 on our awfulness scale, and not the 95 that we are currently perceiving. Decatastrophizing means more than purely acknowledging that our feared situation is unlikely to arise. It means considering the consequences if it should arise, and recognizing that in any event, we would cope.

There are two important things to keep in mind:

**1. Over ninety percent of the things that we fear never eventuate.**
If you were to add up the number of times that you worried about some imminent disaster, and then compared this to the number of disasters that actually occurred, what do you think you would find? Undoubtedly, the vast majority of the things that you worried about never eventuated. In spite of your worst fears, the speech was not the debacle that you had predicted, you survived the dreaded dinner party, and the company restructure did not affect you. Upon reflection, the sky rarely fell, and after each episode of angst, your life continued pretty well as before.

**2. The consequences are rarely catastrophic.**
Even on those rare occasions when your feared situation did eventuate, the consequences were usually not as bad as you had anticipated. Most often there is some discomfort, pain

or inconvenience, but rarely any long-term disastrous consequences. Of course, this is not to make light of the serious situations that sometimes do occur. On rare occasions, our worst fears are realized and have major negative consequences—the diagnosis of a life-threatening illness, abandonment by a partner, the loss of our home, death of a loved one, being seriously maimed in an accident. All of these events can have major long-term consequences and should not be trivialized. The point is, however, that the majority of times when we torment ourselves with worry, the consequences are really not as bad as they seem.

> *Marissa has been feeling particularly low in energy recently and has been drinking a lot of fluids. Her friend told her that she might have diabetes and that she should get herself checked out. The suggestion of a chronic health problem put Marissa into a state of panic. Thoughts of being ill, having to inject herself with insulin and not being in control over her life flooded her mind, and her anxiety subsequently turned to despair. Consultations with her doctor subsequently confirmed Marissa's worst fears—she did indeed have diabetes. While initially this news appeared disastrous, with time Marissa came to accept her situation. She learned how to manage the condition with diet, regular exercise and medication. Although she is not happy to have diabetes, Marissa has learned to live with it, and discovered that what seemed like disaster is not a disaster after all.*

Sometimes situations that appear to be disastrous can have some positive consequences.

> *Alan went through major anxiety as he tried to save his ailing business for two years. Throughout this period he was consumed with worries about his finances and had difficulty sleeping. Finally, after much soul-searching and angst, Alan decided to call it a day. Much to his own surprise, once the decision was made, he felt immediate relief. What's more, over time Alan found himself feeling happier and more relaxed. The closure of the business forced Alan to reevaluate some of his priorities and to make positive changes to his lifestyle. No longer having to work long hours enabled Alan to spend more time with his family, and to do things that he enjoyed. He developed some new leisure interests, including hiking, sailing and golf. The reduction in stress made him happier and easier to live with, and his relationship with his wife improved. So while the closure of the business seemed like a disaster at the time, in retrospect Alan realized that it was actually a good thing.*

## COPING STATEMENTS

Sometimes even a very simple statement can remind us of a more reasonable perspective and so put a stop to catastrophic thoughts. The following list provides examples of coping statements that can be useful to short-circuit catastrophic ruminations. You might like to prepare a statement from the list, to use when you need it. Alternatively, you can create your own coping statement, tailoring it to challenge your own particular thoughts.

> SAMPLE COPING STATEMENTS
> ➤ Relax!
> ➤ This too will pass.
> ➤ I have done what I can. Now it's out of my hands.
> ➤ One day at a time.
> ➤ Not my problem!
> ➤ Whatever happens, I will cope.
> ➤ Wait and see.
> ➤ I have the right to make mistakes.
> ➤ It's a pain in the neck but it's not a disaster!
> ➤ Will this matter in five years' time?
> ➤ How bad is this on the awfulness scale?

To stay mindful of your coping statement, it can be helpful to write it down and strategically display it in a spot where you will see it. The fridge door, the computer screen, the car dashboard or the clear section of your wallet are good locations. Valerie stuck a little "R" on to the face of her watch. Each time she looked at her watch, she received a timely reminder—her "R" stood for "Relax!"

## SOCRATIC QUESTIONING

When we are in a highly anxious state, our cognitions tend to be biased. We selectively focus on our feared situations, overestimate the likelihood of worst-case scenarios and predict catastrophic consequences. Socratic questioning can be a useful tool for addressing biased thoughts because it helps us to objectively evaluate our cognitions and challenge catastrophic predictions. The following Socratic questions are useful for evaluating worrying thoughts:

1. Describe the situation that you are worried about.
2. What specifically do you fear might happen?
3. Rate the likelihood that this will happen (from 0 to 100 percent).
4. What evidence supports your worrying thoughts?
5. What evidence does not support them?
6. If it did happen, what actions could you take?
7. Realistically, what is the worst thing that can happen?
8. What is the best thing that can happen?
9. What is most likely to happen?
10. Are there any useful actions that you can take now?

11. What would you tell a friend who was in your situation?
12. Realistically, re-rate the likelihood that your fears will be realized
     (from 0 to 100 percent).

Sid, a self-employed tax consultant, is extremely anxious over the advice that he recently gave to one of his major clients. He uses Socratic questioning to evaluate and challenge his catastrophic cognitions about this event.

## Socratic questioning

**1. Describe the situation that you are worried about.**
Owing to recent changes in the tax laws, the advice that I gave one of my major clients turned out to be incorrect. This has caused them substantial inconvenience.

**2. What specifically do you fear might happen?**
They may stop using my services, which could mean a decline in my future business. They might also criticize me to other people in the industry, which might have a negative effect on my reputation and income.

**3. Rate the likelihood that this will happen (from 0 to 100 percent).**
50 percent

**4. What evidence supports your worrying thoughts?**
I spoke to their senior partner several times this week, and he expressed his concerns and was a bit curt with me. He pointed out that the error could result in major problems for the firm.

**5. What evidence does not support them?**
After my explanation of the circumstances, he sounded more relaxed. They have always been happy with my services in the past. The problem is fixable. I have spoken to the tax office, and have been given advice on how to resolve it.

**6. If it did happen, what actions could you take?**
If they did stop using my services and my business declined, I would need to rebuild my client base by using the strategies that I used to build up my business in the past.

**7. Realistically, what is the worst thing that can happen?**
I could lose their business, and they could tell some other people in the industry that I am no good. I could lose some other clients as well.

**8. What is the best thing that can happen?**
The problem will be resolved quickly, and they will respond positively to the way I handled it. They will continue to have a good relationship with me, and there will be no negative effect on my reputation or business.

**9. What is most likely to happen?**
They might be concerned, but will not be unreasonable. It won't have any adverse effect on my business or reputation.

**10. Are there any useful actions that you can take now?**

I need to write them a letter restating all the information we discussed on the phone, acknowledging my responsibility and my plan to resolve the problems, and thanking them for their patience. Also, send the senior partners complimentary tickets to the theater as a goodwill gesture.

**11. What would you tell a friend who was in your situation?**

You have a good relationship with the company and with most of your clients. You have taken responsibility for the error and have agreed to cover any costs associated it. Because you have dealt with them for many years, it is easier for your client to stay with you than to start again with another accountant. And even if they do stop using you services, your business might decline, but it is unlikely to suffer significantly.

**12. Realistically, rerate the likelihood that your fears will be realized.**

5 percent

In many anxiety-provoking situations, it is helpful to work on problem solving in combination with Socratic questioning. In the following example, Vesna needs to take greater control over her business, as well as her catastrophic thinking:

> *Vesna has recently started up her own business, importing shoes and bags from Italy and selling them to American retailers. Although she is doing quite well, Vesna is constantly worried. She feels anxious when she wakes up in the morning and thinks about all the things that need to be done. When Vesna gets to work and starts on a particular task, she is often distracted by telephone calls and faxes, and loses track of what she was doing. At the end of each day, several jobs have been commenced but not completed, so she is often unsatisfied. Vesna also gets anxious about having to make decisions. She is aware that she is reasonably inexperienced and has already made some costly mistakes.*

### 1. Problem-solve

Vesna writes down her goals for the business and all the things that she needs to do in their order of importance. She breaks down the larger jobs into small manageable tasks. To help her stay focused, Vesna writes a daily to-do list and displays the list in a prominent position. Listing her most pressing jobs in order of importance gives Vesna a focus to her day, which increases her sense of control, and helps her to feel calmer. Her next challenge is to work her way through the list, staying focused on the top-priority jobs, moving away from distractions and returning to high-priority tasks when distractions are inevitable.

Vesna also calls some of her distributors and asks for practical advice on various matters, including popular stock items, likely demand and ordering practices. She also calls Sam, a friend with extensive experience in running a business. Sam provides her with additional advice on ordering, shipping and tax requirements. Getting information and advice helps Vesna to make more informed decisions, and this also increases her confidence. Next she challenges her worrying thoughts, using Socratic questioning:

## 2. Socratic questioning

**1. Describe the situation that you are worried about.**

I am worried that I am not fully in control of the business, and that ultimately it will collapse.

**2. What specifically do you fear might happen?**

There will be too much work for me to manage. I may not be able to sort out the orders and keep up deliveries, so my cash flow will dry up, and I won't be able to pay my accounts. Then the business will go broke, and I will end up poor.

**3. Rate the likelihood that this will happen (from 0 to 100 percent).**

60 percent

**4. What evidence supports your worrying thoughts?**

I am not very experienced. I have made some costly mistakes.

I have problems with managing stock.

The store room is disorganized, and my ordering system is not up-to-date.

**5. What evidence does not support them?**

I have been operating for six months and am making a profit. My outlets continue to place orders, and the stock is selling well. Feedback from distributors has been positive. I still manage to meet all of my orders, in spite of being disorganized.

**6. If it did happen, what actions could you take?**

If the business failed, I would sell off my remaining stock, either on sale or to my current distributors. I would lose some money, but probably not a huge amount. Then I would have to get a job.

**7. Realistically, what is the worst thing that can happen?**

I will have to close the business and will lose some of the money that I invested.

**8. What is the best thing that can happen?**

As I become more experienced I will manage the business more efficiently, and with time it will become very lucrative.

**9. What is most likely to happen?**

Things will get easier after this initial learning period. As I gain more experience, I should be able to manage it better, and the business will run more efficiently. It will probably do OK.

**10. Are there any useful actions that you can take now?**

I need to keep learning and improving my work practices. I need to spend more time talking to Sam—getting more information and advice. Also, I need to stay goal-focused every day, and avoid getting distracted by low-priority tasks.

## 11. What would you tell a friend who was in your situation?

You are taking greater control over the business as you continue to learn, and things are getting easier. You have been successful in most ventures that you have taken on in the past, in spite of always worrying about them. The business is doing quite well, and as long as you stay focused on your daily goals, it should continue to do well. Even if it doesn't work out in the end, you can sell off your stock and you won't lose too much money.

## 12. Realistically, rerate the likelihood that your fears will be realized.

20 percent

---

**EXERCISE 6.5**

Think of an issue that you are currently worried about. Use the Socratic questions listed above to evaluate and challenge your worrying thoughts about this issue. When you have finished, read over your responses and observe any changes in your level of anxiety.

---

## BUT WHAT IF I AM NOT THINKING ANYTHING?

It is not uncommon for people to experience anxiety without being aware of any particular thoughts. People will often say, "I got anxious, but I wasn't thinking anything." Others may wake up with strong anxiety but do not know why. As we saw in chapter 2, not all cognitions are immediately available to our conscious mind—some are unconscious. Sometimes we can bring unconscious thoughts to our awareness by asking questions such as, "What is happening for me right now? Why am I feeling unsafe?" Once we are able to work out the underlying cognitions, we can challenge them with cognitive or behavioral strategies.

> *Remy is often anxious when she gets home from work but she is not sure why. After some thought, she realizes that her anxiety stems from being alone at home and not knowing how to use her time.*

✳

> *Rupert was unable to identify the thoughts associated with his anxiety until he talked it over with his friend. He subsequently realized that his anxiety was caused by procrastination over outstanding tasks, including some difficult telephone calls and completing his tax return.*

Many people also experience **free floating anxiety**, which may be intermittent or persistent, and not clearly attached to any particular issue. It is a common feature of anxiety disorders, especially GAD. Free floating anxiety is sometimes caused by biological or hormonal processes (e.g., premenstrual hormonal changes, caffeine intake or withdrawal from tranquilizer drugs) and not directly related to cognitions. More often it is the result of *hypervigilance*—our brain is constantly switched onto the possibility of danger. In evolutionary terms, it is the equivalent to having a saber-toothed tiger patrolling the entrance of our cave—we cannot let go of our guard, just in case the tiger enters and attacks. Deep relaxation techniques such as progressive muscle relaxation, breathing exercises and meditation (see pages 141–144) are often useful for managing free-floating anxiety. Identifying and challenging anxiety-provoking cognitions, using graded exposure and disputing are also frequently beneficial

# EXPOSURE

While cognitive strategies are useful for managing catastrophic cognitions that arise in specific situations, when we are dealing with *regular or ongoing fears* (such as public speaking, attending social functions, traveling on public transit, spending time alone or driving on a freeway), exposure exercises are the most powerful tools of all. This is because we learn through direct experience that our fears are unjustified.

## CONFRONT YOUR FEARS

Most of us instinctively avoid the situations that we fear. However, avoidance simply reinforces the perception that the feared situation is threatening, and so it strengthens those fears over time. It also reduces our ability to deal with the situations we fear and lowers our confidence in our ability to solve problems. If we do not confront our demons at some stage, we never learn to overcome them.

*The golden rule when it comes to anxiety—AVOID AVOIDANCE.*

Exposing ourselves to the things that we are afraid of enables us to discover that they are not harmful or terrible after all. The more often you stand up in front of that group of people, get on that dreaded plane, make that phone call or assertively say what you want, the easier it becomes the next time you need to do it.

*Rene has felt anxious about being alone at home at night ever since her husband passed away. She has tried to avoid her anxiety by staying at her daughter's house as often as possible, and sometimes arranging for her adult son to sleep over at her house. This provides a temporary solution, however, it does not solve the problem—she cannot expect her children to be there all the time. By avoiding her most feared situation (being alone at night), Rene actually perpetuates her anxiety. Although she does not like the idea, Rene needs to gradually expose herself to the situation that she fears. By allowing herself to be alone at night, in spite of her anxiety, Rene gradually comes to find the situation less frightening.*

Sometimes, when the situation we need to confront is especially scary, it is a good idea to expose ourselves gradually, one step at a time, using whatever support or resources we can muster along the way. This is called **graded exposure** because rather than jumping into the deep end, we confront our fears gradually. For Rene, it might be useful to initially have one of her children stay with her each evening, but to go home after she has gone to bed. Then, after a week or two, her children might continue to visit each evening, but leave before Rene goes to bed. After another week they might drop in for only an hour each evening or just speak to her on the telephone to reassure her that she is safe. Graded exposure is a gentle way of confronting our feared situation because we give ourselves a chance to adjust as we ease ourselves towards our goal.

*Frances worked as a senior administrator in a government department for five years. While she initially enjoyed her job, some subsequent changes in staffing brought her into direct conflict with a new supervisor. After receiving a negative performance appraisal, followed by some tension and acrimony, Frances finally packed her things and submitted her letter of resignation. As she felt emotionally bruised by the experience, Frances decided to give herself a few weeks to recover before applying for another job. Unfortunately, over this time she lost confidence in her ability to work and now, eight weeks later, Frances still can't bring herself to apply for another job. The problem is that the longer she avoids looking for a job, the more threatening the idea of job-seeking becomes. As difficult as it may seem at the moment, Frances needs to accept her feelings of anxiety, and start taking some action towards getting back into the workforce.*

In order to ease herself in gradually, Frances might initially take on some voluntary work or help out in her brother-in-law's business. Alternatively, she might begin by applying to do some work in an area that she is overqualified for, at a low rate of pay, and then once her confidence has returned, she could apply for more challenging jobs.

## DEALING WITH PANIC ATTACKS

In situations where we are experiencing high levels of anxiety, the accompanying physical symptoms become more intense. Heart palpitations, tightness in the chest, difficulty in breathing, chest pain, tremor, sweating and dizziness frequently accompany high levels of anxiety. This can be experienced as a panic attack. Sometimes the perception of even mild physical symptoms can cause anxiety to increase and consequently trigger a panic attack. For instance, if you feel your heart pounding, your chest constricting or your breathing becoming difficult, you may find yourself panicking. Thoughts like, "I'm going to have a heart attack," "I am going to collapse," "I am going to run out of air," "I am going to lose control and go berserk" or "I'm going to die" cause the anxiety to escalate, which in turn causes your heart to pound even harder, and your breathing to become faster. Rapid breathing often results in hyperventilation—a condition where the level of oxygen in the blood becomes too high relative to the level of carbon dioxide. This causes further chemical changes, which give rise to unpleasant symptoms such as light-headedness, confusion, jitters, dizziness, numbness or tingling in the extremities, chest pain and sweating.

Panic attacks are triggered by unpleasant physical symptoms of anxiety and become more intense as we panic about the symptoms themselves. This is sometimes referred to as the anxiety cycle because the physical symptoms of anxiety become a source of threat, causing our anxiety to escalate. This in turn causes us to panic even more, which causes the symptoms to escalate further.

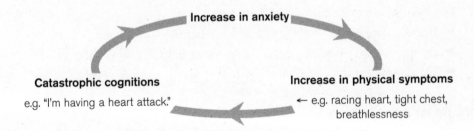

**Increase in anxiety**

**Catastrophic cognitions**
e.g. "I'm having a heart attack."

**Increase in physical symptoms**
← e.g. racing heart, tight chest, breathlessness

In order to short-circuit this process, we need to challenge the catastrophic cognitions that maintain it. Thoughts like "I'm going to lose control" or "I might run out of air" fuel the panic attack and can sustain it for long periods. It is important to realize that the physical symptoms that accompany anxiety and panic are not harmful—they are simply unpleasant. Although you may feel unsafe, the reality is that the physical symptoms you experience during a panic attack are completely harmless. You will not have a heart attack, you will not be unable to breathe, you will not collapse or die, you will not go mad and you will not damage your health in any way. The worst thing that can happen is that you will feel unpleasant sensations.

## Observe the sensations

The most powerful technique for overcoming panic attacks is to observe the physical sensations like a scientist observing an experiment, without trying to control them. Notice how your anxiety feels and remind yourself that it is just the fight-or-flight response. Let your body do what it needs to do and challenge any catastrophic cognitions with rational self-talk (see following page). Most people are amazed to discover that when they stop panicking about the physical sensations, the sensations fizzle out within a few minutes.

Some experts also advocate slowing down your breathing (see the slow breathing exercises on page 144) during a panic attack. This can reverse the effects of hyperventilation and in so doing diminish the unpleasant symptoms that it causes. Slow breathing has the same effect as breathing into a paper bag (which used to be recommended for treating panic attacks in the past), as it reduces the imbalance of oxygen to carbon dioxide in the bloodstream that is caused by hyperventilation. Many people misguidedly breathe *deeply* in an effort to control their anxiety, however, by taking in greater amounts of oxygen, make their symptoms worse. Remember that the aim is to breathe slow normal breaths, not big deep breaths.

While the reduction in symptoms brought about by slow breathing can increase your sense of control during a panic attack, and so reduce your fear, *breathing control is not necessary for stopping a panic attack.* Even if you do no more than observe the physical sensations without catastrophizing, the symptoms will pass within a few minutes.

RATIONAL SELF-TALK DURING A PANIC ATTACK
➤ It's only the fight-or-flight response—it's harmless.
➤ Let my body do what it needs to do—don't fight it, just observe it.
➤ This is unpleasant, but it's not harmful.

## Exposure for panic attacks

In addition to challenging catastrophic cognitions via our self-talk, we can also challenge them behaviorally through systematic exposure to the situations we fear. Exposure exercises for panic attacks involve repeatedly confronting the situations we fear might trigger a panic attack and remaining in those situations until the fear subsides. This process leads to what is called "disconfirmation"—the realization that our catastrophic predictions were incorrect. When it comes to panic attacks, exposure is extremely powerful because we learn directly through our experience that the situation is actually harmless.

*Ben had a disturbing experience when he was shopping in a large department store two years ago. He was feeling unwell at the time, and as he made his way towards the exit he became dizzy and disorientated. Ben became aware of his heart pounding and he struggled to catch his breath. For a moment he thought that he might collapse.*

Ever since that time, Ben has been checking himself, trying to make sure that the symptoms do not return. On occasions when he notices his heart beating faster or his dizziness returning—usually at shopping centers, on public transportation or at the movies—Ben escapes as quickly as he can. In fact, Ben tries to avoid going out to public places because having a panic attack there could be embarrassing and hard to escape. What Ben doesn't realize is that avoiding those situations perpetuates the problem because he does not get the opportunity to discover that his fears are unfounded.

A second problem is that Ben is paying excessive attention to his physical symptoms. Because he is terrified of the prospect of further panic attacks, Ben constantly monitors his body for any sign of arousal. This is called **hypervigilance**, and it is self-defeating because focusing on his physical sensations makes Ben *more* anxious, which in turn *increases* his physical arousal and the likelihood of further panic attacks.

In summary, there are two key strategies for overcoming panic attacks:

## 1. Decatastrophize

During the panic attack, observe the sensations like a scientist observing an experiment, as described earlier. Remind yourself that the symptoms are just the fight-or-flight response—unpleasant, but totally harmless. Use realistic self-talk to help you ride out the sensations without trying to run away from them.

## 2. Graded exposure exercises

Use graded exposure exercises to confront your anxiety. This involves repeatedly entering the situations you fear—working through them from the least to the most anxiety-provoking—and remaining in those situations for long enough to allow your anxiety to diminish.

To prepare a plan for graded exposure, you need to write down all the situations that you avoid—or that generate substantial anxiety—and then order them from the least to the most anxiety-provoking. Write these down in descending order on your Exposure Schedule (see following page). Once your plan is complete, your next task is to commence exposure to the least anxiety-provoking situations—the ones at the top of your schedule. It is important to maintain your exposure until your anxiety drops to a lower level. *It will drop* if you remain in the situation for long enough, so it's important not to run away. Repeat this exercise as many times as it takes for your anxiety to disappear. Usually this requires just a few exposures, but for some deeply held fears many exposures may be necessary. Start working on the next task of your exposure schedule as soon as you feel ready—you can do this even while you are still working on some of the easier exercises.

### Secrets of successful exposure

- **Repetition:** Do the same exercise repeatedly—the more often you practice, the lower your anxiety.
- **Duration:** Don't "dip your toe in and run away." Stay in the feared situation as long as is necessary for your anxiety to diminish. It *will* diminish if you stay there for long enough.

- **Challenge:** Each exposure exercise should be anxiety-provoking but not so overwhelming that it feels unbearable.
- **Daily practice:** Do some exposure exercises every day.
- **Look for spontaneous opportunities** to confront your fears. Take advantage of opportunities to practice exposure whenever they arise, even in unplanned situations.

### EXPOSURE SCHEDULE

| Exercise | Trial 1 | Trial 2 | Trial 3 | Trial 4 | Trial 5 | Trial 6 | Trial 7 |
|---|---|---|---|---|---|---|---|
|  |  |  |  |  |  |  |  |
|  |  |  |  |  |  |  |  |
|  |  |  |  |  |  |  |  |
|  |  |  |  |  |  |  |  |
|  |  |  |  |  |  |  |  |
|  |  |  |  |  |  |  |  |
|  |  |  |  |  |  |  |  |

**Record:** Date, length of exposure, highest level of anxiety experienced (0 = no anxiety; 100 = unbearable anxiety).

In order to work on his fear of being in public places, Ben writes himself a plan for graded exposure exercises. He lists all the situations he has been avoiding. Next he puts them in order, from the least to the most anxiety-provoking. He then sets himself the task of repeatedly confronting each of these situations, beginning with the least anxiety-provoking situations. Here is Ben's exposure schedule:

**BEN'S EXPOSURE SCHEDULE**

| Exercise | Trial 1 | Trial 2 | Trial 3 | Trial 4 | Trial 5 | Trial 6 | Trial 7 |
|---|---|---|---|---|---|---|---|
| Go to supermarket with wife. | May 4 15 mins 70 | May 7 20 mins 65 | May 11 35 mins 45 | May 16 45 mins 30 | May 22 15 mins 10 | May 24 10 mins 10 | |
| Go to supermarket alone. | May 12 15 mins 50 | May 14 25 mins 60 | May 15 10 mins 50 | May 17 25 mins 30 | May 20 15 mins 20 | May 23 25 mins 10 | May 26 15 mins 0 |
| Catch bus for three stops during quiet period. | May 20 5 mins 80 | May 22 5 mins 80 | May 23 5 mins 65 | May 26 5 mins 20 | May 29 5 mins 10 | | |
| Catch bus all the way to the city during quiet period. | May 26 25 mins 70 | May 29 25 mins 50 | May 31 25 mins 60 | June 6 25 mins 30 | June 9 25 mins 10 | June 13 25 mins 0 | June 17 25 mins 0 |
| Catch bus to city during peak hour. | June 10 35 mins 90 | June 12 30 mins 60 | June 15 35 mins 20 | June 16 30 mins 40 | June 19 35 mins 10 | June 22 35 mins 10 | |
| Go to movies. | June 1 1.25 hrs 80 | June 6 1.5 hrs 70 | June 9 1.5 hrs 40 | June 12 2 hrs 20 | June 19 2 hrs 20 | June 26 1.5 hrs 10 | |
| Catch a ferry. | June 14 30 mins 90 | June 19 30 mins 90 | June 25 35 mins 60 | June 30 30 mins 70 | July 3 30 mins 60 | July 5 30 mins 20 | July 10 30 mins 10 |

Doing graded exposure exercises every day enables Ben's fears to gradually dissipate and makes his world safe once again. As the panic attacks disappear, so too do his irrational fears of being in public places and the desire to avoid them.

Graded exposure exercises are useful not just for overcoming panic attacks, but for conquering all types of fear. The same technique is highly effective for overcoming fears such as public speaking anxiety, fear of attending social functions, fear of driving following a car accident or fear of spending time alone. In each case, we need to write down all the situations that we find scary, in relation to that fear, and then order them from least to most anxiety-provoking. As in the above example, we then need to begin exposure to the least anxiety-provoking situations, and gradually work our way through to the more challenging situations.

Although real-life exposure produces the fastest and most effective recovery, sometimes it can be useful to practice exposure through visualizing the situations we fear. This can pave the way for actual exposure, when a situation initially feels too frightening to confront in the flesh. It can also provide the opportunity to practice when our feared situations are difficult to access frequently in real life, such as flying, thunderstorms or snakes.

## Exposure through imagery

Many of our fears are stored inside our mind primarily as images. For instance, if you are anxious about needing to confront someone, you may have a mental image of an angry, abusive confrontation. Or if you are anxious about having to give a speech, you may have a picture of yourself looking flustered as members of the audience "tear you to shreds." Visual imagery can help to reduce anxiety by providing additional exposure and the opportunity to reframe the negative images held in our mind.

Imagery is more powerful when we give it our full attention. For this reason it can be helpful to spend a little time relaxing your body before you start visualizing. Try to evoke all the sensations that characterize the situation, such as the colors, sounds and smells that you associate with it. Spend a few minutes just "being there"—observing the scene and feeling the sensations. Now see yourself coping, doing whatever it is that you need to do, feeling in control. Stay with the imagery for several minutes and finally, when you feel ready, allow it to fade away. As with most of these techniques, coping imagery is most effective when it is practiced frequently—ideally twice daily for at least a week.

> *Ross is anxious about having to present a paper at an approaching World Congress in New York. He worries that he will be so anxious that he won't be able to speak properly, and that people will see how nervous he is. Because much of his anxiety is created by catastrophic thinking ("It could be an absolute disaster") and rigid beliefs ("I must appear totally calm and in control") it would be helpful for Ross to initially challenge his thinking via cognitive strategies such as Socratic questioning.*

In addition, Ross can use visual imagery to expose himself to his feared situation and create positive associations with the event. For instance, he might visualize himself walking into the presentation room, sitting down and awaiting his turn to speak, being introduced, moving up to the podium, facing the audience and then starting his presentation. He can see himself speaking at a relaxed pace, focusing on the points that he has prepared. The speech goes well, and the audience applauds when he concludes. Regular exposure to this image (twice a day for the two weeks leading up to the conference) helps Ross to familiarize himself with the situation, which subsequently becomes less threatening. Having reasonable expectations ("I'll do an adequate job") rather than perfectionist expectations ("I'll be the best") also helps Ross to avoid putting excessive pressure on himself. Combining cognitive techniques with imagery enables Ross to keep his anxiety in check and to cope effectively on the big day.

# RELAXATION TECHNIQUES

As we have already seen, the increase in vigilance and muscle tension that happens during the fight-or-flight response enables us to be more alert and helps us move quickly and efficiently if we need to protect ourselves. However, when we are anxious much of the time, we experience an ongoing state of vigilance, and our muscles tense up for long periods. After a while this may feel normal, and we forget how it feels to relax—physically or psychologically. Practicing deep relaxation on a regular basis (at least once a day) helps to lower physical arousal and enables us to feel more calm and in control. It also teaches us to recognize the tension that we normally carry and in doing so enables us to identify and release tension before it escalates. Learning how to relax our body also gives us a valuable skill that we can use to reduce arousal during periods of high anxiety

Deep relaxation is not the same thing as the normal relaxation that we experience when we put our feet up at the end of the day, go for a walk or listen to our favorite music. It is a deeper, more profound state, which is accompanied by physical changes. These include:

> ➤ a slowdown in the rate of our heartbeat
> ➤ a slowdown in our breathing rate
> ➤ a drop in blood pressure
> ➤ a relaxation of muscle tension
> ➤ a drop in oxygen consumption (metabolic rate).

Notice that these changes are the exact opposite of those that occur during the fight-or-flight response. When we create a state of deep relaxation, we undo the physical changes brought on by high levels of arousal, and consequently release the unpleasant symptoms that accompany anxiety. In fact it is virtually impossible to be deeply relaxed and anxious at the same time.

While deep relaxation is not a "magic bullet," it is one of the useful tools that can help to keep our anxiety under control. It is best thought of as a maintenance technique which, when practiced regularly, helps us to stay relaxed. Regular practice also increases our perception of control over potentially stressful situations.

There are three main techniques that we can use to bring about a state of deep relaxation—progressive muscle relaxation, visual imagery and meditation. In addition, breathing exercises can be used to lower our level of physical arousal at times when we feel acutely anxious.

## PROGRESSIVE MUSCLE RELAXATION

Progressive muscle relaxation is a physical process which involves relaxing the body by systematically working through the major muscle groups—the feet, lower legs, thighs, tummy, chest, shoulders, arms, hands, neck and face. It can be done by sequentially focusing on each muscle group and consciously relaxing the muscles. Alternatively, each group of muscles can be tensed up for a few seconds and then relaxed. Many people find that briefly tensing muscles before relaxing them helps to achieve a deeper state of physical relaxation. After relaxing a muscle group, we need to spend a little time observing the sensations, and allowing the muscles to relax a little more, before moving onto the next area. It is important not to rush this process, as deep relaxation of muscles cannot be achieved in a hurry. A good progressive muscle relaxation exercise takes at least ten minutes.

## MEDITATION

This is a mental process that involves releasing our usual thinking patterns and using the mind to experience inner stillness. The most common meditation techniques involve focusing on a particular object or thing while passively releasing any thoughts that arise during this process. The object of focus may be a part of the body (such as our lungs, heart or the point between our eyes), the breath, a word or sound that is repeated mentally or out loud (mantra), an external sound such as music, waves or bird sounds, a physical object (such as a candle or picture) or a visualized image or symbol. Another technique that has received a lot of attention in recent times is called "mindfulness meditation," which involves passively attending to our experiences, thoughts, feelings and physical sensations in a detached, non-judgmental way. Although it can be practiced in a passive, sitting position, mindfulness meditation can also be practiced while eating, walking, washing or doing any activity (see Recommended Reading).

Most people find meditation to be more challenging than progressive muscle relaxation because the mind is naturally inclined to wander. Maintaining our focus for more than a few seconds at a time is not easy and, like most skills, requires practice. It is therefore important not to become too concerned about intrusive thoughts that inevitably arise during meditation. Once you become aware that your mind has strayed, gently let go of the thoughts and return to the object of your focus.

Meditation has a calming effect if it is practiced for twenty minutes at least once a day, ideally at the same time each day. It is not a good idea to meditate immediately after a heavy meal, as digestion makes us drowsy and increases our chances of falling asleep. For the same reason, it is better to practice meditation in a seated rather than lying position. The aim is to experience a quiet, wakeful state—not to fall asleep. Starting the session with a progressive muscle relaxation exercise can help us to settle, however, it may also bring on sleep. If you frequently fall asleep during meditation, try practicing earlier in the day or soon after physical exercise. It may also be a good idea to increase your level of discomfort by sitting on a firm, upright chair or sitting forwards in the chair so that your back is unsupported. A small degree of discomfort is not detrimental to the meditation experience, and stops you from falling asleep.

## CALMING VISUAL IMAGERY

Visualizing calming imagery can help us to release tension, reduce physical arousal and deepen our level of relaxation. It can be a helpful adjunct to progressive muscle relaxation and meditation or it may be used independently of other relaxation techniques. Some people have a natural ability to visualize easily, while others need to practice in order to acquire the skill.

When using visual imagery, we try to immerse ourselves in a peaceful setting. The most widely used settings are nature scenes (rainforest, beach, countryside, waterfall, beautiful garden), dream-like imagery (floating on a cloud or on a magic carpet) or having a guardian angel or inner guide. The more vivid our imagery, the deeper the experience. For this reason it helps to add as much sensory detail as possible. Try to imagine the sounds, colors, shapes, textures, smells, temperature and physical sensations that you associate with the scene. Hear the crackling of leaves under your feet and the sound of the birds as you make your way through the forest. Smell the damp sweet odor of the undergrowth, see the brightly colored wild flowers that grow near the track, feel the rough textures of the ancient trees ...

While these techniques are most effective when practiced for at least twenty minutes a day, mini-relaxation sessions can also have a calming effect. Short bursts of relaxation or calming imagery can help us to relax at times when we find ourselves becoming tense. Simply close your eyes for a minute or two, relax your body, concentrate on your breathing and use your calming imagery to help you to relax. Even two minutes of relaxation can lower our level of arousal and help us to feel calmer.

There are many CDs on the market that provide step-by-step instructions for practicing meditation, progressive muscle relaxation and calming imagery. Using external guidance from a CD is probably the easiest way to learn these techniques, as it frees us from thinking about what to do next.

## BREATHING EXERCISES

While techniques such as progressive muscle relaxation, meditation and visualization are useful for managing moderate levels of anxiety, they are less helpful for dealing with acute anxiety or a panic attack. When our level of physical arousal is very high, it is difficult to relax using deep relaxation techniques. This is where breathing exercises can be helpful.

The way we breathe generally reflects the way we feel. When we are calm and relaxed our breathing is slow and rhythmic. When we are anxious or panicky our breathing becomes fast and shallow. Intense anxiety can cause hyperventilation which, as we saw earlier, gives rise to a number of unpleasant symptoms. Although not harmful, these sensations often cause anxiety to increase and sometimes bring on a panic attack (see page 134).

While our breathing reflects our level of physical arousal, we can also use the breath to regulate arousal and reduce feelings of anxiety or panic. By consciously *slowing down* our breathing, we can prevent or stop hyperventilation, lower our level of physical arousal, and eliminate many of the unpleasant sensations caused by hyperventilation. In addition, focusing on the breath distracts from catastrophic cognitions and so can prevent the anxiety from escalating.

### Diaphragmatic breathing

This type of breathing involves consciously directing breath down into the lower lungs. To do this we use our diaphragm (the muscle separating our lung cavity from the abdominal cavity) to direct air into the bottom part of our lungs. You can monitor your breath by placing your hands on your chest at the bottom of your rib cage, just above the navel, so that the tips of your middle fingers just touch. As you direct your breath slowly into your lower lungs, you will feel your fingertips being forced apart slightly by the expansion of your abdomen. As you breathe out, you will feel your fingertips touching again. Breathing slowly and rhythmically using diaphragmatic breathing is in itself a very effective technique for controlling high levels of arousal or hyperventilation.

### Slow breathing with a pause

Take in a slow diaphragmatic breath while counting to three, pause for a moment, and then exhale through your nose while counting to three. Repeat this process, continuing to breathe in a slow, regular rhythm, using diaphragmatic breathing.

### Rhythmic breathing

Take in one diaphragmatic breath, and hold it to the count of ten. Breathe out slowly, thinking the word "relax" as you do so. Then breathe in to the count of three and out to the count of three, mentally saying "relax" at the end of each out-breath. Do this for ten breaths, and then take another diaphragmatic breath and count to ten. Keep repeating this process for at least three minutes or until your anxiety drops.

# IN SUMMARY

➤ Anxiety is a feeling of apprehension that comes with the perception that something bad might happen. It is accompanied by physical arousal and increased muscle tension, which are symptoms of the fight-or-flight response—a primal reaction to perceived threat.

➤ Everyone experiences anxiety at times, however, people who tend to be anxious by nature experience frequent or ongoing anxiety. Some people suffer from anxiety disorders, which can have serious effects on their ability to function and feel well. These need to be treated by mental-health specialists.

➤ Problem solving—looking for solutions—is often a helpful first step for resolving anxiety-provoking situations.

➤ Faulty thinking habits that contribute to anxiety include catastrophic thinking, excessive need for approval, perfectionism and excessive need for control. These patterns of thinking can often be challenged effectively through behavioral disputing.

➤ Socratic questions can help us to evaluate and challenge faulty and catastrophic thinking and are particularly useful for worrying thoughts.

➤ Anxiety is fueled and sustained through avoidance. Directly confronting the things that we fear helps us to overcome anxiety. Graded exposure and behavioral experiments (such as shame attacking exercises) enable us to discover that the things we fear are not so terrible after all.

➤ Breathing techniques, deep relaxation practice and meditation can help to induce a state of calm and reduce some of the unpleasant physical sensations that accompany anxiety.

# SEVEN

# Maintaining Self-esteem

One of the main factors differentiating humans from other animals is the awareness of self: the ability to form an identity and then attach a value to it. In other words, you have the capacity to define who you are and then decide if you like that identity or not. The problem with self-esteem is the human capacity for judgment.

MATTHEW McKAY AND PATRICK FANNING, *SELF-ESTEEM*

Our self-esteem is a perception—it is the way that we perceive our own worth as human beings. Of all of our perceptions, our self-esteem is the most important, as it has a major impact on every aspect of our lives. Our self-esteem affects the way we feel much of the time. Poor self-esteem can cause us to feel guilty, inadequate, ashamed, anxious or depressed. It affects our ability to relax and feel comfortable with others and determines who we feel worthy of to have as friends and partner. Our self-esteem may affect the type of work that we do, the risks that we are willing to take and our willingness to be assertive in our dealings with others. Most importantly, our self-esteem affects our ability to feel happy and safe in our world—to know that we have a right to be here, and that we are as worthy and valid as every other person on this planet.

Self-esteem is not the same thing as self-confidence. We may be confident about our ability to do certain things, but still have low self-esteem. For instance, we may feel confident in our ability to do our job, give a speech, repair a computer, run a marathon, host a successful dinner party or perform at a concert. Knowing that we can do some things well does not mean that we perceive ourselves in a positive way. Our self-esteem is the way we appraise our total worth—not just our ability in certain areas.

*Since childhood, Susan has strived hard to be valued and accepted by others. She is bright, competent and attractive. At the age of thirty-four, she had built up her own successful public relations company, and by the age of forty, she could afford to retire. Colleagues respect her and friends admire her, yet in spite of her apparent success, Susan harbors feelings of inadequacy and self-doubt. She is highly sensitive to feedback from other people—even minor criticisms can send her into episodes of self-doubt and rumination. When things go wrong, Susan immediately blames herself and assumes that others must also be judging her harshly. Like many people, Susan has poor self-esteem. In spite of her confident outward appearance, Susan can't help thinking that she's just not good enough.*

# FACTORS THAT INFLUENCE OUR SELF-ESTEEM

Like all perceptions, the way that we think about ourselves is shaped by both our personality and our life experiences.

## PERSONALITY TRAITS

While self-esteem is not genetically determined, some of our inherent personality traits can influence the way that we interpret events, which in turn influence our self-esteem. For instance, a person who tends to be anxious is more likely to notice negative or threatening information (e.g., "She tuned out while I was talking to her') and to interpret such information in a negative way ("She obviously doesn't like me"). A person who is shy may make less effort to connect with other people and may therefore receive fewer socially reinforcing messages compared to someone who is friendly and outgoing. A person who is sensitive to social feedback is more likely to be affected by negative comments compared to someone who is not particularly sensitive.

## CHILDHOOD EXPERIENCES

Events that happened in our childhood can play a significant role in shaping our subsequent perceptions, including perceptions about our own worth. While parents are usually the most important influence, other people (siblings, grandparents, cousins, teachers and even school friends) also play a role. These people provided us with our earliest information regarding how valuable we are.

If, as a young child, the messages that you received suggested that you were defective in some way—inferior to others, worthless or unlovable, this is likely to have had an impact on the way that you perceived yourself then as well as now. How effectively we manage to shake off beliefs about our own inferiority or defectiveness depends on both our subsequent experiences and on our inherent resilience. Developing loving, supportive relationships during our adult lives can sometimes enable us to let go of earlier perceptions of worthlessness. Having a resilient nature—being able to think in a psychologically healthy way—can also protect us from the potentially scarring effects of negative childhood experiences.

## FEEDBACK FROM OTHERS

Our relationships with other people—friends, colleagues, acquaintances, partners and children—can affect the way we perceive ourselves. Feedback from others that informs us that we are loved, accepted and valued helps us to feel good about ourselves. Feedback suggesting that we are insignificant, unlikeable or worthless can make us feel inadequate. Having a partner or friends who tell you that you are wonderful, lovable and important to them helps to reinforce the perception that you are valued. On the other hand, a partner who frequently carps, criticizes and puts you down can make feeling good about yourself a major challenge.

## OTHER EXPERIENCES

Many other events that we experience over the course of our lives can influence the way we perceive ourselves. The loss of something that is an important part of our identity, such as our job, our health, our youth or a role that we play within our family or workplace can change the way we see ourselves. Similarly, experiences of failure in areas that matter to us, such as in our work, business, family role or education can have a negative impact on our self-esteem. Rejection by a significant person, such as a partner, family member or work colleague, can also have a negative impact on our self-esteem by reinforcing the perception that we are defective or unworthy. Positive experiences can have the opposite effect. Success in achieving a significant goal, feeling competent and effective in certain areas or receiving praise and recognition from other people can help us to feel good about ourselves.

While these factors can sometimes influence the way we feel about ourselves, ultimately, whether we feel diminished, uplifted or unaffected by these situations will depend on the way we *think about* our experiences. Realistic, psychologically healthy cognitions protect our self-esteem and enable us to maintain our sense of self-worth in the face of events such as failure, loss or rejection.

## SOCIAL CONDITIONING

In every society certain human qualities and achievements are highly valued, while others are ignored or discounted. As a result, we develop beliefs about how we should look, feel and behave. These beliefs or shoulds contribute to unhappiness in different areas of our lives (see chapter 2). Some of these beliefs play a particularly important role in the way we perceive our own worth. Typically they fall into three main categories:

BELIEFS ABOUT OUR APPEARANCE

➤ I should be slim and attractive.

➤ I should be youthful and sexy.

➤ I should be tall, muscular and have a full head of hair.

BELIEFS ABOUT OUR PERFORMANCE/ACHIEVEMENTS

➤ I should have a high-status, well-paid job.

➤ I should have a college education.

➤ I should be making lots of money.

➤ I should keep a clean, tidy house.

➤ I should have a successful business.

➤ I should have a high libido.

➤ I should be good at sports.

BELIEFS ABOUT OUR SOCIAL RELATIONSHIPS AND INTERACTIONS

➤ I should have lots of friends.

➤ I should be able to connect easily with everyone.

➤ I should be married or in a committed relationship.

➤ I should be going out with lots of people and having fun.

➤ People should like and approve of me.

# PATTERNS OF THINKING THAT DIMINISH SELF-ESTEEM

Many of the beliefs that cause us to feel inadequate or inferior stem from negative patterns of thinking. The most common include comparing ourselves with others, rating our worth through our achievements, having an excessive need for approval and labeling ourselves on the basis of our experiences. These ways of thinking, and strategies for challenging them, are demonstrated in the following section.

## COMPARING

*Recently Kathy ran into Andrea, an old school friend whom she hadn't seen for fifteen years. After some warm reminiscing, Andrea invited Kathy and her husband to come to her house for dinner on the following Saturday night. What a night it was! It turned out that Andrea lives in a beautiful house, in a salubrious suburb. Her husband, a partner in a well-known law firm, is charming and handsome. Their children go to a top private school and are both clever and sociable. The dinner was a culinary delight, beautifully presented on the finest dinnerware. The conversation was stimulating, and Andrea's children entertained the guests with some piano recitals. It had all the makings of a great night. So why did Kathy leave feeling so depressed?*

Kathy fell for the oldest trick in the book—comparing herself to other people. Most of us do it. Like Kathy, we are particularly prone to comparing ourselves to people whom we regard as our peers—those from our own social circle, family members, neighbors, people our own age and people in the same occupation as ourselves. We compare ourselves on things like our achievements, material wealth, appearance, friends, partners and even the successes of our children. Kathy could have left the dinner feeling excited, impressed, pleased for her friend, amazed, inspired or even indifferent. But she left feeling inadequate and depressed because she compared her own achievements and life circumstances with that of her friend, and found herself wanting.

Comparing ourselves with others invariably gets us into trouble. The problem is that there will always be people who are smarter than we are, who are thinner and more attractive, who have more friends, who go out more, who have a better sense of humor, who have more exciting sex, who make more money, who live in nicer houses and own better cars and who have more interesting things to say.

While all of this might sound depressing, keep in mind that the opposite is also true. There are also people who are far less attractive, less clever, less well-off, less sociable and less privileged than we are. The trouble is that we often disregard those who are less fortunate than ourselves, and compare ourselves with those we consider to be better off or more successful.

Some people try to deal with this issue by insisting that the so-called successful people of this world are not really all that happy after all—"Her husband is probably a lousy lover . . . they probably fight when no one is around," "Their children will probably grow up to be boring lawyers and stock brokers." It is true that external appearances can be deceptive—success may be an illusion—but we do not need to convince ourselves that other people are doing badly in order to feel OK about ourselves. A more healthy way of thinking is to acknowledge that some people are especially lucky, gifted or privileged, without begrudging their good fortune or using their success as a yardstick for our own worth. Instead we can set goals that are realistic and life-enhancing for us, and enjoy working towards them without making comparisons between us and them.

*Immediately after their graduation from college, Troy and his friend Peter started working at a large insurance company. In the six years that they have worked there, Peter has had several promotions and was recently promoted to a very senior position. Troy has also had some promotions, however his career has not progressed quite as quickly.*

| SITUATION | Peter told me that he has been promoted to operations manager. |
|---|---|
| FEELINGS | Felt upset—it was like a kick in the guts. |
| THOUGHTS | What about me? I've only had two promotions in the time that Peter has had four. Why wasn't I promoted to operations manager? |
| BELIEFS | Our career paths should move at exactly the same pace. Peter's rapid promotion shows that my progress is poor and that I'm a failure. |
| THINKING ERRORS | Comparing, shoulds, black-and-white thinking, labeling, personalizing. |
| DISPUTE | There is no reason why we must progress at the same pace. Peter is extremely talented and has an affable manner which makes people like him. His ability to do well is his good fortune and it does not mean that my progress is poor. His career success is not an indicator of my own failure. |
| POSITIVE ACTIONS | Focus on my own work. Try to upgrade my skills and set goals that are realistic for me. |

*Julie has developed a friendship with Rob, a work colleague she has known for years. Rob and Julie get on well, but recently Karen has joined the company, and Rob has been showing her a lot of attention. Julie often sees them talking and laughing together, and Rob appears to like her a lot. This makes Julie feel bad about herself.*

| SITUATION | Rob was talking to Karen at her desk for about ten minutes. |
|---|---|
| FEELINGS | I felt threatened and upset. |
| THOUGHTS | He obviously likes her a lot. He'll probably lose interest in me now. |
| BELIEFS | People only like me until someone better comes along. I always end up on the "B" team. The fact that Rob pays attention to Karen means that he thinks less of me and that I am not good enough. |
| THINKING ERRORS | Jumping to negative conclusions, personalizing, comparing |
| DISPUTE | Karen is quite charming—many people find her attractive. That's her good fortune. Rob's friendship with Karen doesn't mean that he thinks less of me. He is still friendly toward me. Even if Rob likes Karen a lot, that doesn't mean that she's better than me. We have different qualities, and I don't need to be like her in order to be OK. |
| POSITIVE ACTIONS | Stop focusing on Rob's behavior; continue to be friendly to both Rob and Karen. |

## RATING OUR WORTH THROUGH OUR ACHIEVEMENTS

In our society, certain accomplishments are frequently perceived as being desirable and important. Achievements related to material wealth, such as having a highly paid job, a successful business or expensive possessions, are status symbols to which many people aspire. Fame, physical beauty and academic status are also commonly sought after goals.

While there is nothing wrong with aiming towards any particular goal, problems arise when our achievements become the basis by which we value our own worth. Consciously or unconsciously, many people practice conditional self-acceptance—I am OK, as long as I make lots of money, have a successful business, have a high powered job, write that book, get that degree, buy that car or lose ten pounds.

In their book *Self-Esteem*, Patrick Fanning and Matthew McKay describe the "empty vessel" syndrome. That is, some people see themselves as empty vessels that are essentially worthless; they can only acquire worth through their achievements—"You might see yourself as essentially worthless, a body that moves and talks. You believe you have no intrinsic value—only the potential for doing something worthwhile and important."

The problem with measuring our worth by our achievements is that it makes us extremely vulnerable. You may feel good about yourself while you are doing well, but what about when things go wrong?

> *Dan has built up a lucrative importing business with an annual turnover of over $30 million. While his business was growing, Dan felt very good about himself. However, recently Dan made some risky investment decisions that resulted in a loss, and this, coupled with rising interest rates and a fall in the value of the dollar, created major difficulties. In the last twelve months Dan has lost a lot of money and has struggled to meet all of his financial commitments. Now Dan is suffering from depression and poor self-esteem. He blames himself for the downturn in his business and thinks of himself as a failure.*

Undoubtedly many people imagine that they would respond in exactly the same way if they were in Dan's shoes, however is it possible to think differently in the circumstances? For instance, could Dan be philosophical about the experience and see it as a learning opportunity? Could he recognize the downside of equating his achievements with his inherent worth and work towards self-acceptance? Although Dan believes that he deserves severe condemnation, does this serve any useful purpose?

While it is appropriate for Dan to go through a period of sadness and reflection, continuing to blame and label himself as a failure is irrational and self-defeating. It is irrational because Dan is rating his entire worth as a human being on the basis of just one criterion—his business performance. It is self-defeating because perceiving himself as a failure makes him feel inadequate and depressed and serves no useful purpose. A much healthier response is for Dan to regret some of his decisions, acknowledge that some unfortunate circumstances also played a role, learn from the experience and return his focus to building his business.

When we make mistakes it is helpful to acknowledge, with the benefit of hindsight, that some of our judgments proved to be incorrect. As we always operate with the limited knowledge and awareness available at the time, it is unavoidable that some of our decisions will lead to unfavorable outcomes. Making mistakes is a normal part of life.

However, it is totally unreasonable and pointless to keep punishing ourselves and to label ourselves as worthless, defective or stupid for those mistakes.

To dispel any lasting doubts about the futility of self-flagellation Dan chooses to use goal-directed thinking. Remember the key question, "Does thinking the way I do help me to feel good or to achieve my goals?"

> *Telling myself that I'm a failure and a loser keeps me feeling inadequate and depressed, and doesn't change the situation. It is totally pointless and self-defeating. I can stay depressed for years by continuing to think this way or I can choose to stop punishing myself and start focusing on the future.*

An additional problem with equating our worth with our achievements is that it often leads to a lifestyle that is unbalanced and stressful. Many people whom we regard as workaholics are in fact desperately trying to earn their worth through their achievements. The constant striving and sacrifice is often accompanied by thoughts that they should be doing more. This makes it difficult to sit back and enjoy their lives or to appreciate all the things that they have achieved. Similarly, people whom we regard as perfectionists are often motivated by the belief that achievements equal self-worth. The problem with perfectionism is that it is based on unrealistic standards. Consequently we never feel satisfied with our performance, and frequently self-flagellate when we fail to meet those standards.

> *Troy works extremely long hours in his job as a corporate lawyer. At age thirty-three he is a very high achiever and hopes to become a partner of the firm within the next few years. In spite of all of his achievements Troy has a self-esteem problem—he only feels adequate when he is performing "brilliantly." Consequently he puts very little store on spending time with his family, maintaining his friendships, reading, participating in leisure activities or doing anything that does not directly contribute to success in his work. Vacations in particular are a grueling experience, and Troy always takes his laptop and some work files when he goes away with the family, to make sure that he uses his time productively.*

It's not that Troy doesn't love his family—in fact he will tell you that they are the most precious things in his life. It's just that in order to feel valuable, Troy believes that he must prove his worth by "being the best." In his mind, that means becoming a partner in the firm and earning buckets of money. Interestingly, even when he does finally become a partner, Troy's perception of himself does not change. Like most people who rely on achievements for their self-worth, the promotion brings him a temporary elevation in self-esteem, which soon evaporates. In addition, his extremely stressful and unbalanced lifestyle is creating other problems, which Troy does not have time to address—his marriage is disintegrating, his children barely know him, he has few friends and he has developed high blood pressure and other health problems.

While for some, self-esteem is contingent on financial success, for others it is about academic achievement or the nature of one's work. The assumption that choosing a particular life path would make us more valuable as people is a common but irrational and self-defeating belief. Take Margaret for example:

> *Margaret has spent most of her married life raising a family. Now that her four children have left home, Margaret feels useless. She believes that she has never achieved very much in her life, and doesn't have any particular talent or abilities. Many of Margaret's friends are college-educated, and have high-status, well-paid jobs. Recently Margaret met up with her friend, Rebecca, for coffee and was struck by her friend's energy and enthusiasm when talking about her job. Margaret immediately thought to herself, "Rebecca must think that I'm boring. I have so little to offer."*

Margaret decides to challenge her assumptions using **Socratic questioning**:

**1. What are facts and what are my subjective perceptions?**
**The facts:** I met up with Rebecca, and she talked enthusiastically about interesting things that she is doing at work.
**My perceptions:** I'm inadequate. I'm not as good as Rebecca. She must look down on me.
**2. What evidence supports my perceptions?**
Rebecca was excited about her job, and she knows a lot of interesting people. I had little to contribute when she was talking about her work.
**3. What evidence contradicts my perceptions?**
Rebecca frequently calls me and always appears to enjoy my company. I have other college-educated friends who also like spending time with me. I usually contribute to conversation as much as anyone else, and my friends don't appear to care whether or not I have a college education.
**4. Am I making any thinking errors?**
I am "shoulding" on myself—telling myself that I should have pursued a certain path and that I'm not OK if I didn't. I am also mind reading—I have no evidence that Rebecca looks down on me.
**5. How else can I perceive this situation?**
People choose different paths, depending on what is meaningful to them. I chose to have a family and bring up my children—that's been important to me. Having a college degree or a high-powered job is right for some people but it's not the path that I could have

managed, as I wanted to be there for my children. The choices I made were valid for me. While it sounds glamorous, having a college degree or a high-powered job would not make me a better or happier person. I don't have to prove my worth with jobs or qualifications. I appreciate my own lifestyle and freedom. I'm very lucky.

## EXCESSIVE NEED FOR APPROVAL

We are all approval-seekers—instinctively, we want to be liked. However, the degree of approval that we need varies. For some, approval from just a few significant people—"my family, my boss and a few close friends"—is enough. They are reasonably indifferent to what most other people think of them. Others need approval from almost everyone. Consequently they may feel embarrassed when buying personal products in the supermarket, when their fellow diners don't leave the waiter a tip or when a stranger in the street hears them thinking out loud. The stronger and more wide-ranging our need for approval, the more prone to anxiety, depression and poor self-esteem we become. In addition, we are more likely to behave in self-defeating ways—trying too hard to impress or please others, and always putting our own needs last. Paradoxically, this behavior frequently has the opposite effect to what we are trying achieve—people sense our desperation and sometimes treat us like the second-class citizen that we present ourselves to be.

Wanting everyone to like you is a tall order. In fact, there are few people in the world who are liked by everyone. All of us have our admirers and detractors, and most of us have had the experience of being liked by some and disliked by others. The trick here is to acknowledge that one size does not fit all. Different people have different preferences, and are attracted to different human qualities. Some people seek out those who are loud and gregarious; others prefer those who are contemplative and good listeners. Some people value honesty and genuineness beyond all other human traits, while others are attracted to people who have social status, wealth or a pretty face. Some people are attracted to intelligent conversation, others to a sense of humor, and others value loyalty and kindness above all else. As we cannot be all things to all people, we need to accept that we will appeal to some and not to others. There may be some people who, for reasons of their own, do like not us. This is actually quite normal—there is no reason why we should appeal to everyone. A psychologically healthy attitude is to acknowledge that some people will like us while others may not, and that we do not need everyone's approval.

Some people worry that they may not fit in or that they're seen to be different from everyone else. They are conscious of things such as looking different, behaving differently, finding different things enjoyable or having different interests and aspirations from the people around them. Concerns about being seen as different usually stem from a need for approval. We want people to like us and standing out from the crowd might cause some to judge us harshly. Perhaps it is better to just go with the flow?

The problem is that sometimes, in order to be genuine or to express ourselves honestly, we need to say or do things that might set us apart. It may be that we take a stand against a prevailing point of view, choose not to go when everyone else is going, choose not to laugh when we do not think something is funny or choose not to care if we do not think it matters. Perhaps it is reflected in the way that we dress or the things that we believe in. Of course, sometimes it is appropriate to compromise—it may be perfectly valid to do things that we do not particularly want to do, out of consideration for others. However, at times it is important to express ourselves honestly, even if this means standing out from the crowd.

- *Sharon isn't interested in going out drinking with her friends on Saturday nights.*
- *Ian doesn't enjoy the jokes shared by the other apprentice mechanics that he works with.*
- *Rita is the only one in her circle of friends who votes for the Democrat party.*
- *Yasmin is a practicing Muslim in a predominantly Christian culture.*

How these people deal with their differences will determine how they feel about themselves. If they are ashamed, embarrassed or worried about how others will judge them, they are likely to feel diminished by their differences. If, on the other hand, they accept that they have a right to be different and are willing to express themselves honestly, they will feel comfortable with who they are.

Whether our differences are major or subtle, there is no rule that says we should all be the same. Variety is the spice of life. A healthy attitude is to accept our differences and to be tolerant of differences in others. Although we may think that people will judge us harshly for not conforming, the reality is often quite the opposite. In fact, people frequently admire those who have the courage to be themselves, to say what they think in spite of social pressure to conform.

## Behavioral disputing

In chapter 6 we saw how behavioral disputing can be used to challenge the excessive need for approval. Instead of trying too hard to please or impress other people, we do exactly the opposite—use shame-attacking exercises and look for spontaneous opportunities to do things that might risk the possibility of disapproval. When we relinquish behaviors based on faulty beliefs, such as "People will only like me as long as I echo their views and do things for them," we learn through experience that our assumptions are incorrect—that we do not need to try so hard to win people's approval. We cannot know that we are inherently likeable until we abandon attempts to please or impress people. In fact, the paradox of trying too hard to be liked is that the harder we try, the less attractive we become (see also Be Honest, page 170).

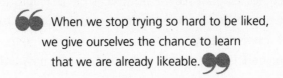

*When we stop trying so hard to be liked,
we give ourselves the chance to learn
that we are already likeable.*

Many of us also live with ongoing dread that at some stage, people will discover our perceived shortcomings, failures or flaws.

*Sean is terrified that people will find out that he has made some mistakes at work.*

✳

*Irving is afraid that people will see how nervous he is when he gives his public presentation.*

✳

*Claude is terrified that people will discover that he is gay.*

✳

*Shirene suffers from social phobia. She is afraid that people will notice her sweating when she feels socially anxious, and will think that she is strange.*

✳

*Joe was charged for driving while under the influence of alcohol four years ago and is anxious that his boss will find out.*

✳

*Nathan suffers from depression and is anxious that his new girlfriend will reject him if she discovers it.*

✳

*Helena has carried huge shame for years—that she was not sufficiently attentive to her father when he was dying of cancer.*

For each of these people, keeping secrets reinforces the perception that their shame is justified, and that catastrophic consequences would follow should others find out. This maintains their anxiety and perception of defectiveness. One of the best ways to evaluate whether our beliefs are correct is to conduct a behavioral experiment—self-disclose to the relevant people and observe their responses. Once we "come out," our anxiety drops because we no longer need to worry that people will find out. In addition, in most cases people do not react with the harsh judgment that we had predicted, and so we get immediate evidence that our perceived failings are not so bad after all.

But what if they do? Behavioral experiments with self-disclosure always involve some risk—sometimes our fears are realized. For instance, when Claude finally disclosed that he is gay, most people were very positive and supportive, however, two of his friends were judgmental. Taking risks invariably involves the possibility of negative reactions—that is what makes them a risk. However, we do not overcome our self-doubts and fears without taking risks. Nothing is gained if we only self-disclose when we have an iron-clad guarantee that people will respond favorably. The most powerful learning occurs when we risk the possibility of disapproval and discover that in most cases it does not happen, and that *even if it should happen, we can cope.*

There may of course be some situations where it is better not to self-disclose, particularly if the stakes are very high. Nonetheless, most of us are too quick to assume that if people really knew us they would see our defects and write us off. Keeping secrets prevents the possibility of disconfirmation—we never discover that our catastrophic predictions are incorrect. It is also harder to modify our negative self-perceptions because we do not get the salutary effects of other people's responses.

## LABELING

At times we all do silly things that have negative consequences, either for ourselves or for other people. Sometimes we handle social interactions badly or make silly comments that we later regret. Sometimes our actions have negative consequences for our work, relationships, health, finances or career, and on occasions we fail to achieve some of our most cherished goals. Sometimes we are just not good at things that we would like to be able to do.

This is the nature of things—human beings are intrinsically fallible, and we all have our strengths and weaknesses. In addition, many people perceive themselves as having certain character flaws that limit their potential. For instance, some people perceive themselves as too shy, too old, too fat, too awkward or too lazy. Others believe they are not clever enough, not successful enough, not capable enough or simply not as good as other people. The extent to which we label ourselves for our perceived flaws or weaknesses largely determines our self-esteem. Many people habitually label themselves as bad or defective on the basis of some perceived shortcomings. The labels that we use are sometimes conscious—"stupid," "weak," "failure" or "hopeless" may be almost audible inside our mind. However, more often our labeling is unspoken—without using words, we have a strong sense of being bad, inferior or defective in some way.

The problem with labeling is that we make gross generalizations on the basis of only some of our characteristics or behaviors. To label yourself as stupid, a loser, a no-hoper or a failure is as irrational as labeling yourself an eater, breather, washer or sleeper. At times we may do silly or bad things. Like washing, eating, breathing and sleeping, they are a tiny subset of the hundreds of things that we do, and they do not define who we are.

> *Vicki unthinkingly passed on some information that was told to her in confidence, which unfortunately got back to her original source. Her friend is furious with her for "shooting her mouth off," and Vicki is beside herself with shame and remorse. She tells herself that she is a traitor and a heel and should never be trusted again.*

Obviously Vicki has some fence-mending to do. It's reasonable for her to conclude that what she did was wrong, and it may take some time before she regains her friend's trust. It's appropriate for Vicki to criticize what she did—to say "I did a very silly thing" or "I behaved very badly in that situation." It's important to acknowledge our mistakes so that we can avoid making them again. Judging some of our behaviors as silly or wrong does not diminish our self-esteem because behaviors can be changed— we can do it differently next time. On the other hand, labeling ourselves as bad or defective impairs our self-esteem because we make a global negative judgment about who we are.

**Don't confuse the things you did with the person you are.**
**You are much, much more than just a few behaviors.**

> *Kim feels like the odd one out at the advertising agency where she works. Although she has been there for almost a year, Kim doesn't feel particularly close to the other members of her team. The other people have different values and interests from her own, and Kim regards much of their conversation to be pretty superficial and banal. Most of the staff seem to get on well with each other, and at times Kim wonders if there's something wrong with her. She labels herself as an outsider. She writes the following on her thought-monitoring form:*

| SITUATION | Sat through a staff meeting—there was lots of joking and carrying on, but I didn't find it funny—couldn't even manage a smile. |
|---|---|
| FEELINGS | After the meeting, I got really down. Felt like an outsider. |
| THOUGHTS | They noticed that I wasn't joining in the revelry—they must think I'm boring or strange. I don't belong—I'm an outsider. Perhaps there's something wrong with me? |
| BELIEFS | I should be like them. I should connect well with all social groups. They must like and approve of me. If I don't connect with them, it means that I am defective. |
| THINKING ERRORS | Mind reading, labeling, shoulds, personalizing |
| DISPUTE | I connect well with some people and not with others. There is no reason why I should connect well with everyone. I got along well with the staff at my last job—people are all different. It would be nice to feel closer to the staff, but it's OK if I don't. That doesn't make me inferior or inadequate. It's OK for me to be who I am—I don't need to be anyone different. |
| POSITIVE ACTIONS | Be friendly and cooperative. Respect their right to be different from me. Focus on having good professional relationships. |

## Be specific

Rather than labeling ourselves, it is much more realistic to think of our behavior or situation in specific terms.

> Claire recently went to a party where she didn't know any of the other guests. As she was too shy to approach anyone to start a conversation, Claire spent much of the evening sitting on the couch, feeling awkward and self-conscious. When she left the party, Claire felt very troubled. "I'm socially incompetent," she thought to herself.

While many of us can empathize with Claire in this situation, the reality is that she did not need to feel that way. Labels such as loser, inferior or socially incompetent make us feel defective. If Claire had been able to think in *specific* rather than *global* terms, she could have told herself, "I'm shy in some social situations, especially when I don't know people" or "I'm not very good at starting up conversations in a room full of strangers." Acknowledging that we have limited skills in some situations does not diminish our self-esteem because we make no global assessment of our overall worth.

## CONVERTING LABELS INTO SPECIFIC STATEMENTS

| LABELS (UNHELPFUL) | SPECIFIC STATEMENTS (HELPFUL) |
|---|---|
| I'm socially incompetent. | I'm shy with people I don't know well. |
| I'm an idiot. | I did a silly thing. |
| I'm a traitor. | I let her down—I made a mistake. |
| I'm a failure. | I didn't achieve some of my career goals. |
| I'm lazy. | I find it difficult to get motivated on some tasks. |
| I'm dumb. | I don't have very good general knowledge. |
| I'm "damaged." | I suffer from depression at times. |
| I'm incompetent. | I'm not very good at using modern technology. |
| I'm pathetic. | I get upset easily. |
| I'm unlovable. | Harry doesn't love me. |

## OVERGENERALIZATION

How do you respond when you make a mistake or fail to achieve a goal? Do you tell yourself that you never get things done? That you always mess things up? That everything is going wrong? A common pattern of thinking that often contributes to poor self-esteem is the tendency to generalize a failure in one area to other areas of our lives.

*Jillian is in her mid-forties and decided to pursue an arts degree as an adult student. Although she believed that she would have no difficulty in coping with the course work, the reality proved to be quite different. Jillian found it difficult to concentrate during lectures or to do the prescribed reading, and worrying about the possibility of failure only made studying more difficult. Finally she decided to defer for a year; however, when she recommenced the course in the following year, the same problem arose. Finally, after much anguish and self-flagellation, Jillian dropped out of the course. Since that time, her self-esteem has plummeted and she has become depressed.*

Jillian's poor self-esteem was largely the result of overgeneralization. Instead of acknowledging that there are some things that she does well and others that she has difficulty with, Jillian told herself that she cannot achieve anything that is worthwhile, and that she is unlikely to do anything useful in the future. By generalizing her perceived failure in one area to other areas of her life, Jillian made herself feel incompetent and useless as a person. In order to recover her self-esteem, Jillian needs to think about her perceived failure as specific to one area of her life. That is, she needs to recognize that she has difficulty in studying, but that this does not make her incompetent in other areas.

Jillian's thought-monitoring exercise:

| | |
|---|---|
| **SITUATION** | Dropped out of a course that I really wanted to do. |
| **FEELINGS** | Feel worthless and depressed. |
| **THOUGHTS** | This means I'm dumb. I'm a failure. I'm hopeless. |
| | I can't seem to achieve anything any more. |
| | I'll never achieve anything worthwhile. |
| **BELIEFS** | My achievements define my worth. If I don't achieve my goals, it means that I'm dumb and hopeless. Not achieving this particular goal means that I'm not achieving anything. I should be able to succeed in everything I set out to do. |
| **THINKING ERRORS** | Labeling, overgeneralizing, predicting catastrophe, jumping to negative conclusions, shoulds |
| **DISPUTE** | Studying is difficult for me at this stage of my life. I find it hard to settle down and get motivated. That doesn't make me incompetent or hopeless. Studying isn't one of my strengths at the present time. There is no reason why I must succeed in everything I attempt. I succeed in some things and not in others. It's OK to not succeed at some things. I don't have to earn my worth. Whether or not I finish the course does not change who I am and does not make me a hopeless person or a failure. |
| **POSITIVE ACTIONS** | Focus on other areas of my life—friendships, interests, health. Set myself new, life-enhancing goals. |

## Be specific

Once again, sticking to the facts encourages us to remain objective, and limits our ability to distort our perceptions with overgeneralizations.

**CONVERTING OVERGENERALIZATIONS INTO SPECIFIC STATEMENTS**

| OVERGENERALIZATIONS (UNHELPFUL) | SPECIFIC STATEMENTS (HELPFUL) |
|---|---|
| I'm not achieving anything. | I haven't achieved a goal that was important to me. |
| Everyone thinks I'm an idiot. | Phil's parents and my mother disapprove of my decision. |
| People reject me once they get to know me. | I have been rejected in three of my relationships. |
| The harder I try, the worse things get. | In spite of trying hard, I couldn't resolve this particular problem. |
| Women don't like me. | I don't connect well with some of my wife's friends. |
| I've been a hopeless mother. | I have made some mistakes in the way I brought up my children. |
| I'm not making any progress. | I have not made as much progress as I would have liked. |
| I have wasted a whole day. | I have achieved substantially less than I had planned. |
| I'm hopeless at job interviews. | I didn't perform very well at my last two job interviews. |

## UNCONDITIONAL SELF-ACCEPTANCE

> 66 The value of human life is that it exists. You are a complex miracle of creation. You are a person who is trying to live, and that makes you as worthwhile as every other person. Whether you are a researcher unlocking the cure for cancer or a person who sweeps the streets, you have known hope and fear, affection and loss, wanting and disappointment. You have looked at the world and tried to make sense of it, you have coped with the unique set of problems you were born into, and you have endured pain. Over the years, you've tried many strategies to help you feel better and deal with pain. Some worked, some haven't. It doesn't matter, you are just trying to live. And in spite of all that is hard in life, you are still trying. This is your worth, your humanness. 99
> MATTHEW MCKAY AND PATRICK FANNING, *SELF-ESTEEM*

The key to healthy self-esteem is unconditional self-acceptance. The above quote describes the essence of what this is. Unconditional self-acceptance means accepting ourselves as valuable for our very humanness; recognizing that we do not need to earn our worth through things like our job, qualifications, achievements, appearance or possessions. It means accepting ourselves—with all our perceived flaws and shortcomings—as inherently as valid and valuable as any other person, believing that we are worthy because we are human and, like everyone else, we are just trying to live.

Learning to accept ourselves does not mean that we should stop setting goals or trying to improve aspects of our life. Learning new skills, embarking on a healthier lifestyle, developing new friendships or taking on new challenges can greatly enhance the quality of our lives. The point is we do not need to achieve these things before we can accept ourselves. Self-acceptance is not conditional—it means knowing that we are valuable, whether or not we succeed or fail in achieving the things that we want.

Self-acceptance also means accepting parts of ourselves that we do not like but are unable to change. This might include aspects of our history, personality, competence or physical appearance.

> *Howard went through a very troubling time when he was diagnosed with schizophrenia ten years ago. While he has managed to get the illness under control with medication, Howard perceived himself as damaged and inferior to others, and this created shame and self-downing. As a result, Howard ended up with two problems—the first was his mental illness (which was largely under control) and the second was his poor self-esteem, which interfered with other areas of his life. It*

*was only when Howard finally learned to accept his illness as a part of him (not liking it, but accepting it) that he stopped perceiving himself as defective and was able to feel comfortable with who he is.*

*Emma has been overweight for most of her life and has hated her body for as long as she can remember. She has spent much of her life desperately fighting fat, trying one weight-loss regimen after another, all to no avail. Finally, at the age of thirty-five, after attending a support group, Emma has learned to accept the body that she has. While she tries to eat a healthy diet and do some exercise every day, she has stopped fighting her body and accepts that she will probably never be slim. By learning unconditional self-acceptance, Emma has released her belief that she must lose weight before she can like herself. This experience has been liberating and has freed her to focus on other areas of her life.*

*Sandra sometimes feels inadequate when she goes out to social functions with her friend, Anne. Anne has a natural warmth and sparkle that draws people to her and attracts admirers wherever she goes. Although Sandra makes an effort to be friendly and to initiate conversations, she does not have Anne's easy, warm social manner. Sandra perceives herself as rather boring when she is in Anne's company, and this makes her feel self-conscious. In order to maintain healthy self-esteem Sandra needs to stop comparing herself with Anne or insisting that she should be like her. She needs to accept that it takes longer for people to get to know her and remind herself that when she is comfortable with people, she can also relate well and have good friendships.*

## Whatever you focus on becomes magnified

We all have things that we do not like about ourselves. Perhaps you are too short or too heavy or have bad skin. Or maybe you are ashamed of some aspect of your past that you cannot put behind you. Or maybe you believe that you are not interesting enough or outgoing enough or clever enough.

Whatever we focus on becomes magnified. Have you ever noticed, for instance, that when you go to a social function and worry about what you are wearing, you give this concern a life of its own? Other people do not notice or care, but focusing on your appearance stops you from having a good time. The more we focus on our perceived defects, the more problematic they become—we create these hang-ups. Paradoxically, it is not the perceived defect, but the attention that we give it that robs our confidence, inhibits our behavior and diminishes our self-esteem.

Most of us are our own harshest critics, and the assumption that others judge us equally harshly is often incorrect. When we can accept the things that we don't like about ourselves, and stop paying them excessive attention, their importance diminishes and our confidence grows. If we can't change it, it is wise to let it go.

*Other people respond to us as we respond to ourselves.*

## EXERCISE 7.1

1 Think of something that you do not like about yourself but which you cannot change.
2 Have you ever noticed that focusing on this thing makes you feel inadequate?
3 What would be the effect of accepting this part of you and releasing it from your focus?
4 What do you need to tell yourself to help you to accept it?

## BE FLEXIBLE

Healthy, adaptive thinking means accepting those aspects of ourselves that we cannot change, and not demanding that we should be otherwise. This involves being flexible about the qualities that we would like to have, without demanding that we must have them. It means not labeling ourselves on the basis of some of our perceived shortcomings and accepting ourselves, with all of our perceived imperfections, as inherently human.

It is often a useful exercise to identify some of the personal characteristics that we believe reflect on who we are, and to examine our beliefs in relation to those characteristics. The table on the next page contains a list of common observations that have the potential to impair self-esteem if they are associated with diminishing beliefs. In the column on the right are examples of flexible beliefs that help to maintain healthy self-esteem. Notice that none of the observations are a problem unless they are accompanied by a belief that we should not be this way.

| OBSERVATION | DIMINISHING BELIEFS | FLEXIBLE BELIEFS |
|---|---|---|
| I'm not as witty as some people I know. | And I should be as witty as they are. | And I don't have to be. Some people have the gift of being very funny. That's their good fortune. There is no reason why I must be as witty as they are. |
| I am not very good at keeping a clean and tidy house. | And I should keep a clean and tidy house. | And I don't have to. I wish I was tidier, but there is no reason why I must be. Keeping my house clean and tidy isn't something that I am interested in or particularly good at. |
| I have a low libido. | And I should have a high libido and I should be having lots of sex. | And I don't have to have a high libido. There is no "correct" amount of libido. Many people don't have a high sex drive—that doesn't make them defective or inferior. People are all different, and sex drive varies from person to person. |
| I don't work. | And I should be working. | And there is no rule saying that I have to work. I'm fortunate that I don't need to work at this stage of my life, so I can enjoy my freedom and spend time on the things I like to do. |
| I'm not a perfect parent. | And I should be a perfect parent. | And I don't have to be. I do my best and usually I do a pretty good job. At times I make mistakes, but then so does everyone else. Perfect parents are hard to find. |
| I take myself too seriously. | And I shouldn't take myself too seriously. | And I have the right to take myself seriously. It would be good for me to lighten up and enjoy myself more but I tend to be a fairly intense person by nature. That doesn't make me bad or defective. |
| I am not achieving as much as I used to. | And I should be achieving as much as before. | And I don't have to achieve as much as I used to. At this stage of my life I can't do all the things that I used to. I'm achieving enough. |
| I don't have a college education. | And I should have a college education. | And I don't have to. Some people have a college education and others don't. There is no reason why I must have a college degree in order to be OK. |
| I'm not very good at sports. | And I should be good at sports. | And I don't have to be good at sports. Some people are good at sports—that is their good fortune, but it isn't one of my strengths. |

## EXERCISE 7.2

Now it is your turn. Make up your own table with columns for "Observation," "Diminishing Beliefs" and "Flexible Beliefs." Write down some observations about yourself that have caused you to feel inadequate—now or in the past. In the diminishing beliefs column, write some of the rigid beliefs that have made you feel that way. Then think about a healthier, more balanced way of perceiving your situation. In the "flexible beliefs" column, write some more realistic ways of thinking about your situation that would help you to maintain healthy self-esteem.

## ACKNOWLEDGE YOUR STRENGTHS AND QUALITIES

In their book *Self-Esteem*, Fanning and McKay refer to the "inner critic"—an internal voice that constantly carps, judges and criticizes us but rarely gives us praise or acknowledgment. It seems that many of us have a harsh inner critic, and consequently we tend to focus on our perceived weaknesses and defects, while ignoring our strengths. An interesting exercise, which helps us to examine our inner critic, is to write two lists— one comprising all our perceived strengths and the other comprising our perceived weaknesses. How easy or difficult it is to think of items for each list tells us a lot about our inner critic. Many people struggle to think of anything good to say about themselves but have no difficulty in coming up with a long list of defects. Others find it easy to think of both their strengths and weaknesses, while some find it easier to think of their qualities and strengths.

People who can think of lots of positive attributes are not necessarily any more gifted or virtuous than those who can think of only a few. They are simply more focused on their strengths. Those who find it easy to think of their perceived defects are more focused on their limitations and tend to ignore their positive qualities. Choosing to focus more on our qualities and to accept the things that we do not like but can't change, can help us to develop a more balanced and healthy self-image.

## EXERCISE 7.3

1. List as many of your positive attributes and strengths as you can think of.
2. Once you have written as many as you can, ask other people to help you by writing up their own list of your strengths and attributes.
3. Refer to your list regularly to remind yourself of the many things that you take for granted.

# BEHAVIORAL STRATEGIES THAT ENHANCE SELF-ESTEEM

We saw earlier that behavioral disputing is a powerful strategy for changing the way we think and feel about ourselves. In addition, strategies such as setting goals and using honest and assertive communication can help us to maintain healthy self-esteem.

## SET LIFE-ENHANCING GOALS

While self-acceptance is essential for good self-esteem, this does not mean that we should avoid striving to improve ourselves in areas where we can make a difference. Whenever we are dealing with a self-esteem issue, it is worth considering whether there are any practical actions that we can take that could enhance our quality of life and help us to feel good about ourselves. For instance, we might consider increasing our general knowledge, extending our social circle, improving our fitness, developing a new interest, learning some new skills, taking on a new challenge or updating our wardrobe.

While pursuing meaningful goals can be very satisfying, doggedly chasing unrealistic goals can be self-defeating. It is therefore important to set goals that are realistic and to remain flexible in pursuing them. Many people underestimate what they are capable of when they really put their mind to it, however, the opposite is also true; some people set themselves unrealistic goals and then feel inadequate and despondent when they fail to achieve them.

*James is seeking Ms. Perfect, with whom he can share his life. She has to be slim, beautiful, clever, gregarious, financially independent and mad about him. While James has occasionally pursued women who looked like Ms. Perfect, none of them has been interested in him. The problem is not that James is unlovable but that his expectations are unrealistic. Modifying his expectations would help James to find a suitable partner and enable him to avoid feelings of failure and inadequacy.*

✳

*Candice is a stocky size 16 build but she desperately wants to get down to a size 10. She has tried various diets, exercise and alternative therapies, but time and again she has temporarily lost weight, only to put it on again. Given her build, it is unrealistic for Candice to expect such a large drop in weight. However, it may be more realistic to aim for a healthy lifestyle, and for a less substantial but more permanent weight loss.*

✳

*Roberto is determined to earn his worth by making lots of money, and his goal is to own a $5 million house on the bay by the time he turns fifty. Given the nature of his business, this goal is unrealistic. Roberto is setting himself up for failure and lots of self-criticism.*

When setting goals, it is important to consider our resources—what we have to work with, what we are capable of and what sacrifices we are prepared to make along the way. Taking those factors into account helps us to set realistic goals, which in turn increases our chances of success. It is also important to remain flexible when pursuing our goals. This means doing our best but at the same time accepting that we may not always succeed. It also means not waiting until we have achieved the things we want before we can accept ourselves. The challenge is to practice self-acceptance at all times, regardless of the things happening in our lives.

In many situations, good self-esteem can be nurtured by both challenging negative beliefs and working towards life-enhancing goals:

*Wendy is shy by nature. Since she moved to New York ten years ago, Wendy has made some new friends, but not as many as she would have liked. One of the women she works with has been in New York for only two years and seems to have made lots of friends in that time. Wendy feels bad about herself for being so shy and for having had such limited success in making new friends. To improve her self-esteem, Wendy needs to accept her shyness as being part of her personality, without labeling herself as defective for being shy. She also needs to accept that it takes her longer than some people to develop new friendships but that she can nevertheless make new friends. Wendy can also make an effort to develop new friendships—this is where goal-setting is important. In spite of her shyness, she might improve her chances of meeting people by getting more involved in social activities, initiating more contact with people she knows and taking more risks.*

Wendy's thought-monitoring exercise:

| | |
|---|---|
| **SITUATION** | It's the weekend, and I've got very few activities planned. |
| **FEELINGS** | Feel depressed and really bad about myself. |
| **THOUGHTS** | How am I going to spend my time? I don't have any friends. Nadia has been here for two years and she knows lots of people. What's wrong with me? I'm just not attractive to people. |
| **BELIEFS** | People don't like me. I should have lots of friends by now. |
| **THINKING ERRORS** | Comparing, personalizing, labeling, jumping to negative conclusions, shoulds |

| DISPUTE | I'm shy with people I don't know—it takes me a while to get close to people. When people get to know me, they often like me. I am capable of making close friends. The friends that I have made over the years like and value me—Jeanette, Sue and Judy really like me. Being shy doesn't make me inferior to other people. It means that I have to work harder than some people in order to make friends. I accept that that's what I need to do. |
|---|---|
| POSITIVE ACTIONS | I'm going to make more effort to take social risks and get to know more people—join Toastmasters and go to bimonthly meetings; join the nature club, and do group walks on the weekends; sign up for lessons in ballroom dancing; invite Cynthia (woman I get along with at work) to see a movie next Friday night; join the local tennis club and take lessons; make more effort to trust people and open up to them when appropriate. |

Joanne has become acutely self-conscious about her appearance. She has aged substantially in the last few years and has put on a lot of weight. These days she avoids going out much because she hates the way she looks. In order to maintain a healthy self-esteem, Joanne needs to accept the physical changes that have come with age and avoid excessively focusing on her appearance (whatever we focus on becomes magnified). In addition, she might consider setting herself some realistic goals in relation to her weight and to doing some behavioral disputing in relation to social activity. The following is her thought-monitoring form:

| SITUATION | Ran into old friend that I haven't seen for years, in the supermarket. She didn't recognize me. |
|---|---|
| FEELINGS | Felt devastated. |
| THOUGHTS BELIEFS | She was probably shocked at how bad I look.<br>I am fat and ugly. I should be thinner and more attractive.<br>People must think that I look disgusting and look down on me. |
| THINKING ERRORS | Labeling, shoulds, mind reading, awfulizing |
| DISPUTE | I prefer to be youthful and slim but I accept that physical change is a part of aging. I will do what I can to lose some weight, but it is unrealistic to expect that I will look the way I used to. My appearance does not define my worth. Most people don't care much how other people look—they mainly worry about themselves. If I don't focus on my appearance, chances are people won't worry about it either. Even if some people think I look unattractive, I can live with that. |
| POSITIVE ACTIONS | Join the gym—start a regular exercise program. Get rid of some of my old clothes and splurge on some new outfits. Initiate some social contact with friends—start going out and participating in social activity. |

## BE HONEST

Feeling connected to others via friendships and intimate relationships can add to our sense of self-esteem because it provides us with direct evidence that we are likeable or lovable. In order to feel comfortable with who we are, we need to be genuine in our dealings with others. Poor self-esteem may cause us to try too hard or to be something we are not. In an effort to be liked we may try to say or do the right thing much of the time. We might also avoid honest communication for fear of making a bad impression. Some people hide behind a happy facade that they believe will make them likeable.

> *For most of her life, Helen strove to be the person she believed others would like. She attempted to win goodwill from her work colleagues by bringing them presents and baking them treats. Even when she felt down, Helen put on a cheerful facade because she believed that people would find this endearing. On the rare occasions when she disclosed a personal problem, Helen always followed up by saying, "But that's OK," in order to reassure others that she's a positive person. Helen tried to present herself as dynamic, knowledgeable and well connected and so she told exaggerated stories about the people she knows and the things that she's been doing. She feigned expertise on subjects she knew little about and used jargon and long words in an effort to impress people.*

Some people regard Helen as a phoney, some like her and some think that she tries too hard. The problem for Helen is that as long as she pretends to be someone she is not, she will always find it difficult to feel good about herself. Even when some people appear to like her, Helen is never sure whether they like the real her or the mask she wears. Most of us appreciate genuineness in others, and we are often turned off by someone who tries too hard to impress us.

> 66 Always be a first-rate version of yourself instead of a second-rate version of somebody else. 99 JUDY GARLAND

An essential ingredient for healthy relationships is honesty—a willingness to take off our mask and be ourselves. It also includes a willingness to reveal our thoughts, feelings and experiences, without manipulating information or trying to impress. It means not putting on airs or false cheerfulness, not exaggerating our achievements and not trying to be all things to all people. Being honest can be scary because we are putting our real selves on the line, but it can be also rewarding. When we discover that people like us without our disguise, we realize that we are valued for who we are—not for who we pretend to be.

Maintaining good relationships with other people involves making an effort—giving our time, initiating contacts, disclosing our thoughts and feelings and being prepared to confront issues that make us feel uncomfortable at times. Moving outside of our comfort zone can be difficult because we risk the possibility of rejection or disapproval. However, it also opens the door to the possibility of greater intimacy and connection to others and a stronger sense of ourselves as valid and likeable human beings.

## USE ASSERTIVE COMMUNICATION

The way we communicate—verbally and through our body language—sends a message to others about how much we value ourselves. Choosing to communicate assertively is a form of behavioral disputing because changing our behavior changes the way we think and feel about ourselves. When we communicate assertively we express our opinions, feelings or needs in a way that also respects the rights of others. We can say what we think and what we want. We are able to look people in the eye and speak in an appropriate tone and volume. Unassertive communication reflects poor self-esteem—the belief that we are not as valid or significant as other people.

### The self-fulfilling prophecy

*Ian believes that he is inferior to others. As a result, he finds it difficult to look people in the eye, to say what he thinks or to ask for what he wants. When he talks to people, he usually looks down at the floor and speaks in a soft voice, as though he really doesn't want them to hear what he has to say. Ian never expresses his thoughts or feelings—he presumes that people wouldn't be interested. He never asks for what he wants because he doesn't believe that he has the right to communicate his own needs. Because Ian's behavior and body language reflect his belief that he is inferior to others, people often treat him as though he really is inferior.*

Ian's behavior is a good example of the **self-fulfilling prophecy**. That is, our beliefs influence our behaviors, which in turn influence our experiences, and these ultimately reinforce our beliefs. So when we believe that we are inadequate or inferior to others, we behave in a way that conveys this message via our body language and the things we do or don't say. As a result, people start to perceive us as inadequate and behave towards us in a way that reinforces our sense of inferiority.

**Belief:** I am not OK. People don't like me.
↓
**Behavior:** Not friendly to people.
Don't initiate conversations or look people in the eye.
Rarely ask for what I want. Sometimes ignore people,
put self down or try too hard to please.
↓
**Feedback:** Other people make little effort to
acknowledge us or be friendly. So the original belief is reinforced.

When we communicate assertively, we give out the opposite message, "I am a person of equal worth to everyone else. I feel comfortable with other people because I know that I am OK. My thoughts, my feelings and my needs matter as much as anyone else's." Not only does this reinforce the belief that we are as significant as every other person, but it also encourages others to treat us with respect. Assertive communication is one of the most valuable tools for maintaining good self-esteem and healthy relationships. It also helps us to get our needs met more of the time. For those of us who struggle with assertive communication, reading more about it (see chapter 10 and Recommended Reading) and, in some cases, doing an assertiveness training program can be extremely beneficial.

## IN SUMMARY

➤ Our self-esteem is the way that we perceive our own worth. This perception has a major impact on many areas of our lives, including our ability to be happy.

➤ Self-esteem is influenced by our inherent personality traits, our childhood and subsequent life experiences, the messages we receive from others and the messages promoted through the mass media.

➤ Common faulty-thinking patterns that diminish our self-esteem include comparing ourselves with others, rating our worth on the basis of our achievements, having an excessive need for approval, overgeneralizing, and labeling ourselves.

➤ Healthy self-esteem is maintained through self-acceptance. This means accepting our perceived flaws or imperfections without labeling ourselves as defective or not OK. In addition, being flexible, accepting that not everyone must like us, and thinking in specific rather than global terms also helps us to maintain healthy self-esteem.

➤ Common symptoms of poor self-esteem include the need to please or impress others and to avoid self-disclosure and honest communication. These can be most effectively challenged via behavioral disputing.

➤ Setting and working towards realistic goals can also help to build up self-esteem. So too can honest and assertive communication.

# EIGHT

# Recovery from Depression

**Life is difficult.**
**This is a great truth, one of the greatest truths.**
M. SCOTT PECK, *THE ROAD LESS TRAVELED*

Everyone feels sad or blue from time to time. Usually experiences of sadness are triggered by a loss or disappointment—things go wrong, people let us down, we fail to get something we wanted, we lose something we valued. Sadness is a normal reaction to life's setbacks and disappointments, and usually passes after a few hours or days or perhaps after a good night's sleep. While we might be able to make ourselves feel better by talking to someone or distracting ourselves with a pleasant activity, sometimes we may simply allow ourselves to experience our sadness, knowing that it is a normal response and that with time it will pass. Occasional episodes of sadness are not usually a problem, however, if it lasts for more than a few days or occurs frequently, it is a good idea to learn some self-help strategies that can help us to keep it in check.

At the other end of the misery spectrum is depression—a debilitating condition that interferes with our ability to experience pleasure, interact with people or actively participate in life. Depression can have negative effects on our health and can even influence our perception of pain and physical symptoms. Unlike sadness, it can last for months or sometimes years.

Depression has been called the common cold of psychological disorders because it is one of the most common problems encountered by mental-health professionals. Nearly ten percent of American adults are suffering from depression at any point in time, and about fifteen percent will experience at least one episode of major depression at some stage of their lives. While both men and women experience depression, women are affected twice as often a men. Many people who suffer from depression also suffer from anxiety at the same time.

The majority of people who become depressed do not seek out or receive any treatment. This is a pity, as depression can usually be treated effectively. While most people eventually recover even without therapy, receiving appropriate treatment from a qualified mental-health professional can speed up recovery by months or years and help to prevent future relapse.

The cognitive behavioral techniques described in this chapter are useful for managing both sadness and mild to moderate depression. However, if you are experiencing more severe depression, these self-help strategies are extremely difficult to implement on your own because the condition itself is debilitating and impairs your ability to think and behave rationally. If this is your situation, it is best to see a qualified mental-health professional, such as a psychologist or psychiatrist. It is particularly important to see someone if your depression interferes with your ability to function, if you are having thoughts about suicide or if you have already tried to use self-help strategies without success. While the information in this chapter will be a useful resource to complement your treatment, it is no substitute for treatment. If you would like to read more about how to manage depression, see the Recommended Reading section at the back of this book.

# TYPES OF DEPRESSION

People experience different types of misery, from fleeting sadness to severe depression. The most common is **depressed mood**, which is a temporary state of sadness that most people experience from time to time. In daily parlance, we often describe ourselves as being "depressed" when we are actually experiencing depressed mood. In this state we feel sad and low, and our self-esteem often diminishes. However, unlike depression, depressed mood rarely lasts for more than a few days.

Because there are various types of depression, mental-health professionals classify them according to some of their specific characteristics. The following are some of the types of depression described in the *DSM-IV,* the manual used by mental-health professionals to identify various psychological problems.

### DYSTHYMIC DISORDER

About three to four percent of the population suffers from chronic mild depression called **dysthymic disorder** (or dysthymia), which causes them to feel constantly sad, pessimistic or down in the dumps. Dysthymic disorder has sometimes been called **depressive personality**, as the person experiences depressed mood for years at a time (at least two years to qualify for the diagnosis). In addition, they experience some other symptoms, such as low energy, low self-esteem, irritability, guilt, poor concentration and difficulty in making decisions. People with dysthymic disorder often see themselves as uninteresting and therefore tend to avoid social situations. Because feeling down has been part of their daily experience, they often do not seek out treatment, assuming that this is just their nature and that there is nothing they can do to change it. People who have dysthymic disorder are at increased risk of experiencing episodes of major depression.

## MAJOR DEPRESSION

**Major depression** (also called **clinical depression**) is a more severe and disabling condition than dysthymia. According to the *DSM-IV*, a person who has major depression experiences at least five of the following symptoms over a minimum of two weeks (including at least one of the first two symptoms listed):

1. Depressed mood for much of the day.
2. Reduced interest in pleasurable activities.
3. Changes in appetite or weight.
4. Changes in sleep patterns.
5. Lack of energy.
6. Feelings of guilt or worthlessness.
7. Agitation or slowing down of physical movements.
8. Inability to concentrate or make decisions.
9. Recurrent thoughts of death or suicide.

Major depression can also be classified as mild, moderate or severe. People with mild depression feel bad, but are still able to function. For instance, they may be able to go to work, do house chores and spend time with people, even though they experience little joy in doing so. Because their depression is not as crippling as the more severe forms, it is less likely to be noticed by others or to be treated. People experiencing moderate depression have a greater degree of social and occupational impairment. For instance, they may go to work but achieve very little because of poor concentration and low levels of motivation. In their social relationships, they may be awkward and withdrawn. People suffering from severe depression experience nearly all of the nine symptoms listed above, and their ability to do things is extremely limited. Even minor tasks like getting out of bed or getting dressed can be extremely challenging when we are dealing with severe depression.

COMMON SYMPTOMS OF DEPRESSION
- ❑ **Emotions:** feel miserable, guilty, irritable, numb, hopeless
- ❑ **Cognitions:** poor concentration, poor memory, feelings of helplessness, dreading each new day, indecisiveness, self-blame, poor self-esteem, thoughts of suicide, self-absorption, loss of interest in the outside world

- ❑ **Behaviors:** inactivity, crying, slowness of movement, social withdrawal, self-defeating behaviors, such as abuse of drugs, alcohol or food
- ❑ **Motivation:** lack of interest in work or hobbies, loss of interest in sexual activities, lack of desire to socialize, go out or talk to people
- ❑ **Physical functioning:** low energy levels, disturbed sleep, disturbed appetite, feeling physically ill, loss of libido.

## DEPRESSION VERSUS GRIEF

Grief and depression are often confused with each other, however, they are not the same thing. Grief is an appropriate reaction to situations that involve a major loss, such as the death of a loved one, diagnosis of a serious illness, loss of a job or breakup of a marriage. Grief is not the product of faulty thinking but a rational response to losing something we value. While the symptoms of grief gradually fade with time (usually within two to six months), the feelings of sadness may last much longer. The grieving person typically experiences symptoms such as depressed mood, insomnia, anxiety and loss of appetite. Many of these are also common to depression, however, the latter is accompanied by faulty thinking, which causes additional symptoms—such as diminished self-esteem, blaming, suicidal thoughts and self-defeating behaviors, such as alcohol and substance abuse.

# CAUSES OF DEPRESSION

Depression is rarely the result of one single factor—rather it is the result of a combination of factors that include a person's biology, personality traits, early and subsequent history, current life circumstances, recent stressful events and their style of thinking. Many mental-health specialists differentiate between depression that is primarily triggered by adverse life events (called "reactive depression") and depression that stems largely from biological causes.

### Reactive depression

The majority of people who experience depression have reactive depression—that is, their depression is in response to some stressful life circumstances. The misery of an unhappy marriage or marital breakdown, social isolation, the loss of a job, the diagnosis of a serious illness, physical disability, bereavement, divorce, loss of reputation and business failure are common triggers for reactive depression. Although the precipitating events for this type of depression are usually specific, sometimes they are subtle. For instance, the existential void brought on by the realization that one's life lacks purpose and meaning or the continual lack of affection from a spouse or family can also lead to reactive depression.

The likelihood of becoming depressed is greater when several negative events occur simultaneously or within a short period of each other. For instance, the loss of a job followed by the breakup of a relationship or the onset of an illness substantially increases the risk of becoming depressed. However, some people are able to get through several major hardships without becoming depressed. This demonstrates the role of resilience factors, which influence how we respond to life's challenges. Resilience factors include things like our patterns of thinking and personality, our biological predisposition and the resources that we have at our disposal, such as friends, communication skills and interests.

## BIOLOGICAL CAUSES OF DEPRESSION

Unhappiness often runs in families. Studies that compared the rates of depression among identical and nonidentical twins have found that genes can play a role in our tendency to experience depression. However, not all children of depressed parents grow up to suffer from depression, and many people who suffer from episodes of depression have no family history of the illness.

Some experts believe that certain types of depression are caused by abnormalities in the delivery of **neurotransmitters**—chemical messengers in the brain. The neurotransmitters most directly involved in the regulation of mood include serotonin, norepinephrine, dopamine, GABA and acetylcholine. It is believed that some people are prone to depression because they have a deficiency in certain neurotransmitters. Antidepressant medications work by increasing the availability of neurotransmitters such as serotonin and norepinephrine to brain cells. However, as depression in itself causes changes in neurotransmitters, some experts argue that the apparent deficiency is the *result* of depression rather than the *cause*. Although the specific biochemical processes are not fully understood, it is clear that certain types of depression have a strong biological basis and are therefore more resistant to counseling or self-help strategies alone.

**Melancholic depression** is difficult to shift with psychological therapy alone but usually responds to treatment with antidepressant medication. People with melancholic depression experience a loss of pleasure in all or most activities and/or a lack of reactivity to usually pleasurable stimuli. In addition they experience psychomotor disturbances, which may include a slowing down in their physical movements and thinking processes or agitation—feeling restless, irritable and distressed. Early morning waking (typically between 2 and 4 am) and depressed mood that is worse in the mornings is also common for this disorder.

**Premenstrual dysphoric disorder.** About three percent of menstruating women suffer a monthly depression in response to hormonal changes associated with their menstrual cycle. While up to fifty percent of women experience some emotional, physical or behavioral changes prior to their monthly period, those who suffer from this disorder experience more severe symptoms for anything between a few days and two weeks each month prior to menstruation. Symptoms include severely depressed mood, marked anxiety, irritability or anger, decreased interest in activities, social withdrawal and impaired ability to function.

**Postpartum depression** (PND) is much more severe than the more common "baby blues" that affect most mothers for a few hours or days shortly after childbirth. Postnatal depression occurs within three months of childbirth and affects about twenty percent of mothers. It can last for a few weeks to years or, if untreated, can become a chronic disorder. In addition to symptoms of depression, mothers suffering from postpartum depression may also experience fluctuations in mood, anxiety or panic attacks, sleep and appetite disturbance, feelings of guilt, shame, anger, incompetence and hopelessness, suicidal thoughts and unrealistic fears regarding themselves, their baby or their partner.

**Bipolar disorder** (sometimes called **manic depression**) affects about one percent of the population. This disorder involves cycles of severe depression followed by mania (being too happy, hyperactive, talkative, fast, unreasonable thoughts and inability to sleep). Bipolar disorder is influenced by genetic factors, and is sometimes passed down from one generation to the next. For most people with bipolar disorder, mood stabilizing medication is an essential part of their treatment.

## Other biological causes of depression

Very occasionally, depression may be brought about by physical illness or drugs. Certain endocrine disorders (e.g., lupus, Cushing's disease, diabetes), neurological disorders (e.g., Parkinson's disease, epilepsy, multiple sclerosis) and allergies may for some sensitive individuals cause depression. The use of certain prescribed medications (e.g., anti-hypertensive drugs, analgesics, migraine medication), and the abuse of both legal and illicit drugs (e.g., alcohol, nicotine, cocaine, cannabis, amphetamines) can also trigger episodes of depression. Depression is also a common withdrawal symptom of many addictive drugs.

In some situations, changes in hormone levels can cause depression. For instance, depression sometimes occurs when an underactive thyroid gland produces too little thyroxin, a condition known as hypothyroidism. Fluctuations in sex hormones (estrogen and progesterone) can trigger depressive symptoms in women who are premenstrual, pregnant, premenopausal or who have recently given birth. Even seasonal reductions in daylight during the winter months can cause depression among some sensitive individuals—a condition known as Seasonal Affective Disorder, or SAD. This condition is rare in America but affects people who live in countries that have little sunlight during the winter months.

Different types of depression frequently require different types of treatment. In order to get the most appropriate treatment, accurate diagnosis is essential. For this reason it is a good idea to avoid self-diagnosis but rather to consult with a qualified mental-health practitioner.

## THE DEPRESSION SPIRAL

If it is left unchecked, depressed mood can escalate into depression. In fact, some of the symptoms of depression actually serve to reinforce and exacerbate the condition. When we feel down, we lose motivation to do things, including some of the things that would normally be pleasurable. Inactivity, avoiding people and spending much of our time alone makes us feel more despondent. The more we withdraw, the more self-absorbed and miserable we become. Consequently depressed mood or an episode of mild depression can easily spiral into more severe depression that may take months to overcome.

Depression is often hard to hide. It may be visible in the way we look, move and talk. Our voice becomes flat and our facial expression is glum. Friends or family members may lose patience with us and tell us to pull ourselves together or stop moping. As we recognize that people find us depressing to be around, we choose to withdraw even further into our shell, thus making recovery even more difficult.

## RECOGNIZING DEPRESSION IN OTHERS

People have different ways of carrying their misery. Some people look unhappy, talk in a flat, emotionless tone and cry easily. Some talk openly about their despondency to friends and family, while others conceal their unhappiness by putting on a brave face. Although severe depression is hard to hide, people with mild depression may be more successful in covering it up. The problem with hiding our feelings is that we miss out on the support that friends and family members could otherwise give us if they were aware of how we feel.

## OVERCOMING DEPRESSION

Although thinking in an irrational, self-defeating way increases the risk of depression, negative thinking is rarely the sole cause. Depression results from a combination of factors, which may include stressful life events, inadequate social support, rigid patterns of thinking and poor coping strategies. Whatever the cause, there are two main paths to recovery from depression:

1. **Change our cognitions:** challenge the depressive, self-defeating thoughts and beliefs that perpetuate depression.
2. **Change our behaviors:** do things that enhance our mood and help us to feel good again. Helpful behaviors include engaging in pleasurable activities, talking to supportive friends and family members, doing physical exercise, problem solving and goal setting. Improving our social support network and developing interests can protect us from a relapse into depression further down the track.

## COGNITIVE STRATEGIES FOR MANAGING DEPRESSION

Whatever the cause, one thing always happens when we become depressed—our thinking becomes negative. Aaron Beck observed that depressed people have an "information processing bias" that causes them to selectively perceive things in pessimistic, distorted way. In fact, once we start to feel depressed, the negative cognitions that accompany it can cause a downward spiral into deeper depression.

Beck observed that depression causes people to take a negative view of:

> ➤ themselves
> ➤ the world
> ➤ the future.

When we feel depressed, we interpret our experiences in the most negative light. We assume too much responsibility for things that go wrong and blame ourselves for things that are beyond our control. We ruminate—that is, we think about issues over and over again—and find it hard to get on with other things. Our negative thinking occurs automatically and without awareness. We assume that the way we perceive things is the way they really are.

## HOPELESSNESS

One of the most debilitating aspects of depression is the sense of hopelessness that accompanies it—the perception that our problems are huge, numerous and insurmountable, and that things will never get better. The negative cognitions that accompany depression fuel feelings of hopelessness, which in turn make the depression harder to shift. In fact, an important step on the path to recovery is to acknowledge that although we feel bad at the moment, this feeling will eventually pass. (This can be terribly hard to believe when we feel depressed.) We do not know how long it will take—it may be weeks, months or possibly longer, but eventually we will recover.

## HELPLESSNESS

In addition to hopelessness, depression also brings with it a sense of helplessness—the perception that we have no control over what happens to us. Our life seems full of overwhelming problems that we cannot solve. We have very little energy or motivation, and we find it difficult to think clearly or make decisions. This sense of helplessness discourages us from trying. The best thing that we can do to regain a sense of control is to make decisions and act on them, even though we may lack the energy or confidence to do very much at all. Doing things to help ourselves—whether it is getting out of bed, initiating contact with friends, doing some exercise or seeking out treatment—helps us to feel better, partly because it increases our perception of control.

## POOR SELF-ESTEEM

Depression and low self-esteem go hand in hand. Having low self-esteem increases the likelihood that we will become depressed in the first place, and once we feel depressed, our self-esteem plummets. Depression causes people to perceive themselves as defective and worthless. We blame ourselves for not being more in control and we attribute negative events to our own perceived deficiencies, such as laziness, incompetence or lack of effort. We may even condemn ourselves for the very symptoms that depression brings about. So for instance, we may view our lack of motivation as laziness and our tendency to ruminate as self-centredness. If we are unable to experience pleasure or any positive emotions, we condemn ourselves for being cold and loveless. Even though we judge ourselves harshly, we do not necessarily hold the same standards for other people. In fact, we often accept other people's flaws more readily than our own. An important step to recovery from depression is self-acceptance. This means not criticizing or condemning ourselves—accepting that we are inherently human and that we are doing the best that we can.

## DISPUTING DEPRESSIVE THINKING

It is not so much the absence of positive thoughts but the pervasiveness of negative thoughts that perpetuates depressed mood. For this reason, trying to think positively is less effective than identifying and challenging the negative, distorted aspects of our thinking.

Faulty-thinking patterns, such as awfulizing, labeling, blaming, overgeneralization, jumping to negative conclusions and predicting catastrophe, make us vulnerable to emotional upsets such as anxiety, anger, guilt and low self-esteem, however, they play a particularly important role in the maintenance of depression. The more depressed we feel, the more distorted are our cognitions. Depression generates a sense of global pessimism—the perception that everything is bad and pointless, that we are totally defective and that nothing will ever improve. We make overgeneralizations about ourselves, other people and the rest of the world. We see things in black and white and we blame and label ourselves as bad and defective.

TYPICAL COGNITIONS ASSOCIATED WITH DEPRESSION
- ➤ Everything is hopeless.
- ➤ Things will never get better.
- ➤ Life is not worth living.
- ➤ It's impossible to solve my problems.
- ➤ I am defective.
- ➤ Everything is my fault.
- ➤ I'm inferior to other people.

➤ Life is meaningless.
➤ Nobody cares.
➤ I have nothing.
➤ I am a failure.
➤ I'm a burden to everyone.

Although our thoughts are distorted and unrealistic, they feel one hundred percent true. An important step in the process of taking control over depression is to examine our negative cognitions and to identify the errors in our thinking. The questions below can serve as a useful checklist.

IS MY THINKING FAULTY?

➤ Am I assuming the worst here? (jumping to negative conclusions)
➤ Am I condemning myself as a person, on the basis of one or two events? (labeling)
➤ Am I ignoring my strengths and focusing on my weaknesses? (filtering)
➤ Am I focusing on the negative aspects of my situation but ignoring the positive aspects? (filtering)
➤ Am I seeing things in black and white while ignoring the gray in between? (black-and-white thinking)
➤ Am I blaming myself for things that aren't my fault? (personalizing)
➤ Am I making gross generalizations on the basis of just a few experiences? (overgeneralizing)
➤ Am I overreacting about something that isn't really all that bad? (awfulizing)

## THE TWO-COLUMN TECHNIQUE

Depression generates a whole series of negative cognitions—not just one or two. When we have lots of cognitions to challenge, a useful alternative to the thought-monitoring form is the two-column disputing form. In the left column we record our negative cognitions and the type of faulty-thinking patterns that underlie them. In the right column we write some disputing statements or rational cognitions that challenge our faulty thinking.

*At the age of forty-four, Victor has sunk into deep depression. As he looks back on his life, Victor perceives that his goals and ambitions were never fulfilled. In the search for his true vocation, Victor worked in several areas, but none of these led to the career success that he had dreamed of. Working very long hours has put Victor's marriage under strain, and he has had little time to spend with his wife and children. Years of neglecting his health have also taken their toll, and he suffers from high blood pressure and frequent headaches. When Victor thinks about his life, the word "failure" resonates in his mind. To Victor it seems that he has failed at everything that matters—his career, his family and his health. The thoughts that go through Victor's mind include, "Nothing has worked out the way I would have liked. I have wasted my life; I have achieved nothing. I am a failure ... What's the point of trying? I can never make it work."*

Like all depressed people, Victor's faulty cognitions contribute to and perpetuate his depression. It is therefore important for him to examine his cognitions objectively, identify the distortions in his thinking and reframe his thoughts into more rational and helpful cognitions. Victor fills in his two-column form as follows:

| NEGATIVE COGNITIONS | RATIONAL COGNITIONS |
|---|---|
| Nothing has worked out the way I would have liked. *Black-and-white thinking* | I have achieved some of my goals but not others. I have done quite well in some of the vocations that I pursued and I provided a comfortable living for my family. Some things have not worked out the way that I had hoped. |
| I have wasted my life; I have achieved nothing. *Black-and-white thinking* | My life has been full of learning experiences—none of it has been a waste. Many of the things I did were worthwhile. In retrospect I can see that I made some mistakes and could have done some things differently. I can learn from these experiences and make the rest of my life more satisfying. |
| I am a failure. *Labeling* | It is ridiculous to label myself on the basis of some of my past actions. I have done well in some things and not so well in others. I don't need to earn my worth or to achieve all of my goals to be a worthwhile person. |
| What's the point of trying? I can never make it work. *Jumping to negative conclusions* | I can't change the past but I can learn from my experiences and work on making my life better from now on. I have no reason to believe that I can never make it work. |

In addition to challenging his negative cognitions, Victor also needs to think about practical steps that would enable him to take greater control over his life. For instance, it may be useful for Victor to reevaluate his current lifestyle and to set some new life-enhancing goals. These might include taking better care of his physical health, working to improve his relationships with his wife and children, and increasing his leisure activities.

*Andrea completed her studies in law two years ago and has been working for a large law firm over the last six months. The firm holds regular performance appraisals for the junior lawyers, and Andrea has just received her first appraisal. She was totally unprepared for the degree of criticism that the report contained. It stated that Andrea was often sloppy in her work and paid insufficient attention to detail. She had failed to follow up on important matters and at times communicated poorly with her colleagues and clients. It also stated that she had not been responsive to feedback and had failed to act on specific instructions from her supervisor. To add insult to injury, there was even some criticism of the way that she dressed and presented herself.*

Andrea could not recall any previous event that had left her feeling so utterly demoralized. She was devastated. While initially she believed that her performance appraisal was totally unfair, after a few days Andrea admitted to herself that many of the comments were true. Her mind was filled with thoughts about impending catastrophe—"This has ruined my entire career. I'll never recover from this; no one will ever employ me again. I'll have to resign. I will have to leave the legal profession. I'm no good. Everyone thinks I'm hopeless."

Because she was feeling so shattered, Andrea decided to objectively examine each of her thoughts to see if there is any other way that she can look at her situation. She filled in the two-column form as follows:

| NEGATIVE COGNITIONS | RATIONAL COGNITIONS |
| --- | --- |
| This has ruined my entire career. I'll never recover from this. *Black-and-white thinking* *Predicting catastrophe* | This is a setback, but it's only one appraisal. If I improve my performance over the next six months, the next one will be better. It is very disappointing, but I still have my job. This is not likely to have any long-term consequences if I substantially improve my performance from now on. |
| My life is falling apart. This is a complete disaster. *Awfulizing* *Overgeneralization* | It is very upsetting, but I can deal with this. Nothing is actually falling apart—I'm just upset. It is terribly disappointing but it's not a disaster. |
| Everyone thinks I'm hopeless. *Jumping to negative conclusions* *Overgeneralization* | My supervisor obviously doesn't have a high opinion of my performance, but I have not received negative feedback from other people. In fact some of my colleagues have been very supportive. I have no evidence that everyone thinks badly of me. |
| I am no good. *Labeling* | My value as a person does not depend on how I perform in one job. I have not done very well in this job over the last six months, but this has been a useful learning experience for me. I will make sure I do things more effectively from now on. |

In addition to challenging her negative cognitions, Andrea would also benefit from looking at practical things that she could do in order to improve her situation. This might involve speaking to her supervisor, asking for clarification on some of the items that she did not agree with or understand, and telling her supervisor that she is taking all of the feedback very seriously and intends to act on it. Andrea may also choose to set herself specific work-related goals so she can be sure that her performance will improve.

## SOCRATIC QUESTIONING

Because our thinking is highly error-prone when we feel depressed, Socratic questioning can be a useful tool to help us stay objective. The following Socratic questions can be used to evaluate depressive thinking:

1. What are facts and what are my subjective perceptions?
2. What evidence supports my perceptions?
3. What evidence contradicts my perceptions?
4. Am I making any thinking errors?
5. What is an alternative, more balanced view of this situation?

> Helen's partner, David, has recently broken off their relationship, and Helen has been depressed for weeks. She has written the following thoughts on her thought-monitoring form: "I'm unattractive. I'm unlovable. I'll never find a partner. I'll never be happy again."

Helen decides to examine the evidence for her cognitions:

**1. What are the facts and what are my subjective perceptions?**
The facts are that David has ended our relationship.
My subjective perceptions are that there is something wrong with me, that I'm unattractive, and that I'll never find a partner or be happy again.

**2. What evidence supports my perceptions?**
David broke up with me.

**3. What evidence contradicts my perceptions?**
I had boyfriends in the past who found me attractive and some males occasionally show interest in me even now, so I can't be totally unattractive. Also, I have friends who love and care about me, so I can't be an unlovable person. I was happy for the first thirty-three years before I met David, so I must be capable of being happy without him. I felt this way before when I broke up with Ben, and I also thought I could never be happy again. But I did get over it, so I will probably get over this as well.

**4. Am I making any thinking errors?**

❑ Personalizing—assuming that David's decision to break up the relationship means that I am not OK.

❑ Overgeneralizing—assuming that no one else can find me attractive.

❑ Predicting catastrophe—assuming that I'll always be alone and that I'll never be happy.

**5. What is an alternative, more balanced view of this situation?**

David has chosen not to be with me, but that doesn't mean that no one else would want to be with me. He is not the final arbiter of my lovability. I feel miserable now because I'm grieving the loss of our relationship, but that doesn't mean that I won't be happy again or that I'll never find another partner. I was happy before I met David, so it's quite likely that I'll be happy again, although it may take me a while to get over it.

> *Rosa is a workplace trainer for several large companies. Recently APL, one of her largest customers, informed her that they intend using their own in-house trainers from now on, and therefore no longer require her services. Upon hearing the news Rosa's mood plummeted. Her mind was filled with anxious ruminations about why they are no longer using her, and she concluded she is a failure, and that her business will never succeed.*

**1. What are the facts and what are my subjective perceptions?**

The facts are that APL did not renew my contract for future training work.

My subjective perceptions are that they must think that I am no good, that I am a failure, and that my business will never succeed.

**2. What evidence supports my perceptions?**

APL has stopped using my services for staff training.

**3. What evidence contradicts my perceptions?**

The majority of the evaluations for the workshops that I ran there were positive, and the feedback from Tracy (the training manager) was also quite positive. I also get lots of positive comments from the other firms that I do work for. APL has been going through cost-cutting measures on a number of fronts, and Tracy said that this is one of those measures.

**4. Am I making any thinking errors?**

I am personalizing—assuming their decision was because they are unhappy with me. I am also predicting catastrophe, assuming that my business will never succeed, and labeling myself as a failure.

**5. What is an alternative, more balanced view of this situation?**

This is a set-back, but set-backs are a normal part of life and are common for people who are self-employed. You win some and you lose some. I have no evidence that these changes are based on dissatisfaction with my work. In fact I have lots of evidence that I am highly regarded by my clients. Even if it were true that they are not a hundred percent happy with me, that still wouldn't make me a failure. I need to speak to Tracy to find out if there is anything that I could have done differently but I also need to accept that things go wrong at times and it's not always within my control.

## SECONDARY DEPRESSION—DEPRESSION ABOUT DEPRESSION

It might sound strange, but it is quite common for people to become depressed about their depression. While the initial depression may be triggered by things like stress, rejection, loss or loneliness, once it sets in, irrational thoughts about the symptoms of our depression can contribute to a further, secondary depression. Secondary depression is caused by negative cognitions about our experience of depression. We condemn ourselves as bad or weak for becoming depressed and for not recovering more quickly. We might castigate ourselves for making life difficult for others, for being preoccupied with our own problems and for being unmotivated and idle. Of course blaming ourselves only makes us feel worse.

The following are examples of common cognitions that contribute to secondary depression. Notice that these cognitions focus on the symptoms of the depression and involve a judgment that we are bad or blameworthy for being this way. Giving ourselves a hard time for feeling blue does not magically motivate us to get over it. On the contrary, self-condemnation simply makes us feel worse and perpetuates the depression. Sometimes we need to give ourselves permission to feel down—to accept that it is OK to be depressed. While challenging ourselves to dispute some of our negative thinking will help us to feel better, damning ourselves for feeling depressed will only make us feel worse.

### NEGATIVE COGNITIONS

| THOUGHT | BELIEF |
|---|---|
| This is my own fault—I'm a weak person for becoming depressed. | I should never get depressed—only weak people get depressed. |
| I should have recovered by now—I'm not trying hard enough. | If I don't recover quickly, it means that it's my own fault and that I'm not trying hard enough. |
| I'm causing other people to suffer. | If other people feel upset on my account, it means that it's my fault and that I'm a bad person. People should never suffer on my account. |
| I'm totally egotistical—I don't care about anyone but myself. | Thinking about myself means that I'm egotistical. If I were a better person I wouldn't be thinking of myself—I'd be thinking about others. |
| My brain is deteriorating—I'll never be able to think normally again. | Because my ability to concentrate and to make decisions is poor, this means that there is something permanently wrong with my brain. |
| I'm so lazy. I just don't do anything. | I should be doing more. It's bad to be inactive, and it means that I'm lazy. |
| I'll never get over this. I'll be depressed for ever. | If it's taking a long time for me to recover, it means that I'll never recover. |
| I shouldn't feel like this. | It's a bad, shameful thing to be depressed. |

Just as it is important to identify and challenge the faulty cognitions that cause our primary depression, it is also important to challenge the negative, self-damning thoughts that are associated with secondary depression. Here are some examples of how the cognitions listed above might be challenged.

| NEGATIVE COGNITIONS | LOGICAL STATEMENTS |
|---|---|
| This is my own fault—I'm a weak person for becoming depressed. I should never get depressed—only weak people get depressed. | Depression can affect anyone. It is not a measure of character or personal value. I prefer not to feel depressed and I will do my best to recover, but being depressed does not mean that I am a weak or flawed person. |
| I should have recovered by now—I'm not trying hard enough. If I don't recover quickly, it means that it's my own fault because I'm not trying hard enough. | There is no set time period for recovery from depression. It is often a slow process, and it may take quite some time before I am fully recovered. That doesn't mean that I'm not trying hard enough or that it's my fault. I am doing the best that I can. |
| I'm causing other people to suffer. If other people feel upset on my account, it means that it's my fault and that I'm a bad person. People should never suffer on my account. | People who care about me are concerned about my welfare, and may be worried about me at times. That's the price we pay for caring about each other. If our roles were reversed I wouldn't condemn them for being depressed. All of us would like me to recover, and I am doing the best that I can, but it's not totally within my control. |
| I'm totally egotistical—I don't care about anyone but myself. If I were a better person, I wouldn't be thinking of myself—I'd be thinking about others. Thinking about myself means that I'm a bad person. | Ruminating on my problems is a symptom of the depression. It does not mean that I am egotistical or conceited. It is true that I would feel better if I focused on other things or other people, and I will try to do this. However, at times when I do become self-absorbed, I don't need to condemn myself. |
| My brain is deteriorating—I'll never be able to think normally again. Because my ability to concentrate and to make decisions is poor, this means that there is something permanently wrong with my brain. | Depression affects people's ability to think clearly and to make decisions. Not sleeping well also affects brain function. These symptoms may last as long as the depression but they are not permanent changes and do not cause brain damage or deterioration. |
| I'm so lazy. I just don't do anything. I should be doing more. It's wrong to be so inactive, and it's all my own fault. | Lack of motivation and lethargy are normal symptoms of depression. They don't mean that I am lazy or bad. It is true that I would feel better if I became involved in more activity and I will try very hard to do this. However, I don't need to condemn myself for not feeling motivated—that is the nature of depression. |
| I'll never get over this. I'll be depressed for ever. If it's taking a long time to recover, it means that I'll never recover. | Most people who get depressed have times when they think it will never end. Feeling hopeless is a common aspect of depression. People do eventually recover, although some remain depressed for several months. I'm doing what I can, one step at a time. Recovery is a long slow process, and I need to be patient. |
| I shouldn't feel like this. It's a bad, shameful thing to be depressed. | Depression is one of the many conditions that affects some people. I prefer not to feel depressed, but there is nothing shameful or immoral about being depressed. |

**EXERCISE 8.1**

Make up your own form with columns for "negative cognitions" and "rational cognitions." Write down some of your negative thoughts and beliefs about feeling depressed in the "negative cognitions" column. Then write down some more positive or reasonable ways of thinking about your depression in the "rational cognitions" column.

## BEHAVIORAL STRATEGIES FOR MANAGING DEPRESSION

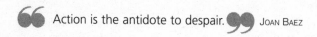 Action is the antidote to despair. JOAN BAEZ

We have already seen that there are two main paths to lifting our mood—change our cognitions and change our behaviors. Behavioral strategies are particularly useful at times when we feel down or depressed. Certain behaviors, such as doing physical exercise, listening to music or spending time with friends can have a direct mood-enhancing effect—doing them can make us feel better. In addition, some behaviors have an indirect effect on our mood by influencing our cognitions. For instance, communicating honestly with a friend can help us to challenge the belief that no one likes or cares about us, which in turn gives us a psychological boost. Fixing something, cleaning out a cupboard or cooking a meal can challenge the belief that we are completely useless, and this can also make us better. In fact, any behavior that gives us a feeling of achievement can lift our spirits. In the section below, we will look at the specific types of behavior that are most helpful for overcoming depression.

### ACTIVITY

As simple as it may sound, being active is one of the best remedies for depression, as well as a good way of protecting ourselves from relapse. The problem with depression is that it makes us introspective and self-absorbed. Our mind becomes preoccupied with thoughts about the hopelessness of our situation, our perceived shortcomings, injustices and other people's indifference to our plight. Depression drains our energy and depletes our motivation so that even minor tasks like getting dressed or making breakfast can feel like hard work. Our inability to get things done adds to our sense of helplessness and hopelessness, which in turn makes us even more depressed. The more depressed we feel, the less we want to do—and the less we do, the more depressed we become.

One way to break out of the depression spiral is to engage in some activity, despite the overwhelming desire to do nothing. By shifting our focus away from negative thoughts out to the world around us, activity gives us a break from depressing ruminations and so makes us feel better. Activity scheduling is also a form of behavioral disputing because as we take some control over our lives we realize that we are not completely helpless after all. Sometimes our motivation increases after we start doing things, so it is important to push ourselves to do things, even when we cannot be bothered.

> 66 Do the opposite to what your depression tells you to do. If you are inclined to stay in bed, then get out. If you do not want to go to the concert, then go. It's important not to let your down moods take control and guide the way you act. 99
> SUE TANNER AND JILLIAM BALL, *BEATING THE BLUES*

## SCHEDULE POSITIVE EVENTS

Two types of activity are particularly helpful for overcoming depression—activities that give us a sense of pleasure and achievement.

### Pleasure

Activities that are intrinsically pleasurable improve our mood and lift our spirits. It is helpful to prepare a list of pleasurable activities that you enjoy, which you can choose from at times when you feel down. For example:

- *talk on the telephone*
- *have a bath*
- *look through some old photos*
- *watch a funny video*
- *write poetry*
- *go for a swim*
- *play computer games*
- *play a musical instrument*
- *work on a puzzle*
- *cook a nice meal*
- *listen to a relaxation CD*
- *play cards*
- *go for a walk*
- *listen to music*
- *have a massage*
- *write in a diary*

- *do some dancing*
- *sit in the sun*
- *go shopping*
- *say a prayer*
- *play golf*
- *read a good book or magazine*
- *have a meal with a friend*
- *do some stretching*
- *play with your pet*
- *work on a hobby*
- *sing*
- *visit a neighbor*
- *do some art work*
- *sexual activity*
- *see a play*
- *Internet chat room*

## Achievement

Activities that give us a sense of achievement are also good spirit-lifters. Getting things done is intrinsically satisfying and helps to reduce the feelings of helplessness that so often accompany depression. Again, prepare a list of achievement activities, including items such as these:

- *get out of bed before 9 am*
- *repair something*
- *work in the garden*
- *finish an incomplete job*
- *make an appointment*
- *drive someone somewhere*
- *do the ironing*
- *work on some special project*
- *make a phone call*
- *mow the lawn*
- *initiate some social contact*
- *do some knitting*
- *do a routine chore*
- *do some sewing*
- *write a letter*
- *clean up the bedroom*
- *do some exercise*
- *pay a bill*
- *clean out a cupboard or spare room*
- *cook a meal*
- *initiate some activity with your children*
- *wash the dishes*
- *go to work*
- *help someone else*

When we feel down or depressed, it is important to increase our involvement in activities that give us a sense of pleasure and achievement, even though they may give us little satisfaction at the time. It is quite normal to find things less enjoyable than usual when we feel depressed but it is important to persevere.

*Doing something is always better than doing nothing.*

*Carol used to enjoy singing in the community choir, but since the onset of her depression she gets little pleasure from her singing. It is tempting for Carol to think, "What's the point? I'm not enjoying it anyway." However, when she compares the way that she feels when she goes to choir practice with the way she feels when she stays at home, Carol can see the value of making the effort.*

## DAILY ACTIVITIES SCHEDULE

A daily activities schedule is a plan of the things that we intend to do each day. Preparing a schedule can provide us with a practical guide during times when we feel particularly low and unmotivated. It is also a useful way of ensuring that we engage in some mood-enhancing activity every day.

### How to use a daily activities schedule

First of all, make several copies of the daily activities schedule form on the next page. If your mood is particularly low in the mornings, it is best to plan your activities the evening before, and begin the day with easy, lead-in activities that motivate you to get out of bed. If your mood does not follow any particular pattern during the day, you may prefer to plan your activities each morning. If you are feeling particularly low it is a good idea to plan for every hour of the day, even if you do not end up doing everything that you had planned. Be sure to include activities for pleasure and achievement every day.

At the end of each day, look at your activities schedule to reflect on the things you planned and the things that you did. Write "as planned" for all the activities that you completed according to your plan. When you digressed from your plan, write down the activities that you actually did. Score each activity that you did out of ten on "P" and "A," to indicate how much *pleasure* or sense of *achievement* you experienced. When rating yourself on achievement, make sure your score reflects your sense of achievement given how depressed you felt at the time, rather than an objective measure of how much you accomplished. For instance, getting out of bed or having a shower may be a major achievement on days when you feel very low.

> KEEPING A DAILY ACTIVITIES SCHEDULE HAS VARIOUS BENEFITS
> 1. It provides a structure to our day and motivates us to stay active.
> 2. It increases our sense of control when we find that we were able to do many of the things that we had planned.
> 3. By scoring our pleasure and achievement activities out of ten, it helps us to identify activities that make us feel good. This gives us useful information about the things that we can continue to do to enhance our mood in the future.

## DAILY ACTIVITIES SCHEDULE

**Date** _____

| Time | Planned activity | Actual activity | P-score | A-score |
|---|---|---|---|---|
| 7:00–8:00 am | | | | |
| 8:00–9:00 am | | | | |
| 9:00–10:00 am | | | | |
| 10:00–11:00 am | | | | |
| 11:00 am–noon | | | | |
| 12:00–1:00 pm | | | | |
| 1:00–2:00 pm | | | | |
| 2:00–3:00 pm | | | | |
| 3:00–4:00 pm | | | | |
| 4:00–5:00 pm | | | | |
| 5:00–6:00 pm | | | | |
| 6:00–7:00 pm | | | | |
| 7:00–8:00 pm | | | | |
| 8:00–9:00 pm | | | | |
| 9:00–10:00 pm | | | | |
| 10:00–11:00 pm | | | | |

*Leonie has been struggling with depression ever since the last of her children left home last year. She has decided to use a daily activities schedule to motivate her to stay active. Each evening she plans her activities for the following day. At the end of each day, she reflects on what she did that day, filling in the "actual activity" column and scoring each activity out of ten on pleasure and achievement. The following are two pages from Leonie's daily activities schedule.*

### DAY/DATE: Monday, August 1

| Time | Planned activity | Actual activity | P-score | A-score |
|------|------------------|-----------------|---------|---------|
| 7:00–8:00 am | Get up. Put on track suit. Go for walk. | Stayed in bed. | 0 | 0 |
| 8:00–9:00 am | Have shower, get dressed, have breakfast. | Stayed in bed. | 0 | 0 |
| 9:00–10:00 am | Go to the library. | Stayed in bed. | 0 | 0 |
| 10:00–11:00 am | Go the supermarket. | Got up. Had a shower. | 1 | 1 |
| 11:00 am–noon | Tidy up the house. | Sat around. Watched TV. | 1 | 0 |
| 12:00–1:00 pm | Lunch with Marilyn. | As planned. | 5 | 3 |
| 1:00–2:00 pm | Lunch with Marilyn. | As planned. | 5 | 3 |
| 2:00–3:00 pm | Go home. Do some gardening. | Did gardening for half an hour. | 4 | 6 |
| 3:00–4:00 pm | Make some phone calls. | Lay down in bed. | 1 | 0 |
| 4:00–5:00 pm | Cook dinner. | As planned. | 2 | 5 |
| 5:00–6:00 pm | Have dinner with Sam. | As planned. | 5 | 0 |
| 6:00–7:00 pm | Go to support group. | As planned. | 5 | 5 |
| 7:00–8:00 pm | Support group. | As planned. | 5 | 5 |
| 8:00–9:00 pm | Come home. Watch TV. | Talked to Sam until almost 10 pm. | 4 | 0 |
| 9:00–10:00 pm | Read in bed. | Watched TV in bed. | 3 | 0 |
| 10:00–11:00 pm | Go to sleep. | Tried to sleep. Stayed awake until about 1 am. | 0 | 0 |

**DAY/DATE: Tuesday, August 2**

| Time | Planned activity | Actual activity | P-score | A-score |
|---|---|---|---|---|
| 7:00–8:00 am | Get up.<br>Put on track suit.<br>Go for a walk. | Stayed in bed. | 1 | 0 |
| 8:00–9:00 am | Have shower,<br>get dressed,<br>have breakfast,<br>read the paper. | Stayed in bed. | 1 | 0 |
| 9:00–10:00 am | Go to supermarket. | Went for a short walk. | 4 | 6 |
| 10:00–11:00 am | Do the laundry. | Had a shower;<br>had breakfast. | 4 | 4 |
| 11:00 am–noon | Tidy up the house. | Did the laundry. | 3 | 6 |
| 12:00–1:00 pm | Make lunch. | As planned. | 2 | 3 |
| 1:00–2:00 pm | Pick up Emma from kindergarten and drop her off at Katy's. | As planned. | 6 | 5 |
| 2:00–3:00 pm | Go shopping. | Stayed and talked to Katy. Played with Emma. | 6 | 4 |
| 3:00–4:00 pm | Come home. Relax. | Came home. Watched TV. | 2 | 0 |
| 4:00–5:00 pm | Cook dinner. | Watched TV. | 2 | 0 |
| 5:00–6:00 pm | Dinner with Sam. | Watched TV. | 2 | 0 |
| 6:00–7:00 pm | Do the ironing. | Had takeout with Sam. | 4 | 0 |
| 7:00–8:00 pm | Work on my patchwork quilt. | Phone calls—Marilyn, Kim. | 4 | 3 |
| 8:00–9:00 pm | Read my book. | Watched TV. | 2 | 0 |
| 9:00–10:00 pm | Watch TV in bed. | Watched TV. | 2 | 0 |
| 10:00–11:00 pm | Go to sleep. | Went downstairs.<br>Watched TV till 3 am. | 2 | 0 |

Leonie finds that keeping a daily activities schedule makes her feel more confident about facing each new day, as she has a structure and purpose in mind. When Leonie reflects on her P and A scores, she notices that she experienced the greatest pleasure when she was spending time with people she likes—her friend Marilyn, her husband Sam grand-daughter Emma, and the women at her support group. She also noticed that activities like going for a walk, gardening and doing household chores such as laundry, ironing and working on her patchwork quilt also made her feel better. On the other hand, she felt at her worst when she stayed in bed, watched TV or just sat around. Leonie can now apply this information when planning her use of time over the next few weeks.

Some people prefer to plan their activities weekly rather than daily. The weekly activities schedule below provides a template for making a weekly plan.

| Time | Monday | | Tuesday | | Wednesday | | Thursday | | Friday | | Saturday | | Sunday | |
|---|---|---|---|---|---|---|---|---|---|---|---|---|---|---|
| | A | P | A | P | A | P | A | P | A | P | A | P | A | P |
| 7:00–8:00 am | | | | | | | | | | | | | | |
| 8:00–9:00 am | | | | | | | | | | | | | | |
| 9:00–10:00 am | | | | | | | | | | | | | | |
| 10:00–11:00 am | | | | | | | | | | | | | | |
| 11:00 am–noon | | | | | | | | | | | | | | |
| 12:00–1:00 pm | | | | | | | | | | | | | | |
| 1:00–2:00 pm | | | | | | | | | | | | | | |
| 2:00–3:00 pm | | | | | | | | | | | | | | |
| 3:00–4:00 pm | | | | | | | | | | | | | | |
| 4:00–5:00 pm | | | | | | | | | | | | | | |
| 5:00–6:00 pm | | | | | | | | | | | | | | |
| 6:00–7:00 pm | | | | | | | | | | | | | | |
| 7:00–8:00 pm | | | | | | | | | | | | | | |
| 8:00–9:00 pm | | | | | | | | | | | | | | |
| 9:00–10:00 pm | | | | | | | | | | | | | | |
| 10:00–11:00 pm | | | | | | | | | | | | | | |

# GENERALLY UNHELPFUL BEHAVIORS

Although individuals find different activities to be helpful, there are some behaviors that are generally unhelpful for most people who feel depressed.

THE MOST COMMON UNHELPFUL BEHAVIORS INCLUDE:
- staying in bed for hours during the day
- inactivity—watching TV for hours or sitting around unoccupied
- avoiding people—isolating yourself
- avoiding any situation that reminds you of your problem
- short-term comfort activities, such as eating snack foods, drinking alcohol or taking drugs (other than prescribed drugs)
- discouraging people who care about you from giving you their support.

## PROBLEM SOLVING

> 66 We must accept responsibility for a problem before we solve it. We cannot solve a problem by hoping that someone else will solve it for us. I can solve a problem only when I say 'This is my problem and it's up to me to solve it.' 99
> M. SCOTT PECK, THE ROAD LESS TRAVELED

Whether you are experiencing major depression or just a period of the blues, chances are that a particular set of circumstances initially triggered your descent into gloom. Sometimes the precipitating event is specific—a relationship breakdown, the death of a loved one, the failure of a business, the loss of a job, the diagnosis of a life-threatening illness. At other times the circumstances that lead to depression are background factors that are not related to any particular event—loneliness, poor self-esteem, an unsatisfactory marriage or family life, the absence of meaning or purpose. Whatever the cause, once depression sets in, a number of additional problems invariably present themselves.

To respond effectively to our depression, we need to not only challenge the negative thoughts and beliefs that fuel it but also to address the specific problems that contribute to our unhappiness. A good way to begin is by writing down a list of the specific problems that we are currently facing. This process imposes some order on our sense of chaos—a mass of distressing experiences can be reduced to a number of specific difficulties. Avoid writing vague statements such as, "My life is a mess" or "Nothing is working out." Using precise descriptions helps to make the situation feel manageable.

*Since I have separated from Tim:*
*I'm afraid that I won't be able to find somewhere to live.*
*I am avoiding people.*
*I am unable to sleep.*
*I feel financially insecure.*
*I have poor self-esteem.*
*I'm afraid of being alone for the rest of my life.*

Once we have defined our problems, the next step is to commence problem solving. This will involve examining each of the specific problems and working out ways in which they can be addressed. When dealing with problems for which there are no clear answers, we will need to brainstorm a number of possible solutions and subsequently identify those which are most viable (see chapter 9). It is a good idea to get other people's input during this process, as depression impairs our ability to think creatively. By focusing on the changeable aspects of our situation, deciding what needs to be done and then following through with specific actions, we can often improve our circumstances substantially and feel a greater sense of control over our lives.

> *Tina has been an active and energetic woman for most of her life. In her earlier days Tina did lots of ballroom dancing and by the age of thirty she was a proficient dancer. She also enjoyed writing, reading books and entertaining friends. Early in her marriage, the family home was always full of interesting people wining, dining, exchanging ideas. After her three children left home, Tina started to focus on her own career and eventually set up a successful public relations consultancy. When her marriage broke up ten years later, Tina sold her business and her house, and went traveling overseas for three years. After she returned, Tina rented an apartment by the beach and set herself a new goal—to write a book about her travels.*

Tina was totally unprepared for the depression that descended on her shortly after she moved into her apartment. For weeks she had difficulty sleeping and found it hard to get out of bed before the early afternoon. She lacked the motivation to do even basic things and found it impossible to work on her book. Tina soon realized that writing is a solitary business and without an outside job or reason to leave the house, she had few opportunities to meet with other people. In addition, being away for so long had caused her to lose contact with many of her old friends and now that she was depressed she felt incapable of calling them. Tina was also reluctant to call on her children because she did not want to burden them with her own problems.

Tina defined her problems in the following way:

➤ I have lost my motivation to do anything, including to write.
➤ I feel lonely and disconnected from people—I'm spending too much time alone.
➤ My days have very little structure—I have too much time on my hands.
➤ Other than writing, I have no interests.
➤ I have difficulty sleeping.

Her next step was to explore possible solutions for each of the problems that she identified. After doing some brainstorming and generating additional ideas from talking to a friend, Tina resolved to take the following steps:

1. Get a part-time secretarial job, for two to three days per week.
2. On the days when I'm not at my job, work on my book each morning until 1 pm.
3. Call up some of my old friends. Reestablish contact. Invite them over for dinner and make more effort to see them.
4. Talk to my children. Tell them how I'm feeling at the moment and ask for their support.
5. Arrange to babysit my granddaughter two afternoons a week.
6. On the days when I work on my book, go to the gym at 3 pm every afternoon. On the days I work in my secretarial job, go to the gym in the evenings.
7. Take up dancing again—go along to the dance club on weekends and two evenings per week.
8. Get back into reading. Join the local library and start reading books again.
9. Join a women's support group.
10. If I still have too much time on my hands, consider doing some courses through the local adult education center.

As Tina involved herself in more activities and reestablished contact with some of her old friends, her mood improved dramatically. Now, two years later, Tina has reestablished an enjoyable lifestyle that gives her personal satisfaction and protects her from falling back into depression.

## SOCIAL SUPPORT

> 66 And in the sweetness of friendship
> Let there be laughter and sharing of pleasures
> For in the dew of little things
> The heart finds its morning and is refreshed. 99
>
> KAHLIL GIBRAN, *THE PROPHET*

Strong, supportive relationships are one of the best safeguards against depression. In fact, studies have found that good social support helps to protect both our psychological and physical health. Sharing our lives with others is pleasurable and helps us to feel better at times when we feel down. The process of talking about our problems and being listened to by someone who cares can be healing in itself.

FRIENDS PROVIDE US WITH MANY IMPORTANT THINGS:
➤ emotional support
➤ practical assistance and information
➤ a different perspective on our problems
➤ a sense of personal worth and belonging
➤ ideas for problem solving.

Being depressed often makes us feel alone. Normal conversation and interaction with people becomes difficult, and there is a heaviness in our heart that can make even basic communication feel like hard work. As we assume that we have nothing to offer, it is tempting to withdraw—physically and emotionally. While curling up into our shell makes us feel safe, it also gives us more opportunity to dwell on our problems. The more we ruminate, the worse we feel.

Most people we interact with can usually guess that something is wrong, although some people might misinterpret our withdrawal as snobbery, rudeness or even rejection of them. For this reason, it is usually helpful to talk to the people in our lives and to explain that we are going through a difficult time. Letting people know that we feel down or depressed can relieve a lot of pressure and sometimes brings additional unexpected support. It is particularly important to talk honestly with the people who care about us the most—our family members and close friends.

Talking is therapeutic, and sharing our concerns can make us feel better. However, sometimes a problem arises when we talk about our issues—people who tell us what we should do. "Why don't you leave that bastard? I would!" or "You've got to be more assertive" or "Lose some weight, buy yourself some new clothes and start flirting!" The problem with receiving advice is that other people's solutions may not be right for us—it may not even be right for them. It is easy to give advice when you do not have to take it yourself! This is not to say that suggesting possible solutions is not useful. Getting suggestions and brainstorming strategies can be helpful, as long as we do not feel pressured or directed on what we should do.

The best way to avoid gratuitous advice is to tell people how they can help. Let them know that you appreciate their support and their willingness to listen, and that this in itself helps you to feel better. Let them know that they cannot solve your problems for you (although you might value some suggestions) as only you can work out what is right for you. This may actually come as a relief—once people realize that all they need to do is listen, they can relax and just be there for you.

A second thing to be aware of is other people's limits. Talking too much and for too long about our own misery can sometimes drive people away. While some friends are happy to listen to our problems indefinitely, others have a short listening span. It is important to be sensitive to people's limits and to know when to stop. (If you feel a strong need to talk about your issues but do not want to push the friendship, try writing in a diary, talking into a tape recorder or seeing a therapist.)

One of the best ways to use our available social support is to do things with people, that is, combine social interaction with an interest or activity. Go to the movies, meet someone for coffee, go for a walk with a friend, go out for dinner or go along to see a show. If you feel well enough, challenge yourself to do something more physically active, such as a game of tennis, a jog in the park, a swim or a game of golf. Activities such as these provide the opportunity to enjoy the company of others without focusing exclusively on our problems. If you can also pay attention to the activity itself and to the lives of the people you are sharing it with, the experience will be all the more satisfying for both you and your friend.

> ❝ The depressed person is constantly chewing on himself. He needs to find something else to chew on. The form of diversion is not important, but the act of diversion is. ❞ PENELOPE RUSSIANOFF, *WHEN AM I GOING TO BE HAPPY?*

## RELAPSE PREVENTION STRATEGIES

Effective management of depression is more than responding to the depression once it has set in. It is about creating a lifestyle that minimizes the likelihood of further episodes and actively responding to any signs of depression the moment they appear. Prevention is always better than cure, and immediate action as soon as symptoms arise is always preferable to seeking treatment after the depression has spiraled.

## DEVELOP MEANINGFUL INTERESTS—FIND YOUR PASSION!

>  Develop interest in life as you see it—in people, things, literature, music. The world is so rich, simply throbbing with rich treasures, beautiful souls and interesting people. Forget yourself. HENRY MILLER

We all know someone who has a passion for something that they love. We know that it is a passion because they talk about it with great excitement, they love doing it and they want to do it as often as they can. The object of their enthusiasm may be totally remote from anything that we can relate to—steam trains, sky diving, seventeenth-century baroque music, model airplanes. It may be a political cause or scuba diving, poetry or football, playing guitar or bird watching. It is not the actual activity that defines a passion, but the joy and enthusiasm with which it is pursued.

*To know what we love doing and to do it often,*
*That is a life well lived.*

In his book, *Flow*, Hungarian-born psychology professor Mihalyi Csikszentmihalyi describes a state of total involvement and immersion in an activity that is satisfying and meaningful. In this state of "flow" we are so absorbed in what we are doing that we are barely conscious of other things around us. For instance, we might not notice noises, other people's presence or the passing of time. We feel in harmony with the object of our attention. Any activity we love doing or that absorbs us in this way also gives protection against depression. Activities that involve active participation (rather than mere observation) and some interaction with other people tend to be the most enjoyable and protective.

Ask yourself, "What do I love doing? What is my passion?" If at this stage your answer is "Nothing," it is a good time to consider your options. Think about some activities that you might enjoy. Keep in mind that a passion is something that we develop over time—not necessarily overnight. It starts as an interest and develops into something more fulfilling as we do it more and more. It may take months or even years to find something that we love doing. That's OK. In the meantime, simply enjoy exploring different things. A good place to start is by choosing one or two courses offered by an adult education center or activities that are offered by clubs and interest groups. Look in the Yellow Pages under "Clubs," check the "What's happening?" section in your local paper, search the Internet, and get a catalog of courses from an adult education center near you. Choose one or two activities that sound interesting and commit yourself to giving it a go for at least six months.

To start you thinking, here are some activities that some people get passionate about:

- play tennis
- sail
- weight-lift
- go to the gym
- play baseball
- fish
- do pottery
- do print making
- quilt
- act in amateur theater
- write short stories
- play card games
- play computer games
- join Internet chat sites
- go to the movies
- play a musical instrument
- join a support group

- play golf
- roller-blade
- scuba dive
- play soccer
- row
- bird watch
- do stained glass
- sculpt
- do computer graphics
- sing in a choir
- write poetry or plays
- collect stamps
- play chess
- join a political party
- go to the theater
- join a foreign language club
- join a singles club

- hike
- dance
- ski
- play softball
- play touch football
- sketch
- do woodwork
- embroider
- read books
- cook
- visit the art gallery
- do public speaking
- paint
- dine out
- join a bridge club
- become active in a movement or political group
- do yoga

> One common reason for suicidal depression is the absence of purpose. The suicide rate fell dramatically as America became involved in the war effort. A national purpose—inspired by America's marching off to war—had transmitted itself to individuals. Suddenly their lives were given a meaning that they might not have found by themselves. Being swept up in a historic time and event put purpose into their existence. But we don't need World War III to overcome personal depression. We need to find something that engages us and lends meaning to our lives. As in the war effort, when we commit ourselves, particularly together with other people, we become part of something larger than ourselves. And we are distracted from the despair of a life lived in solitary, obsessive fixation on ourselves. Our headlights again are turned outwards, illuminating the wonder of the world around us, instead of inward, blinding us to everything but our own unhappiness. PENELOPE RUSSIANOFF, *WHEN AM I GOING TO BE HAPPY?*

## PHYSICAL EXERCISE

Doing regular physical exercise, such as brisk walking, jogging, swimming, weightlifting exercises or working out in a gym, enhances our mood and helps to protect us from depression. Several studies have found that regular physical exercise can be as effective as antidepressant medication for resolving depression among people with mild to moderate depression. There are different theories on how it works, from boosting the production of endorphins (our body's natural opiates) to increasing neurotransmitters such as norepinephrine and dopamine, which in turn elevate mood. Regular exercise also increases our available energy, which gives us greater reserves to deal with stressful situations that arise. In addition, by changing our environment and activity we distract ourselves from negative thoughts. Exercise also enhances our self-efficacy, as the commitment to participate in something difficult, yet important, helps us to feel good about ourselves and increases our perception of control. The commitment to regular physical exercise can also be a symbol of our active participation in life—the willingness to work on something that makes us feel physically and psychologically well.

## DEVELOP YOUR RESOURCES

Everyone experiences negative events at times, but not everyone gets depressed. How we respond to negative events largely depends on the resources that are available to us. These are the things that we can use to help us cope during difficult times, to help us to feel good and protect us from spiralling down into depression.

> OUR RESOURCES INCLUDE:
> ➤ **adaptive thinking:** the ability to think in a psychologically healthy way, and to challenge irrational, negative thinking patterns
> ➤ **good self-esteem:** the belief that we are as important and worthwhile as everyone else, and that we deserve to be happy
> ➤ **self-efficacy:** the belief in our ability to solve our problems and achieve the things that we want
> ➤ **effective communication skills:** the ability to express our thoughts, feelings and wants in a clear and reasonable manner
> ➤ **social support:** the friends, family and social networks that we can access for emotional and practical support
> ➤ **interests:** the things that we engage in beyond our regular commitments, for pleasure and stimulation.

Our resources are not fixed at birth—they are accrued over the course of our lives. We can make a deliberate decision to develop or enhance some of our resources. For instance, we can develop our ability to think in a more psychologically healthy way by reading books, monitoring our thinking on a daily basis and challenging unhelpful thoughts and beliefs by writing disputing statements. We can work to improve our self-esteem by challenging some of the beliefs that cause us to feel inadequate at times (see chapter 7). We can improve the quality of our existing relationships by using effective communication strategies (see chapter 10). We can develop a more extensive and supportive network of friends by participating in more interests and activities, taking social risks, improving our communication skills and initiating social contacts. We can develop new interests by searching for activities that appeal to us, enrolling in courses and joining clubs. Much of the information presented in this and other self-help books provides strategies for increasing our resources and motivating ourselves to access and utilize them in a way that will make our lives richer. It is useful to think about the resources that we already have, and to identify any areas that we would like to improve.

---

### EXERCISE 8.2

1  Describe the resources that you already have which help you to feel good and protect you from becoming depressed.
2  Describe any additional resources that you would like to acquire. What would you need to do in order to develop these resources?

---

## GOAL SETTING

Setting goals is the means by which we move towards the things that we want. Goals give us a sense of direction and purpose and provide us with a structure to help us achieve the changes we want to make. There are two main ways in which goals can help us in relation to depression:

### 1 A safeguard against depression

Working purposefully towards a particular goal keeps us focused and motivated. The sense of purpose makes us feel good and reduces our risk of becoming depressed.

### 2 A tool for overcoming depression

When we feel depressed, setting goals helps us to take control over aspects of our lives and reduces feelings of helplessness. Setting and achieving our goals gives us a sense of mastery, which enhances our mood.

While it is always important to set goals that are attainable, this is particularly the case when we feel depressed. Setting unrealistic goals can lead to failure and then reinforce feelings of helplessness. For this reason, it is important to set modest goals when we feel depressed. These might include things like:

➤ Get out of bed and shower by 9 am.
➤ Walk around the park.
➤ Have a massage.
➤ Cook dinner.

➤ Monitor my thoughts.

➤ Initiate a social activity with someone.

➤ Go to a yoga class.

➤ Practice relaxation.

➤ Eat breakfast, lunch and dinner.

➤ Work in the garden.

➤ Visit a friend.

➤ Reread this chapter.

When we feel depressed, having a daily plan to guide the way we spend our time keeps us motivated. A daily activities schedule provides a good format for setting daily goals. In addition, some people also find it useful to set weekly goals. A weekly goals statement helps to keep us focused on the things we want to achieve over the following week. It is not generally recommended to set goals for more than a week in advance when we feel depressed, as we need frequent reinforcers to lift our spirits. (Longer-term goals provide less frequent reinforcement.)

WEEKLY GOALS STATEMENT

1. Get out of bed and shower by 8 am each day.
2. Go to work each day.
3. Eat dinner with my family each day, even if I'm not hungry.
4. Answer the telephone when I am home.
5. Do two sketching sessions for at least an hour each time.
6. Listen to music for half an hour before going to bed.
7. Go to bed by 10 pm each evening.
8. Reread chapters 7 and 8 of this book.
9. Go to the movies on Friday night.
10. Make an appointment to see a therapist.
11. Enrol in an adult education course.
12. Make telephone calls to two people.

When setting goals, it is important to express them in a way that is objective and measurable. This means defining specific behaviors that we can undertake, rather than vague notions of self-improvement.

Setting goals such as "I'm going to be more positive," "I'm going to improve my eating habits" or "I'm going to be calmer" can be problematic because they are vague and difficult to measure. On the other hand, defining specific behaviors gives us concrete steps that are more easily implemented and achieved. Below are some examples of vague versus objective goals:

| VAGUE GOALS | OBJECTIVE GOALS |
|---|---|
| Be more positive. | Do my thought monitoring every day. |
| Improve my eating habits. | Eat three meals every day. |
| Try to get out more. | Go for a walk each morning, go to classes on two evenings a week, babysit my niece once a week and go out for lunch with a friend at least once a week. |
| Stay calm. | Practice meditation at least four times per week. |
| Take more social risks. | Make telephone calls to at least three people each week. Initiate two social outings each week. |
| Increase my leisure activities. | Go to the movies once a week, go sailing each weekend and do my sketching for at least two hours per week. |

In addition to short-term goals, it is also valuable to think about life goals. These are the goals that keep us focused and motivated in the longer term. As we saw earlier, pursuing life goals gives us a sense of purpose and protects us from getting depressed later (see also chapter 11).

### Relapse prevention example

*Because Anna has suffered previous episodes of depression, she is familiar with the symptoms that signal the possible onset of a new episode. Anna has learned that when she is on the precipice she can often prevent the depression from taking hold by implementing relapse prevention strategies. Anna has written down the following plan, which she starts to implement the moment even a hint of depression emerges.*

1. Get out of bed by 7 am, no matter how I feel. *This is not negotiable.*
2. Start each day with a walk—at least 45 minutes.
3. Call my supportive friends, Susie, Bronny or Jill, and tell them how I feel. Don't isolate myself.
4. Listen to my favorite music.
5. Stay active—keep going to work, write in my journal, talk on the phone, play computer games, cook dinner and clean up my room.
6. Read *Change Your Thinking*.
7. Fill out thought-monitoring forms every day and use Socratic questioning when I find it difficult to dispute.
8. If I'm not feeling better in a few days, see my counselor as soon as possible.

## MEDICATION

People's ability to respond to counseling therapy like CBT depends on the type of depression they are experiencing, as well as their coping resources and personality traits. While many people find CBT to be useful, not everyone recovers with counseling or self-help strategies alone. For those who experience little or no improvement or only partial recovery, the option of antidepressant medication needs to be considered. Mental-health practitioners often recommend medication for people who have moderate to severe depression and/or anxiety, for those whose depression severely impacts on their ability to function, and for those who have not responded to psychological treatment.

Doctors and psychiatrists can prescribe antidepressant medications. The majority of antidepressants are prescribed by general practitioners—usually the first port of call for people who are depressed. Sometimes depressed people are referred to psychiatrists, who have expertise in diagnosing the specific type of depression, and the most suitable medication to prescribe. Clinical or counseling psychologists have expertise in the use of counseling therapies for treating psychological problems and disorders, but they cannot prescribe medication. Thus psychologists who believe that antidepressant medication is appropriate will normally refer clients to their family doctors for medication. Antidepressants are usually given as a temporary measure, with the length of treatment depending on the nature of the depression (frequently six to twelve months). For people who have suffered previous episodes of depression, longer treatment is often recommended—sometimes two years or longer (longer treatment reduces the risk of relapse).

People who are severely depressed, and those who do not respond sufficiently to CBT alone, often benefit from a combination of antidepressant medication and counseling. A major advantage of adding CBT to treatment with medication is that it reduces the likelihood of future relapse. For some people, antidepressant medications produce side-effects, such as dry mouth, agitation, insomnia, nausea, headache, tiredness, mild tremor and diminished libido. Although most antidepressant medications help to reduce anxiety as well as depression, some can cause an increase in anxiety in the short term. While the majority of side effects decrease or disappear after a few weeks, some people find the side effects to be intolerable and may need to try different medications before they find one that suits them.

Over the last twenty years, a huge amount of research has gone into the development of new antidepressant drugs. There are now various types of medication available which, although chemically different from each other, all work through increasing the availability of certain neurotransmitters within the brain. The main classes of medication are:

### Monoamine oxidase inhibitors (MAOIs)

These are an earlier generation of antidepressant drugs (e.g., Nardil, Parnate). MAOIs work by inhibiting the production of an enzyme—monoamine oxidase (MAO)—which in turn increases the availability of neurotransmitters such as dopamine and noradrenaline within the brain. MAOIs are highly effective in treating depression, especially depression that does not respond to other types of medication, however, they tend to produce more side effects, which for some people makes them difficult to tolerate. In addition, people who take MAOIs must adhere to strict dietary restrictions (e.g., no cheese, yeast extracts or soy products, limited alcohol), which also makes them difficult to use. A newer MAOI, Emsam, delivers the medication through a patch worn on the skin. Emsam appears to produce fewer side effects and, at low doses, does not require dietary restrictions.

### Tricyclic antidepressants (TCAs)
Up until the 1990s, TCAs (e.g., Anafranil, Sinequan, Tofranil, Norpramin, Amoxapine) were the standard medication for the treatment of depression. TCAs are frequently effective in treating some of the more resistant types of depression. Because there is no need for dietary restrictions, TCAs are easier to use than MAOIs. However, TCAs also tend to produce side effects and are therefore prescribed mainly for depression that does not respond to treatment with newer types of antidepressants.

### Selective serotonin reuptake inhibitors (SSRIs)
Introduced in the early 1990s, these drugs (e.g., Paxil, Celexa, Lexapro, Luvox, Prozac, Zoloft) are the most frequently prescribed category of antidepressant. They work by increasing the availability of serotonin within the brain. The main advantage of SSRIs is that they produce fewer side-effects than the earlier types of drug and are therefore better tolerated by many people.

### Other types of antidepressant drug
Some newer types of antidepressant drugs are similar to SSRIs but work in different ways. These include SNRIs (serotonin–norepinephrine reuptake inhibitors) such as Effexor, and postsynaptic serotonin receptor blockers and reuptake inhibitors, such as Serzone. Because they are chemically different to the other types of medication, they have slightly different side effects, which make them preferable for some people.

The decision as to which particular antidepressant medication should be prescribed is usually based on the individual's specific symptoms, and what has worked in the past. For instance, some antidepressant medications also have a sedating effect and are therefore useful for people who have trouble sleeping. Some appear to have less adverse effects on libido, which makes them suitable for people who are particularly concerned about impaired sexual function. Certain antidepressants have also been shown to be effective in the treatment of other disorders, such as bulimia and obsessive-compulsive disorder, and are therefore prescribed for people who also have those disorders. Some medications are not suitable for people who have cardiac disease, and a few have negative interactions with other medications and are therefore not prescribed for those particular individuals. Certain types of depression do not respond well to treatment with SSRIs but can be effectively controlled with MAOIs or TCAs. The doctor or psychiatrist who is prescribing an antidepressant normally takes these issues into account when selecting a suitable medication.

Medications are helpful for the majority of depression sufferers, but not all. Studies have found that between fifty percent and ninety percent of depressed people respond to treatment with antidepressant medication. From the time of commencing medication, it often takes two to four weeks before a substantial improvement is felt, although most people who will respond to a medication usually feel some improvement in the first ten days. As people react to different levels of medication, sometimes the dose needs to be increased before the full benefits can be felt. Any change in the recommended dose should only be done with the supervision of a doctor or psychiatrist.

When an antidepressant medication starts working, its effects can be dramatic—people often report feeling significantly better. If you have been taking antidepressant medication for three to six weeks but have not experienced any improvement, you need to see your doctor or psychiatrist to have the dose adjusted or the medication changed. It is not uncommon for people to try two or three different types of medication before they find one that suits them.

## ELECTROCONVULSIVE SHOCK TREATMENT (ECT)

For many people ECT treatment still brings to mind images from *One Flew Over the Cuckoo's Nest*, where the Jack Nicholson character was "zapped" into a zombie-like state in order to make him docile and compliant. In spite of the bad press, ECT can in fact be a highly effective treatment for certain types of severe depression and is particularly effective for treatment of depression that is accompanied by psychotic features (presence of delusions or hallucinations). Modern procedures have eliminated most of the unpleasant effects that used to be associated with ECT. The patient is given a short-acting general anesthetic and a muscle relaxant before an electric current is applied to a carefully selected site on one side of the brain. The convulsive spasms caused by the current are barely perceptible to onlookers, and the patient awakens a few minutes later, remembering nothing about the treatment. To reduce the risk of relapse, ECT is given in a series of treatments (usually between four and fifteen) about two or three times per week. The most common side effects are loss of short-term memory and confusion. ECT works more rapidly than antidepressant drugs and is generally regarded as safe and effective, however, its use is limited to the most severe types of depression.

# IN SUMMARY

➤ Depression is often triggered by stressful life events; however, biological factors, personality, cognitive style and coping resources also play a role in its onset and duration.

➤ Depression causes cognitions to become increasingly negative and self-defeating, which in turn perpetuates or exacerbates the depression. It can also lead to secondary depression, where negative thoughts about the depression itself further intensify the depression.

➤ The negative cognitions that accompany depression can be challenged by using a thought-monitoring form, Socratic questioning and the two-column technique.

➤ Although depression decreases our energy and motivation, it is extremely important to stay active. Any activity that provides a sense of achievement or pleasure reduces despondency and elevates mood. Social activities and physical exercise are particularly helpful.

➤ More severe depression is difficult to treat with self-help alone, and it is important to see a qualified mental-health practitioner. In some cases, antidepressant medication is required for successful treatment of the depression.

## NINE

# Taking Charge

**It is in the process of meeting and solving
problems that life has its meaning.**
M. SCOTT PECK, *THE ROAD LESS TRAVELED*

Life is full of problems! Some are minor irritations that arise during the course of the day, while others are major hardships that can trouble us for years. We have problems in our relationships, finances, health, work and home. On top of that, there are the normal demands and frustrations of everyday life: deadlines, traffic, teenage kids and mounting bills. As some problems get resolved, new ones appear. That is the nature of things.

- *Henry has high blood pressure. Following his recent medical assessment, he has been told by his doctor that he is at serious risk of having a heart attack.*
- *Lee is struggling with his repayments on his mortgage, due to rising interest rates.*
- *Simon has made some incorrect statements on his tax return and has been summoned by the tax department for an audit.*
- *Helen's daughter has dropped out of school and spends her time watching TV.*
- *Ross has been caught driving under the influence of alcohol and is likely to lose his driver's license.*
- *Mary has discovered that she is pregnant following a casual Saturday night liaison.*
- *Lucy has lost her job.*
- *Eleni will have to sell her lovely house in order to finance her divorce settlement.*
- *Nancy has had a fiery argument with her boyfriend, and now it seems that the relationship is over.*

One of the great challenges of being human is to confront and solve problems as best we can. How well we are able to resolve our problems determines how well we live. When we see our problems as a challenge, we feel in control. Taking action is powerful, as the very act of planning and implementing a strategy increases our sense of control and makes us feel better. This is important, as it is the feeling of not being in control that makes problems stressful. Feeling helpless drains our energy and makes us miserable.

This chapter is all about taking charge—learning to look for solutions when problems arise and being prepared to do whatever is necessary to implement them. Taking charge helps us in two ways:

1. It increases the likelihood that we will solve our problems and so helps to get our needs met more often.
2. It gives us a psychological boost. We feel better when we take control.

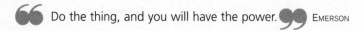 Do the thing, and you will have the power. EMERSON

But what if there's really nothing we can do about it?

Sometimes, we find ourselves in situations where there is nothing that we can do to fix or modify a problem. In those circumstances, our greatest challenge is to practice acceptance—to acknowledge that the situation is beyond our control and to accept that this is how it is. (In fact, the ability to accept situations that are beyond our control is actually a way of exercising some control—we choose to let it go.)

In the vast majority of situations however, there are things we can do to either resolve the problem or, at the very least, reduce its effect. Sometimes the solutions are obvious—at other times we need to explore lots of options before we find out what will work. While the answers are not always clear-cut, the secret is to see each new difficulty as a puzzle waiting to be solved. When you think of yourself as a problem-solver, you are more likely to find solutions.

*If it's going to be, it's up to me!*

## SOLVING PROBLEMS

Our ability to successfully overcome our difficulties depends partly on the nature of the problem itself and partly on the personal resources that are available to us. These include our attitudes, beliefs, strategies and problem-solving skills.

## PRESUME THAT SOLUTIONS EXIST

An exercise that I occasionally do in my workshops is to ask participants to come up with fifty possible uses for a paper clip. Sounds impossible at first, but when I reassure people that our record is 102, the creative juices start to flow. After some time, I ask participants to join up with four other people and continue brainstorming in groups. At this stage, the ideas come flooding in. Not only can we draw upon the ideas of others, but there is an additional synergy that happens when we bounce our ideas off others. The list of ideas grows and grows.

There are two main lessons that we can learn from this exercise. Firstly, when we believe that solutions exist, we are much more willing to look for them and, as a result we are much more likely to find them. Secondly, when we recruit the support of other people we can usually come up with more ideas, and better ones, than if we try to find the answers by ourselves.

## FINDING SOLUTIONS

Some situations lend themselves to problem solving more easily than others. Sometimes the solutions are obvious and, while we may not always be keen to make the effort, we know what we need to do. Henry, for instance, who has recently discovered that he is at risk of a heart attack, knows exactly what he needs to do—stop smoking, improve his diet, embark on a regular exercise regime, and make some lifestyle changes to reduce his stress levels. Lee, who is struggling to keep up his mortgage repayments also has some options—renegotiate the terms of his bank loan, borrow some money from his father or sell some of his shares to give himself some breathing space.

But what about the tough ones—those difficult situations for which no obvious solutions exist? These really test our mettle. Just like the exercise with the paper clip, these situations challenge us to think creatively. Once again, brainstorming possible options, and then narrowing them down to a short list, is the best way to work out what needs to be done.

## SETTING GOALS

To solve a problem, we need to decide what we want to achieve and how to go about it. Setting clear goals is the single most important step to getting the things that we want. Sometimes the steps we need to take may be as simple as "call and explain"; more often, working towards our goals requires thought and planning. The following steps can be useful when we are dealing with more complex problems:

**1. Define the problem clearly.** When we feel overwhelmed by life's circumstances, the problem may appear to be huge and insurmountable. Clearly defining the problem makes the situation feel more manageable and draws our attention to the things we need to work on.

**2. Brainstorm possible solutions.** When the solutions are not obvious, we need to think creatively. Brainstorming helps us to explore a wider range of options and can lead to better solutions. Because brainstorming is a creative process, it is important to think laterally and to write down all your ideas, even those that initially seem silly or impractical (silly ideas can sometimes lead to clever ideas). It is also helpful to ask other people for their suggestions and to add their strategies to your list.

**3. Identify the best solutions.** The next step is to think about the ideas that you have generated and to eliminate those that are not feasible or realistic. Identify the most potentially workable solutions—the ones that are worth considering seriously. Once again, it may be helpful to talk to other people during this process.

**4. Set clear goals.** From your list of potentially workable solutions, write down specific goals. These goals will become the focus of your future actions.

**5. Break down your larger goals into subgoals.** For more complex goals or those that require some planning, it is often helpful to break them down into small chunks or "subgoals." These subgoals are the stepping stones to your main goals. Setting a deadline for each step can provide an additional psychological boost.

> *Chris has been running a busy real estate agency for the past ten years. For most of that time the business has been successful, however, in the last two years sales have plummeted. While part of the problem has been a downturn in the economy, the biggest contributor to the problem has been low morale and lack of motivation among the sales staff. Chris knows that unless things improve, he will be facing financial ruin in the next twelve months.*

Chris decides to do some problem solving to come up with strategies that will help him to turn things around. He invites a colleague who also works in real estate to help him to brainstorm and discuss options. Chris writes the following notes:

1. **Define the problem clearly.**
   - Large drop in sales over the last two years.
   - Currently operating at a loss.
   - Poor performance and low morale among the sales team.
   - High staff turnover.
2. **Brainstorm possible solutions.**
   - Sack the entire sales team and employ a whole new team.
   - Sack two employees who are performing particularly badly.

- Implement more financial incentives for staff to work harder.
- Talk to other real estate agencies and find out how they deal with this type of problem.
- Do a major restructure of staff positions, responsibilities and salaries.
- Invite a management consultant to come in, assess the problem and give advice.
- Offer a voluntary redundancy package to staff and see who takes it.
- Team building—invite sales team and their partners to come sailing on the weekend.
- Organize motivational workshops.
- Schedule weekly staff meetings to discuss performance and productivity issues.
- Send some of the sales team off to do training programs.
- Revise their pay structure to create greater incentive to sell.
- Close the business and invest the money in managed funds.
- Lay down the law: "If your sales fall below our minimum level over three months in a row, you're out."
- Initiate social activities with sales team on a more regular basis.
- Talk to each employee individually and get their perspective on the problem.

3. **Identify the best solutions.**

After exploring each idea generated in the brainstorming session, Chris identified the following as the most viable solutions:

- Call a staff meeting and talk to them as a group—ask them for their suggestions.
- Talk to each employee individually and get their perspective on the problem.
- Schedule weekly staff meetings to encourage more open communication.
- Revise pay structure to create greater incentives to sell.
- Run motivational workshops to build up enthusiasm and team spirit.
- Provide funds for training in sales and marketing.
- Be open to making other changes, based on feedback from staff.

4. **Set clear goals.**

Once he had compiled his list of possible solutions, Chris noticed that they fell into three main areas. From these, Chris identified three goals:

- *Goal number 1*: Substantially improve communication with sales team.

- *Goal number 2*: Create greater financial incentives for sales team to boost their sales.
- *Goal number 3*: Provide additional training programs.

**5. Break down your larger goals into subgoals.**

Chris then proceeded to write subgoals for each of his three main goals:

- *Goal number 1*: Substantially improve communication with sales team.

  Monday to Thursday: Talk to each member of sales team individually and get their perspective on our current problems.

  Friday: Call a staff meeting for the sales team and get their joint feedback and suggestions. Schedule weekly staff meetings to encourage more feedback and open discussion.

  From now on: Try to communicate more openly with staff. Be friendly and remind them that my door is always open. Be open and responsive to their ideas—don't dismiss anything out of hand.

- *Goal number 2*: Create greater financial incentives to boost sales.

  Wednesday: Talk to accountant about revising salary structure. Work out structure that provides greater rewards for higher sales. Announce additional bonus to employees who achieve quarterly sales above our target figure.

  Next week: Consult individually with each employee regarding revised packages.

- *Goal number 3*: Provide additional training programs.

  Monday: Get Rosemary to call Training Solutions to find out about training programs in sales and marketing. Bring up training at next staff meeting.

  Tuesday: Arrange motivational program for next month for entire staff.

  July : Review staff training needs. Arrange further training if necessary.

Now that Chris has worked out his goals and subgoals, he faces the greatest challenge of all—the follow-through. To achieve his goals, Chris will need to act on each subgoal that he has set. This means that he will communicate more openly with his staff from now on, arrange regular meetings, talk to his accountant, change the salary packages, arrange training programs and be more open to receiving feedback from his employees.

Following through with action does not mean that we must never deviate from our plan. At times when obstacles arise or new ideas emerge, it is appropriate to revise some of our plans and to set new goals. However, if we do choose to deviate from our original goals, this should be based on a considered decision to modify our approach rather than merely a lack of staying power or low frustration tolerance.

# IDENTIFYING THE OBSTACLES

The question arises, if it is only a matter of exploring solutions, planning appropriate actions and then taking the necessary steps, why don't we all just do it? Why do so many people remain stuck in unhappy, frustrating, soul-destroying situations when there is a better way? Why can't we simply do what needs to be done to make life easier for ourselves?

The truth is, when it comes to action, most of us are not go-getters. We are not in the habit of looking for solutions and even when we know what needs to be done, we are often reluctant to give it a go. When obstacles arise we give up too easily. We procrastinate, we make excuses, we rationalize, "What's the use? It won't work anyway." The idea might be there, but not the drive to follow through. Obstacles get in our way.

> 66 The elusive goal is translating intentions into action and resolutions into results. The gap between knowing and doing remains a weak link in most of our lives. 99 DAN MILLMAN, *NO ORDINARY MOMENTS*

There are two types of obstacle—psychological obstacles and logistical problems. The psychological obstacles are the most challenging—things like lack of confidence, fear of failure, inertia and low frustration tolerance. Sometimes we also have to deal with logistical problems, such as other people's needs, lack of time, money or skills. Logistical problems are like roadblocks that we need to negotiate in order to get what we want. Solutions usually exist, but we need to look for them and be prepared to do whatever is necessary to implement them. Sometimes we will need to encounter some frustration or discomfort along the way. Allowing ourselves to experience frustration without running away from the task will help us to get what we want.

To achieve our goals we need to be aware of our obstacles—both psychological and logistical—and plan strategies to overcome them.

## PSYCHOLOGICAL OBSTACLES (MIND BLOCKS)

These are the thoughts, feelings and attitudes that stop us from making progress on our goals.

### Fear

Fear is the greatest obstacle of all—it stifles our motivation and can keep us stuck in unhappy situations for years. Common fears include fear of failure, fear of disapproval, fear of discomfort, fear of making the wrong decision, fear of change and fear of stress and hassles.

### Low frustration tolerance

Getting what we want often requires us to move outside our comfort zone. A low tolerance for frustration causes us to procrastinate and sometimes to give up because we are reluctant to endure the discomfort that comes with working towards our goals. Some of that discomfort is created by anxiety, especially when we know that we need to get going but our motivation is low. Low frustration tolerance makes it difficult to start and to persevere, especially when we need to put substantial effort into achieving the things we want.

### Inertia

Humans are creatures of habit. We have a tendency to continue doing the things that we have always done. Creating change requires us to challenge our natural tendency to stick to our old ways.

### Low self-efficacy

Self-efficacy is our belief in our ability to get things done. When our self-efficacy is low, we lack confidence in our own ability, and therefore are not motivated to try or to persevere.

### Poorly defined goals

Knowing that something is wrong and wanting things to change is not enough. Vague or poorly defined goals are a common obstacle to success. To get what we want, we need to clearly define what it is that we want to achieve.

### Poor task approach

Defining what we want is important, but so too is knowing where to start and how to go about getting it. Poor planning and defective strategies limit our chances of success.

### Indecisiveness

Indecisiveness stems from a fear of making the wrong decision. It is supported by the belief that some decisions are right and others are wrong, and as we do not know which are which, our choice might lead to disastrous consequences. It is true that some options may eventually lead to better outcomes than others, however, we can only ever make choices on the basis of information that is available to us at the time. While it is important to consider the possible outcomes of major decisions and at times to delay our actions until we have more information, in some situations we just have to go ahead and decide. Failing to do anything can be the worst decision of all.

# LOGISTICAL PROBLEMS

To overcome psychological obstacles, we need to change the way we think. On the other hand, logistical problems often challenge us to take some sort of action, for instance, communicate with someone, reorganize the way we spend our time or change aspects of our lifestyle.

### Time constraints

Having limited time in which to do all the things that are necessary to get what we want.

### Financial constraints

Having insufficient money to be able to afford some of the things that we need to achieve our goals.

### Low energy

Lacking the stamina needed to do what needs to be done, as a result of things like stress, fatigue, illness or a demanding lifestyle.

### Needs of other people

The time and commitment involved in pursuing some goals can get us into trouble with our partner, family members, work colleagues or friends. The needs or desires of other people can make it difficult for us to work towards our goal, especially if they do not support what we want to achieve.

### Conflicting goals

Pursuing some goals makes it more difficult to pursue others. For example, you may want to develop a business (which requires working long hours) and at the same time to maintain a healthy lifestyle (which requires making time for regular exercise and not pushing yourself too hard). Or you may want to become closer to your children (which involves spending more time with them) but you also want to make your family more financially secure (which may involve working long hours).

### Lack of skills

Sometimes we simply do not have the skills to enable us to get what we want. We may initially need to learn some new skills. Depending on what it is that we want, acquiring skills, such as effective communication, time management, budgeting, cooking or learning to use the Internet, can help us to achieve our goal.

# CONFRONTING OUR OBSTACLES

Once we have defined our obstacles, our next step is to plan strategies to overcome them.

- *Leonard has tried to give up smoking on a few occasions but has not succeeded.*
- *Steve would like to ask his friend to repay the $1000 which he lent him more than two years ago.*
- *Ruth needs to do an evening course at college to upgrade her qualifications but she keeps putting it off.*
- *Helen would like to initiate a friendship with a woman at work.*

All of these people would like to solve problems or improve their lives in some way yet they are all procrastinating. Some are aware of why they are stalling, while others have a vague sense of wanting things to change but they have not made clear decisions about what they need to do. The first step is to set clear goals—define what they want to achieve and how they plan to achieve it. The second step is to identify the obstacles that might get in their way and plan strategies to overcome them.

## DEALING WITH LOGISTICAL PROBLEMS

Logistical problems are rarely insurmountable but they do test our resolve. They tell us that we need to do something to smooth the path ahead. We need to make decisions and follow through with action. Sometimes we will need to reprioritize—put some of our goals on hold while we work towards our highest-priority goal. Sometimes we may need to forgo a comfortable lifestyle for a period of time, take out a loan, get into the habit of rising early in the morning or do a stress management program. Sometimes we may need to get advice from other people, do some research or just try doing things differently for a while. Sometimes we may need to communicate with the people who will be affected by our actions to try to win their support. Every problem has its own potential solutions and the strategies we choose will ultimately depend on our situation and the resources that are available to us.

For instance, Leonard may need to change the way he spends his leisure time for the next six months so that he can avoid the people and situations that arouse his desire to smoke. On top of that, he could use nicotine patches to help reduce his cravings for cigarettes and exercise on a daily basis to remind his lungs how good it feels to breathe. Leonard might also reward himself with a treat every two weeks, using the money that he has saved by not buying cigarettes.

Steve would find it easier to ask his friend to repay his debt if he was more confident of his ability to communicate. It may therefore be helpful for him to read about assertive communication and to carefully plan what he is going to say. He might also consider doing an assertiveness training course so that he can learn to ask for what he wants without feeling guilty.

Ruth will need to cut down on some of her other commitments so that she can concentrate on her college course over the next two years. She will also need to talk to her family, to help them understand why her studies are important and how they can best support her.

Working out what needs to be done is usually not the hard part. Far more challenging is the follow-through—taking the necessary action. Usually this involves moving outside our comfort zone and acting in spite of our internal resistance. Psychological obstacles (mind blocks) such as fear, low frustration tolerance and low self-efficacy can tempt us to say that it is all too hard. When we resolve our psychological obstacles, the logistical problems become far less daunting. When self-doubt and fear dissipate, problem solving becomes much easier.

## DISMANTLING MIND BLOCKS

Mind blocks can be tricky. Sometimes we know exactly why we are procrastinating. At other times we have no idea—we simply know that we cannot get started. Our first task is to identify the source of the problem—the limiting thoughts and beliefs that fuel our resistance. This will involve writing down our thoughts and beliefs. Ask yourself, "Why am I putting this off? Why don't I just go ahead and do what needs to be done?"

Communicating our thoughts directly onto paper or the computer helps us to tap into cognitions that are otherwise difficult to recognize. Writing them down heightens our awareness and helps us to see the specific thoughts that need to be challenged.

| AREA OF PROCRASTINATION | LIMITING THOUGHTS |
|---|---|
| Leonard—giving up smoking | I should give up smoking, but it's so damn difficult! I've already tried so many times—let's face it, I'm not going to succeed now. It's just too hard. |
| Steve—asking for a debt to be repaid | He may not like being reminded about his debt. He might get annoyed if I bring it up. It would be very unpleasant if he got annoyed with me. It makes me feel anxious. |
| Ruth—updating qualifications | At this age, I might not have what it takes. I may end up doing all that work and then failing in the end. It's going to involve making a lot of changes to my lifestyle. There could be many hassles. Do I really need this now? |
| Helen—initiating social connection with woman at work | What if she's not interested? If she says no, I'll feel like a real loser. She might think that I'm desperate—I'd hate her to think of me as needy or vulnerable. |

Once we have identified the limiting thoughts that keep us stuck, it is also very helpful to look at the limiting beliefs that accompany those thoughts.

| LIMITING THOUGHTS | LIMITING BELIEFS |
|---|---|
| Leonard—It's just too hard. I'm not going to succeed. | Things should be easy. I shouldn't have to do things that are difficult. (Low frustration tolerance) Past failure means that it's impossible to succeed this time. (Low self-efficacy) |
| Steve—He might not like it. He might get annoyed with me. | People must always like and approve of me. I should never do things which someone might disapprove of. (Fear of disapproval) |
| Ruth—I might not succeed. I might go to a lot of trouble and fail anyway. | I should always avoid the possibility of failure. I should not attempt things unless I am certain of success. The consequences of failure would be catastrophic. (Fear of failure) I should avoid hassles at all costs. My life should always be easy and comfortable. (Low frustration tolerance) |
| Helen—If she says no, I'll feel like a loser. She might think that I'm desperate. | I'd hate her to think of me as needy or vulnerable. If she's not interested or available it means that I'm not OK. I should always appear confident and self-assured. (Fear of rejection and disapproval) |

## CHALLENGING LIMITING THOUGHTS AND BELIEFS

Identifying the limiting thoughts and beliefs that keep us stuck can be motivating in itself. When we look at our negative cognitions, we can often see the lack of logic in our thinking. However, this is still not enough. The most important step of all is to write down statements that directly challenge our limiting thoughts and beliefs. These positive statements are not based on magical thinking but on realistic perceptions regarding what we can achieve. The process of writing and reading over these statements (several times if necessary) increases our motivation and inspires us to challenge limiting cognitions and get on with the job (see table below).

| LIMITING THOUGHTS AND BELIEFS | POSITIVE STATEMENTS |
|---|---|
| It may be hard or unpleasant. I should always avoid things which might be hard or unpleasant. | It may be hard or unpleasant, and that's OK. There is no reason why I must always avoid things that are hard or unpleasant. Confronting things that are difficult makes it easier to deal with difficult things in the future and makes me stronger. |
| It might involve lots of stress or hassles. I should avoid situations that may involve hassles. | It might involve stress or hassles, but hassles are a normal part of life. It's OK to experience hassles in the process of working towards what I want. Confronting hassles is a good learning experience. If I can achieve my goal, it's worth the hassles. |
| It's too much work. | It's a lot of work, but it's not too much work. If I take one step at a time, and have reasonable expectations of how much I can achieve each day, it's manageable. |
| I might not succeed. It would be awful to try and fail. I should never attempt things unless I'm guaranteed success. | I have no guarantee of success but I'm guaranteed that nothing will change if I don't give it a go. I prefer to succeed but I can cope with failure if it should happen. |

| LIMITING THOUGHTS AND BELIEFS | POSITIVE STATEMENTS |
|---|---|
| I can't do it. I don't have the ability to succeed. | I can achieve some things when I put my mind to it. I have achieved lots of things already. If I'm willing to try more often, I am more likely to experience success more often. |
| I've already tried and failed in the past. Past failure means that it's impossible to succeed in the future. | Some things require several attempts before we finally succeed. Just think of how many times Thomas Edison failed before he finally succeeded in inventing the light bulb. |
| The problem is too complex. Complex problems can't be resolved. I shouldn't deal with complex problems. | Complex problems can be resolved by breaking them down into small manageable chunks. If I break down the problem into small sections and do one step at a time, it won't be too complex. It's OK to tackle complex problems. |
| If I fail I'll feel awful. Failure is a terrible thing. | Better to have tried and failed than to never have tried. There is no shame in failure—only in not giving things a go. If I try, at least I'll know that I've given it my best shot. |
| Other people might not like it. I should never do anything that some people may disapprove of. | Some people may not like it but if they have my best interests at heart, perhaps they will support me. I need to explain to them why this goal is important and try to recruit their support. I prefer people to approve of what I do but I can choose to do some things, even if certain people don't approve. |

# THE PLAN OF ACTION

So now that we have defined the problem, brainstormed some possible solutions, set goals and identified the obstacles that are likely to get in our way, we are ready for the final stage—writing our plan of action. This is a blueprint of what we want to achieve, and the steps we will take to achieve them. Our plan of action also includes a list of the obstacles that we will need to overcome, and the strategies that we will use to overcome them.

PLAN OF ACTION
- ❏ statement of goal
- ❏ specific measurable targets
- ❏ target date
- ❏ how I will benefit from achieving this goal
- ❏ specific steps to achieve this goal.

Overcoming the obstacles
- ❑ logistical problems
- ❑ strategies to overcome them
- ❑ limiting thoughts
- ❑ motivating thoughts.

*Janice is in a rut. Until her mid-thirties, Janice used to be a picture of health and fitness, however, in the last few years she has stopped paying attention to her health. She has developed the habit of eating lots of unhealthy takeout food and drinking wine every evening to relax. Drinking at night makes it difficult for Janice to get out of bed the following morning, and it also makes her feel tired for much of the day. As she has little time to exercise, Janice has become unfit and has put on weight. She feels particularly frustrated at not being able to get into some of her favorite clothes.*

After many months of concern about the direction that her life is taking, Janice decides that it is time to do something about it. She writes the following plan of action:

## PLAN OF ACTION

### 1. Statement of goal
I want to have a healthy lifestyle—lose weight, improve my fitness, and eat healthy food.

### 2. Specific measurable targets ■ Target date
- Lose 10 pounds in the next three months—*by November 1.*
- Jog around the park (3 miles) on five mornings per week—*from next Monday.*
- Eat home-cooked healthy meals on at least five evenings per week—*from today.*
- Stop eating deep-fried foods, rich desserts and high-fat snacks—*from today.*

### 3. How I will benefit from achieving this goal
- I will be healthier.
- I will feel more in control over my life.
- I will look better.
- I will be able to wear some of the clothes that I can't fit into at the moment.
- I will have more energy—will feel better physically and mentally.
- I will feel good about myself.

### 4. Specific steps to achieve this goal
- Get up at 6 am each morning on Monday to Friday and go for a jog around the park.
- Buy some healthy lifestyle cookbooks to give me ideas for making healthy meals.
- Go to the market every Saturday morning and buy lots of fruit and vegetables.
- Say no to temptations of junk food and high-fat snacks. When I feel like a snack, eat fruit, yogurt or other healthy alternatives.

- Cook healthy meals on at least five nights a week. Use recipe books and ideas from friends.
- Eat out on weekends only. Be selective with the type of restaurants that we go to and the meals I order. Try to choose more healthy dishes.
- Stop drinking wine during the week—drink only on weekends or special occasions.
- Relax in the evenings by listening to my favorite music and talking on the phone to friends.

## OVERCOMING THE OBSTACLES

| LOGISTICAL PROBLEMS | STRATEGIES TO OVERCOME THEM |
|---|---|
| I find it very hard to get up early in the morning to exercise because I am usually very tired. | I will need to go to bed earlier from now on. Go to bed at 9:30 and read for half an hour each night. (I tend to get sleepy when I read.) Also, I'm going to stop drinking wine during the week (except on special occasions) as that also makes me tired the next day. |
| Jason (husband) enjoys eating out and he may not like my home-cooked meals as much. | Talk to Jason—tell him how I feel. Get him to understand why I need to make these changes. Ask him to support me. Try to encourage him to also take an interest in healthy food and lifestyle. Agree to eat out on weekends. |
| Don't get much time to shop during the week. | Go to the markets early on Saturday mornings. Buy the fruit and vegetables for the entire week. |

| LIMITING THOUGHTS | MOTIVATING THOUGHTS |
|---|---|
| I enjoy drinking wine at night—it helps me to relax. I'll find it hard to stop that now. | It may be hard at first, but not too hard. It's good for me to do things that are difficult at times. Once I get used to feeling well and energetic on the following morning, it will be much easier to keep doing it. |
| I don't believe that I can really change much. This could be beyond my control. | Some situations are beyond my control, but this one is not. I used to have good control over my lifestyle, and there is no reason why I can't do it again. I just need to get back into the routine. |
| I feel impatient—like I need to get instant results. | No change happens overnight. Losing weight slowly is the best way to keep it off. If I monitor my progress weekly rather than daily and if I have reasonable expectations, I'm more likely to succeed. |
| The way I'm living has become a habit. It's hard to change my lifestyle because I'm used to it. | I've changed many of my habits over time and I can continue to change some of them now. There will be some frustration in the beginning, but that's OK. Once I get used to a healthier lifestyle, feeling good will be my biggest reward. New habits are easier to maintain once I've had them for a while. |

## BEHAVIORAL DISPUTING

We have already seen that behavioral disputing—using specific behaviors to challenge our cognitions—is an extremely powerful way of changing our perceptions. So for instance, we might challenge the belief that certain people deserve our contempt, by deliberately being helpful or pleasant towards them; we can challenge the belief that we must always be in control by deliberately choosing to relinquish control in some situations; or we might challenge the belief that rejection would be unbearable by taking social risks and experiencing the possibility of rejection.

Behavioral disputing is particularly useful when we are dealing with cognitions that stifle our motivation, such as "It's too hard," "I can't do it" and "I'll probably fail." A good way to dispute these cognitions is to make a start, in spite of the desire to put it off for another day. Once we make some progress on the things we thought we could not do, our cognitions tend to change. Experiencing even a small degree of success challenges beliefs such as, "It's too hard" or "I can't do it," and increases our motivation. We develop confidence in our ability to succeed as we realize that it is not so hard after all.

> 66 Courage is not the absence of fear. It is the willingness to act, in spite of the fear. 99 M. Scott Peck, *The Road Less Traveled*

INGREDIENTS FOR SUCCESS
➤ a belief that change is possible
➤ self-efficacy—the belief in our ability to succeed
➤ clearly defined goals
➤ a plan of action
➤ a willingness to confront obstacles.

## EXERCISE 9.1

Describe a goal that you would like to achieve or an issue that you want to resolve.

1. Are there any logistical problems that you need to overcome? If so, write them down.
2. Suggest some actions that could help you to overcome these logistical problems.
3. Are there any psychological obstacles that might impede your ability to succeed? If so, write them down.
4. Suggest some positive statements that can help you to challenge those psychological obstacles.
5. Can you do any behavioral disputing to challenge the obstacles that have held you back so far?

# SELF-EFFICACY

Self-efficacy refers to the belief in our ability to get things done. It is the confidence that we feel in our ability to achieve things, from cooking a nice meal to writing a best seller. Our self-efficacy varies from one task to another. For instance, you might feel confident when it comes to using a computer, fixing an electrical appliance or building a boat but not when it comes to making friends or selling yourself at a job interview.

Our self-efficacy plays an important role in the things that we are willing to attempt and our motivation to persevere. It determines how hard we try and how long we are willing to persist. So for example, if you have little confidence in your ability to stop smoking, improve your diet, make new friends, get a college degree, or set up your own business, low self-efficacy will be a major obstacle to success.

Our self-efficacy is largely influenced by our experiences—the things that we have been able to achieve in the past. Whenever you experience success in a particular area, your self-efficacy grows for this type of task. It may even encourage you to extend yourself to more challenging tasks. Experiences of failure often have the opposite effect. To try and fail can reduce our self-efficacy, and so diminish our willingness to try again. This is particularly the case if we have experienced failure on several occasions. Repeated episodes of failure can demolish our confidence in our ability to succeed. Ultimately, not achieving what we want may have a lot more to do with low self-efficacy than with lack of talent. Once you believe that you cannot do it, chances are that you won't.

 Whether you think you can or you think you can't, you are right.
HENRY FORD

## BUILDING SELF-EFFICACY

Self-efficacy is a perception. Like many of our perceptions, it can be modified and sometimes radically overhauled. Many motivational writers suggest using affirmations to reinforce our ability to succeed. Affirmations can be useful, but their content needs to make sense to us. Simply repeating statements like, "I deserve success and I am a winner" or "I am achieving everything that I set out to do" does not magically increase your self-efficacy if you do not believe that what you are saying is true. There is, however, a more practical way to affirm our belief in our ability to succeed—use realistic thinking. Recognize the skills and abilities that you already have. Acknowledge your past achievements and dispute some of the negative thinking that diminishes your belief in your ability to succeed.

## ACKNOWLEDGE YOUR SKILLS AND PAST ACHIEVEMENTS

When it comes to thinking about their performance, many people self-sabotage. Unrealistic standards and high expectations can cause us to undervalue our skills and achievements. Perfectionist thinking makes us aware of our faults and failures but causes us to ignore our strengths, abilities and past successes. Perhaps self-criticism and flagellation is our way of trying to motivate ourselves to try harder? While this may intuitively seem like a good idea, in reality it is about as effective as trying to motivate a child with constant criticism, telling her how hopeless she is and that she will never amount to anything. Do you really believe that focusing on your deficiencies will encourage you to try?

A basic rule of human motivation—we are far more likely to achieve what we want when we believe in our ability to succeed. For this reason, it is much better to think about our successes, strengths and achievements than to focus on our shortcomings. Acknowledging our skills, abilities and past successes reinforces the perception that we have the ability to succeed on this occasion.

> 66 No matter how well you do, it only becomes an accomplishment when you tell yourself that you did well. 99 BOB MONTGOMERY, *THE TRUTH ABOUT SUCCESS AND MOTIVATION*

### EXERCISE 9.2

Do the self-efficacy booster exercise below and notice how your perceptions change when you recognize your existing strengths and abilities.

SELF-EFFICACY BOOSTER

1. Write down a goal—something that you would like to achieve.
2. List all the skills, abilities and strengths that you already have that will help you to achieve this goal.
3. Write down any of your past achievements which provide evidence that you are capable of achieving this type of goal.
4. Describe the limiting thoughts or beliefs that cause you to doubt your ability to succeed and, next to each of these, write some statements that directly challenge those cognitions.

*Bob has worked as an architect at a large firm for the past fifteen years. While he doesn't mind the work, Bob believes that he is poorly paid and, at times, taken for granted. For this reason, a recent job advertisement for a highly paid position at another company caught his eye. Bob would dearly love to apply for the position but he is not sure that he has what it takes. It has been a long time since Bob has gone for a job interview, and he thinks that he might find it hard to demonstrate his abilities or impress the panel. In addition, he is not sure whether he is good enough to do the job. Perhaps they want someone younger, with more management experience?*

The problem is that while Bob's self-efficacy is low, he is not likely to get very far. Even if Bob does manage to get to the interview, his lack of confidence will be reflected in his tone, body language and the things that he says. His performance at the interview is likely to suggest that he is not up to the job. It would therefore be useful for Bob to consider his skills and realistically reflect on some of his strengths and abilities. To help him do this Bob decides to do a self-efficacy booster:

SELF-EFFICACY BOOSTER

1. Write down a goal—something that you would like to achieve.
   - I would like to get the advertised position at Design Solutions.
2. List all the skills, abilities and strengths you already have that will help you to achieve this goal.
   - I have lots of experience—I have done this type of work for the last fifteen years.
   - I am self-disciplined and hardworking and I enjoy doing this type of work.
   - I pick up new information and concepts quickly.
   - My designs have led to many new contracts at my current workplace.
   - My performance appraisals have always been positive.
   - I get on well with the people I work with.
   - I am highly regarded by the people in management.
3. Write down any of your past achievements that provide evidence that you are capable of achieving this type of goal.
   - I secured that highly lucrative government contract, when most people thought it was impossible.
   - I have made a good impression on our new clients.
   - I made some useful connections at the conference last year.
   - I learned to use some of our new technically complex computer software.
   - In the days when I used to apply for jobs, I succeeded in about fifty percent of my applications.
4. Describe the limiting thoughts or beliefs that cause you to doubt your ability to succeed and, next to each of these, write down some disputing statements that directly challenge them (see table following page).

| LIMITING THOUGHTS AND BELIEFS | DISPUTE |
|---|---|
| This position must require someone with a lot more ability than I have. | I already have lots of skills and abilities—I am pretty highly qualified. I'll be honest with them at the interview, and if I'm not what they're looking for, that's OK. |
| To earn so much money, I would have to be a super-performer. | I am used to getting paid less, but that doesn't mean that I am not worth more. Many people who are paid more than me are not particularly outstanding performers. |
| I am forty-five years old—perhaps that's too old to take on a new, high-powered position? Am I still smart enough to learn all the new things that I'll have to learn? | Being forty-five gives me the advantages of experience, maturity and accrued skills. I know that I can learn new concepts, ideas and systems without difficulty. |
| I haven't gone for a job in such a long time—I'm not sure I'll be able to sell myself. | I can sell myself effectively when I believe in my own ability. For this reason I need to focus on my strengths and achievements. I also need to put together a good resume and prepare myself for the interview. |

You might be saying to yourself, "That's all very well for Bob, he's performed really well throughout his career. Now all he needs to do is realize it. But what about those of us who have made some major mistakes or experienced failures along the way?" It all comes down to how we think about "mistakes" or "failure."

## LOOK AT MISTAKES AND FAILURE AS A LEARNING EXPERIENCE

The trouble with mistakes or failure is not the event itself but the negative beliefs that it can generate—"I've screwed up in the past, so I'll screw up again." Repeated failures are discouraging because they can reduce our expectations of future success.

Developing self-efficacy involves more than recognizing our strengths and achievements. It also involves acknowledging our past mistakes and failures without exaggerating or distorting their importance. The challenge is to learn from our past mistakes and to use those lessons in our new endeavors so that we increase our chances of future success.

> 66 Let's expect to make some errors in judgment and welcome them as part of the learning process. Also, if we don't take ourselves too seriously, it is a whole lot easier to live with a few mistakes. 99 ANDREW MATTHEWS, *BEING HAPPY*

## AVOID PERFECTIONISM

Although perfectionism is a common trait of many ambitious people, those who excel are rarely perfectionists. More often they are people who aim for excellence and set themselves challenging goals but remain flexible enough to accept mistakes and setbacks as a normal part of the process. In fact, perfectionism has the potential to destroy our self-efficacy and crush our motivation as we are rarely able to meet the high standards that we set for ourselves.

Having unrealistic expectations of how well we should perform and how much we should achieve can leave us feeling frustrated and discouraged. On the other hand, realistic expectations allow us to experience success more often, which in turn boosts our self-efficacy and motivates us to stay on the job.

 Anyone who has never made a mistake has never tried anything new.
ALBERT EINSTEIN

## USE A REALISTIC DEFINITION OF SUCCESS

What does success mean to you? Does it mean achieving everything you set out to do each day? If so, chances are that you are feeling pretty discouraged by now. You are far more likely to achieve what you want and to feel good about what you do when you define success realistically.

Several writers have provided definitions of the word "success," but probably the best one I have come across is that of Dr. Bob Montgomery in his book *The Truth about Success and Motivation*. He defines success as having "done your personal best at this stage, given your genes, past experiences and present situation." Note that this does not mean that you always get things right or achieve what you want. It means that you do your best, given the information, abilities, energy, skills and life circumstances that are available to you at the time. When we are able to accept that we can only do our best, given our available resources, we can be kinder to ourselves and feel successful more often.

## USE SUBGOALS

Facing the challenge of an important new goal can be daunting. It is easy to feel overwhelmed and discouraged by the sheer size of the task, especially when the rewards of success are a long way off. Working towards a goal that takes months or years to achieve, such as getting a college degree, launching a new business, changing careers or expanding our social network, can be hard work if there is little to keep us going along the way.

This is why setting subgoals is so important. Breaking down our main goal into small chunks makes the task more manageable and increases our opportunity to experience a sense of achievement along the way. While our final target may be a long way off, our subgoals are within reach. Consequently, subgoals keep us motivated as we work our way towards the bigger target, and as we reach our subgoals, our self-efficacy grows. Achieving subgoals gives us a sense of making progress, even if it happens at a slower pace than we would ideally like.

## SET REALISTIC SUBGOALS

As with our main goals, it is also important to be realistic with the subgoals that we set, otherwise our self-efficacy will suffer.

> *Mary is hoping to write her history essay over the next week. She has planned to do the background research on Monday, develop a rough draft on Tuesday, write the main section on Wednesday and finish off the remainder on Thursday. Like many students, Mary is finding that her essay is taking much longer to write than she had planned, and as a result she feels frustrated and discouraged. Today Mary spent the entire afternoon working on the discussion section of her essay but she has completed only half of what she had planned. Mary thinks to herself, "Today was a total waste of time—I barely achieved anything."*

Setting overly ambitious subgoals can leave us feeling discouraged. Mary could have saved herself a lot of frustration by setting more realistic subgoals. In addition, telling herself that she had "wasted the entire day" is counter-productive. Mary would have felt much more motivated if she had acknowledged that she has made some progress, despite the fact that she did not achieve as much as she would have liked.

Telling ourselves "I didn't do as much as I had planned but I did make some headway" helps to reinforce the idea of success and makes it easier to return to the task on the next occasion. Remember, the time that we spend working towards a goal is never a complete waste, even if we achieve no more than discovering what does not work.

## WRITE A DAILY TO-DO LIST

A very simple yet amazingly effective tool for getting things done is to write a daily to-do list. This is a list of the tasks that we plan to do each day. Crossing off the items on our list as they are accomplished boosts our self-efficacy because we acknowledge our progress as we get things done. It also enables us to realistically reflect on what we have achieved each day and to adjust our expectations over time.

If we are not achieving the tasks that we had planned, it may be worth examining the reasons why. Just as it is useful to identify the obstacles to achieving our greater goals, it is also useful to reflect on the obstacles that stop us from achieving our daily goals. The following are common obstacles to achieving our daily goals:

**Unrealistic expectations**—We were overly ambitious in what we had planned to achieve in one day.

**Low frustration tolerance**—We lacked the self-discipline to confront the tasks because we find them difficult, challenging or boring.

**Anxiety**—We know what we need to be doing, however, the thought of doing it makes us feel anxious, so we procrastinate.

**Depressed mood**—We feel too low to motivate ourselves to work on our goals.

**Giving way to distractions**—We allow ourselves to get distracted by emails, phone calls, TV or conversations.

**Lack of focus**—We lose sight of our set tasks because we do not refer to our to-do list.

**Lower priority tasks**—We engage in other, lower-priority activities because we can mentally justify them to ourselves (after all, they need to be done), however they are not the things that we need to be working on right now.

**Low energy**—We find it hard to work on our tasks because we feel tired or low in energy.

**Other people's expectations**—Other people make demands on our time, and we respond to them.

---

## EXERCISE 9.3

Write a daily to-do list for the next two weeks. At the end of each day, cross off the tasks that you have achieved. For every task you do not achieve each day, fill in the following form:

TASKS THAT WERE NOT ACHIEVED TODAY: _____

| WHAT WERE THE OBSTACLES? | LESSONS LEARNED? STRATEGIES TO OVERCOME THESE OBSTACLES IN THE FUTURE? |
|---|---|
| Unrealistic expectations | |
| Low frustration tolerance | |
| Anxiety | |
| Depressed mood | |
| Giving way to distractions | |
| Lack of focus | |
| Lower priority tasks | |
| Low energy | |
| Other people's expectations | |
| Other | |
| _____ | |
| _____ | |
| _____ | |
| _____ | |

## KEEP IT GOING—REINFORCEMENT

Once we start to make some progress, we feel good—we are on the way! It is easy to feel inspired in those initial days or weeks, but what about later? One of the biggest obstacles to getting what we want is losing sight of our goals over time. We get distracted. We forget. We stop trying. We give up.

Whether or not we succeed depends largely on our willingness to persist—to continue working towards our goals for as long as it takes to get there.

> 66 Persistence is a secret. Successful people know the secret.
> They realize that it is the main ingredient in winning at anything …
> Most people are quitters. 99 ANDREW MATTHEWS, *BEING HAPPY*

To remain motivated over the longer haul, it is important not to lose sight of our goals. Just as certain strategies can inspire us to get started, others can help us keep up the momentum over time.

### 1. DISPLAY GOAL PROMPTS

The very act of defining our goal and writing down a step-by-step plan for its achievement boosts our motivation—that is why preparing a plan of action is so important. In addition, writing down and displaying goal prompts helps us to stay on track. A goal prompt is a word or short phrase that represents our goal and serves as a reminder of the things we want to achieve. For instance, the word "vitality" may remind us of our decision to build up our fitness; "lighten up!" may remind us of our plan to take things a little less seriously; and "communicate" may remind us of our decision to remain open and available whenever our partner brings up an issue that needs to be resolved. Display your goal prompts in prominent places to remind you of your commitment. Consider sticking them on the fridge door, the telephone, the inside of your closet door, the toilet door, a business card in the clear section of your wallet or as a screen saver on your computer.

Every time you see your prompt, stop and ask yourself, "Have I done anything today in relation to my goal? What can I do today or tomorrow that will bring me closer to achieving my goal?"

### 2. DISPLAY PHOTOS AND PICTURES THAT REMIND YOU OF YOUR GOAL

Visual images can evoke powerful emotional responses that inspire us on a deeper level. A photograph or drawing that captures the spirit of what you want to achieve can serve as a powerful impetus to persist. A picture on the fridge of the divan you would like to buy can remind you of the need to keep saving. A photo of you and your partner during happier times can serve as a motivator to keep working on that relationship. A picture of a dream holiday from a travel agent's brochure can remind you of the reward that you will give yourself after you finish that important project.

## 3. VISUALIZE

Visualizing successful outcomes is widely used as a motivational tool for reinforcing goals. After you have defined your goal and made a plan of action, visualize yourself working towards it, going through each of the steps that you will need to take along the way. The more senses you employ within your imagination—sounds, textures, images, colors and smells—the more vivid the experience and the more powerful the effect. After visualizing yourself working towards your goal, see yourself having achieved it, enjoying the fruits of your success. For example, you might see yourself studying at home, cramming in the library, taking your exams and checking the Web site for your grades. Then see yourself on graduation day, stepping up to the podium as you are about to receive your diploma. Finally, see yourself working in an exciting and rewarding job—the product of persevering with your studies.

## 4. TALK ABOUT IT

Talking about our goals reinforces our commitment and helps to keep us focused. Talking with people who share similar goals, or to those who strongly support our desire to succeed, is particularly inspiring. It is also important to talk to the people who will be affected by our efforts—those whose goodwill we will need to nurture along the way. When people understand what we want to achieve and why our goal is important they are more likely to come on board, particularly if they have our best interests at heart. Accordingly, recruiting support from your partner, children, friends, boss or work colleagues can help to smooth the path further down the track.

## 5. FOCUS ON THE REWARDS THAT YOU STAND TO GAIN

The desire to receive rewards and to avoid punishment is at the essence of all human behavior. When we perceive the punishment associated with a course of action to be greater than the rewards, we are not motivated to act. So focusing on the possible problems, difficulties, frustrations and hassles that you might encounter as you work towards your goal is a guaranteed turn-off. On the other hand, acknowledging that there may be some difficulties along the way, but keeping them in perspective while focusing largely on the rewards, will have the opposite effect. Stay mindful of all the benefits that you stand to gain—write about the rewards and visualize them on a regular basis. Be sure to include all the incidental rewards that will come with success, such as improved self-efficacy and self-esteem, admiration from others and a sense of personal satisfaction.

## 6. REWARD YOURSELF

Although the joy of achieving a goal is usually its own biggest reward, sometimes setting an additional prize that is conditional upon the completion of your goal can provide extra incentive. Make the size of your reward proportional to the amount of effort that you will need to put in. Rewards such as a massage, a new outfit, a night out at a special restaurant, a weekend away, an overseas holiday or a new car may be appropriate, depending on the effort involved. Be sure to make your reward conditional on achieving your goal—if you plan to reward yourself regardless of your achievement, it will not be an effective motivator.

## 7. USE QUOTES THAT INSPIRE YOU

Just as certain pictures can arouse strong emotional responses that intensify our desire to succeed, so too can words. A poem, a quote or a short piece of prose that is meaningful to you can provide additional inspiration to strengthen your desire to persist.

Below are examples of quotes that some people find inspiring. If any of these move you, use them for your own spark of inspiration. Alternatively, you might prefer to look at other sources for quotes that are meaningful to you.

**Do the thing, and you will have the power.**
EMERSON

**Just do it!**

**Action is the antidote to despair.**
JOAN BAEZ

**If it's going to be**
**It's up to me.**

**Don't wait for a light to appear at the end of the tunnel**
**Stride down there ... and light the bloody thing yourself.**
SARAH HENDERSON

**Life is made up of a series of choices**
**For which I am largely responsible.**

**The way we live is determined**
**not by what we read or hear or think**
**but by the things that we do.**

**Victims spend their time pointing to the problems.**
**Winners spend their time looking for solutions.**

**Persistence is a secret ...**
**Most people are quitters.**
ANDREW MATTHEWS

# IN SUMMARY

➤ Problems are an unavoidable part of life. Taking responsibility for solving problems increases our perception of control and enables us to get our needs met more often.

➤ It is important to accept situations that are beyond our control and to focus our efforts on situations that are changeable.

➤ For more complex problems, a systematic process of problem solving can help us find optimal solutions. Once we have identified useful goals, it's helpful to break them down into small steps and work through them, one step at a time.

➤ When people fail to achieve their goals, it is because certain obstacles get in their way. Obstacles can be psychological (such as low self-efficacy, fear of failure, inertia and low frustration tolerance) or logistical (such as other people's needs, lack of time, money or skills). We can increase our likelihood of success by recognizing our obstacles and planning strategies to overcome them.

➤ A plan of action can keep us focused and motivated while working towards our goals. Other motivational strategies include goal prompts, visualization, focusing on the rewards, and inspiring quotes.

## TEN

# Effective Communication

A sweet life is a shared experience. Our greatest joys, our most precious moments, our toughest challenges and our most loving times are mostly shared with people ... To have a memorable stay on this planet we must be prepared to knock down some barriers—make a special effort to meet, be with, get close to people.

ANDREW MATTHEWS, *MAKING FRIENDS*

Communication is the process through which we connect with people, share information, disclose our concerns and negotiate solutions to our problems. Good communication is essential for successful relationships. It enables us to make friends and develop bonds. Without communication, we would be isolated in our own solitary world. We would also be unable to solve many of our problems or get our needs met most of the time.

*Dennis is constantly getting into trouble in his personal relationships. Whenever he needs to resolve a problem, his attempts at communication invariably end in unpleasant confrontations that upset both himself and the other person. Over time Dennis has managed to alienate many of the people that he deals with, both at work and in his private life. Finally he concludes that trying to resolve issues by communicating only makes things worse and he decides on a new strategy—say nothing. Although this enables Dennis to avoid unpleasant confrontations, it also prevents him from getting his needs met and causes him to feel frustrated and resentful much of the time. "No matter what I do, I just can't win," he thinks to himself. Like many people, Dennis doesn't realize that it is not communication in itself, but the way that he communicates that gets him into trouble.*

Being an effective communicator is much more than having a good command over the English language—in fact, many people have a great vocabulary but do not communicate well. Effective communication means expressing ourselves in a way that increases mutual understanding and promotes goodwill. When we communicate effectively, people understand what we think and how we feel, and do not feel threatened or under attack. Although other people will not always agree to do what we want, effective communication increases our likelihood of getting our needs met.

Throughout our lives, we experience hundreds of thousands of situations in which we need to negotiate or resolve a problem by communicating with someone—a partner, family member, friend, work colleague, supervisor, neighbor, tradesman, shop assistant or stranger. The issue may be as minor as having to ask someone to move their car or as significant as informing a partner that the relationship is over. Regardless of the circumstances, the way in which we communicate will determine the tone of our discussion, how effectively we resolve the problem, how we feel afterwards and how amicable our relationships remain in the longer term.

## GUIDELINES FOR EFFECTIVE COMMUNICATION

Many people have poor communication habits and so, like Dennis, they frequently find themselves alienating people and experiencing tension within their relationships. Others communicate pretty well most of the time but get into difficulties when they need to confront someone or ask for what they want. Applying the techniques that are described in this chapter can make a big difference to the way we interact with people and can determine whether our relationships are based on mutual understanding or distrust.

## POOR COMMUNICATION HABITS

When we look at the reasons why people experience problems in their relationships, we invariably find poor communication habits. The most common of these are avoidance and alienating messages.

### AVOIDANCE
Good communication involves saying what we think, feel or want in a way that increases mutual understanding and reduces the perception of threat and the likelihood of conflict. When we are dealing with an issue that we believe other people will not approve of, the idea of communication often makes us feel anxious or uncomfortable. Low frustration tolerance and fear of conflict or disapproval may cause us to withdraw, procrastinate and

avoid the issue. We put off saying what we need to say to avoid the discomfort that comes with tackling potentially unpleasant situations. The trouble with avoidance is that it prevents problems from being discussed and resolved, and consequently it leads to tension and resentment. So, while we evade the short-term pain of raising issues that make us uncomfortable, we sabotage our greater goals—to solve problems and have healthy relationships.

Some people habitually avoid any possibility of confrontation. They are loath to initiate discussion about issues that they are concerned about and refuse to engage in conversations that make them feel uncomfortable—they may literally walk out of the room when someone brings up issues that are potentially distressing. While it is reasonable to occasionally postpone discussion when we feel very angry or upset, sooner or later issues need to be dealt with, even those that make us feel uncomfortable. The trouble with refusing to discuss important issues is that they do not get resolved, and consequently resentment grows, tension increases and relationships deteriorate.

Some of us choose to avoid the possibility of conflict by giving incomplete messages—conveying only part of the story. Instead of clearly saying what we think, feel or want, we drop hints, mutter under our breath or make vague comments alluding to the issue and hope that the other person will work it out. For instance, we might bring up an issue but avoid saying how we feel about it or we might agree to do something that we don't want to do and then express our objection through brooding, withdrawal or unfriendly body language. Incomplete communication is another form of avoidance because we steer away from saying what we need to say.

COMMON BELIEFS THAT CAUSE AVOIDANCE
➤ Raising the issue will result in conflict and disapproval.
➤ I must avoid conflict or disapproval at all costs.
➤ Everyone should like and approve of me.
➤ If someone is hostile towards me, it's awful and I can't stand it.

CHALLENGING BELIEFS THAT CAUSE AVOIDANCE
➤ Raising the issue does not necessarily result in conflict. Good communication skills can help to minimize the likelihood of conflict.
➤ It is important to discuss certain issues, even if there's a chance that doing so may generate some conflict or disapproval.
➤ I prefer to be liked but I can cope even if some people don't like or approve of me.
➤ I prefer to avoid conflict but I can cope with conflict if it should arise. If someone is hostile towards me, it's unpleasant, but I can stand it.

## ALIENATING MESSAGES

While avoidance stems from fear of conflict or disapproval, alienating messages stem from anger, defensiveness or lack of skills. Alienating messages are expressed in a hostile, uncompromising or threatening way and therefore put others on the defensive. When others feel threatened, they stop listening to what is being said because they start planning their counterattack. As a result it is not possible to achieve mutual understanding and goodwill. Typical alienating messages are designed so we get our way or win an argument. It is not only the things we say but the way we say them that can alienate other people. Our facial expressions, body language and tone of voice play a huge role in the way our messages are perceived. Speaking in a belligerent tone or using hostile gestures makes people feel threatened, which in turn causes them to respond defensively or aggressively. In this atmosphere, tension escalates, and ultimately no one wins. Although we may sometimes believe that we have won the argument, it is a hollow victory if we are unable to solve problems or have good relationships.

In some situations alienating messages can intimidate others into submission or cause them to withdraw from communicating altogether. In families and workplaces we occasionally see individuals who rule the roost through threat and intimidation. While the frequent use of alienating messages gives those people power over others, the resentment and bitterness that it generates makes for an unhappy environment and unhealthy relationships.

Alienating messages are usually expressed as "you-statements." Metaphorically speaking, we point our finger at the other person and suggest that they are wrong or bad. This tends to put them on the defensive and frequently triggers a hostile response. Typical alienating messages include:

LABELS
- ➤ You only think of yourself.
- ➤ You're a hopeless communicator.
- ➤ You're stingy.
- ➤ You're so neurotic!
- ➤ You're manipulative and deceitful.
- ➤ You need professional help!

OVERGENERALIZATIONS
- ➤ You're never happy until you get things your own way.
- ➤ Every time you say you'll do something, you never do it.
- ➤ You always take, but you never give.
- ➤ Whenever I suggest anything, you're always negative and critical.
- ➤ You're always telling me what to do.

INFERRED MOTIVES (MIND READING)

➤ You conned me into doing all that extra work because you knew you could get away with it.

➤ You're just jealous because I've met someone and you're still single.

➤ You feel threatened when you see me with other people because you're insecure; you'd prefer it if I had no friends.

➤ You tried to make a fool of me in front of all those people.

SARCASM

➤ You're just so clever—you know everything.

➤ When was the last time you had your hearing tested? You obviously have a hearing problem.

➤ That's great! I really like the way you take my needs into account!

THREATS

➤ If you don't change your attitude, I'm going to leave you.

➤ If you ever treat me that way again, I'll tell everyone about your big secret.

➤ You do that again and you can get out of the car and walk!

Threats are not conducive to good relationships because they are based on power and intimidation rather than negotiation. One person tries to make another do what they want by threatening to hurt them in some way if they do not comply. This is the opposite of good communication, which involves respect for the other person's rights. There are, however, some occasions where it may be appropriate to point out the consequences of another person's actions. When all reasonable communication has failed and we believe that our current message is not being heard, it is appropriate to describe the consequences if things do not change—"If you continue to lie to me, I'm not willing to stay in this relationship," "If you're not prepared to complete the job satisfactorily, I'm going to lodge a claim with the small claims court," "If you don't clean up your room, I'm not going to give you any allowance this week." Pointing out the negative consequences can be a useful strategy after more conciliatory negotiation has failed. However, it is effective only if it is used sparingly and if we are fully prepared to act on the consequences that we describe.

## EFFECTIVE COMMUNICATION HABITS

Steering away from poor habits such as avoidance and alienating messages is an important aspect of good communication. In addition, using the following principles and communication strategies can make a substantial difference to the quality of our communication.

## BE CONCILIATORY

Good communication enables us to maintain goodwill in our relationships with other people. This means that we avoid messages that are alienating. We look for win-win solutions in our negotiation with others, so that both parties feel good and no one feels disadvantaged. The secret is to always be reasonable, even when it seems that the other person is not. We do not make demands or idle threats, we do not blame or finger-point and we accept that we may not necessarily get what we want. However, we are willing to communicate how things are from our point of view.

Conciliatory = I want what's fair for all of us.

"But why should I be conciliatory, when they're not the slightest bit concerned about my feelings?" asks Dennis. The answer is that being conciliatory increases your chances of getting what you want. It gives you power. It also lets you avoid the stress and agitation that come with a bad-tempered exchange or an escalation of conflict. It is in your interests to be conciliatory, Dennis! While sometimes it may seem easier to lash out and say what's on your mind, ultimately this doesn't help you to get what you want. Conciliatory communication enables you to avoid stress and to get your needs met more often.

## BE ASSERTIVE

Many people think that being assertive simply means standing up for your rights. While this is one aspect of assertive communication, it is not the whole story. Being assertive means that we are willing to honestly express our thoughts, feelings and needs in a way that also takes into account the rights of other people. The spirit of our communication is "we both matter—let's try to understand each other." Assertive communication enables people to have healthy relationships based on mutual respect.

The willingness to communicate assertively comes from recognition of our own self-worth. We do not see ourselves as superior to others but we recognize that our needs are just as valid as anyone else's. This does not mean that we are inflexible and insist that we must always get our own way—good relationships involve negotiation and compromise. However, we are willing to express ourselves honestly and clearly and we are prepared to ask for what we want.

## MAKING REQUESTS

An important aspect of assertive communication is the ability to make requests or express our needs to others. Often all that is required is a brief statement describing what we want:

- *Marcella, I'm taking the train into work today, so would you be able to pick me up from the station this afternoon?*
- *I'd like to spend the weekend with my daughter. Is that OK with you?*

- *Lorraine, I need to talk to you about the project. Will you be available at 10:00 this morning?*
- *I have to work until late this evening. Can you cook the dinner tonight?*
- *Luc, I'm finding it difficult to concentrate with all the noise—could you please turn the TV down?*
- *Tony, I need those accounts by this afternoon. Could you have them ready by then?*
- *Ricki, it worries me that you spend so much time on the Internet. Could you finish your homework first, before you do that?*

In the majority of situations, asking for what we want is reasonably straightforward. However, sometimes we may expect that others will feel threatened, annoyed or put out by our request. In these situations, the way we communicate can make the difference between a happy resolution or a major brawl. The following techniques are particularly useful when more skilful negotiation is called for.

## I-STATEMENTS

I-statements are a simple and effective technique for communicating messages in a conciliatory way. When we use I-statements, we describe our own feelings and preferences without blaming or criticizing the other person. By pointing the finger at ourselves, we reduce the likelihood that others will feel threatened, which then opens the door for conciliatory negotiation.

When someone has said or done something that we are unhappy about, making an I-statement can help to communicate our concerns in a nonthreatening way. Typical I-statements describe the person's behavior that is problematic to us, the way we feel about it and the alternative behavior that we would prefer:

When you ... I feel ... I'd like (or prefer) ...
- *Bill, when you criticize me in front of other people, I feel embarrassed and upset. I'd like you to treat me with respect, whether we're with other people or on our own.*
- *Sally, when you keep giving me extra jobs while I'm still working on earlier projects, I feel overwhelmed. I'd prefer it if some of those new projects were distributed among our support staff.*
- *Dad, when you tell me that I'm neglecting my children, I feel angry and upset. I'd like you to have faith in my ability to look after my kids.*
- *Jimmy, when you stay out late without letting me know where you are, I feel very worried. I'd like you to call me if you are going to come home after 12 o'clock.*
- *Sarah, when you interrupt me when I'm telling a story, I feel frustrated and annoyed. I'd like to you allow me to finish what I am saying, without trying to edit it.*

A major advantage of using I-statements is that they focus on behaviors rather than the person. This is an important distinction because behaviors are something that people can change. When we focus on behaviors, we are not attacking the person but describing the way their actions affect us and the changes we would like. As a general rule, when people know how we feel and what we want and they do not feel under attack, they are more likely to respond in a conciliatory way. Although there are no guarantees, in most situations clear, nonthreatening statements increase the likelihood of getting our needs met.

## WHOLE MESSAGES

I-statements are useful for conveying our feelings and preferences in situations that are reasonably straightforward. However, some situations are more complex, and using an I-statement may not adequately convey why we think and feel the way we do. In these situations it is often useful to provide a more complete picture of how things look from our point of view. This is particularly the case in potentially threatening situations, where we want to minimize the likelihood of conflict.

In their book *Messages*, McKay, Davis and Fanning describe the use of whole messages for communicating in a clear and conciliatory manner.

WHOLE MESSAGES DESCRIBE OUR:
➤ observations
➤ thoughts
➤ feelings
➤ needs.

Whole messages are a form of I-statement, in that they describe the problematic behavior, how we feel about it and what we want. However, they also provide a description of our own observations and thoughts, and therefore convey a more complete picture of how things are from our point of view.

Communication using whole messages is particularly useful at times when we need to discuss issues that we believe might generate disagreement, disapproval or conflict. A whole message clearly communicates what we need to say in a reasonable and non-threatening way. This increases the likelihood of constructive engagement with the other person. As we develop confidence in our ability to use whole messages, we discover that discussing contentious issues does not necessarily result in conflict. In fact, very often it helps to clear the air and enables potential conflicts to be resolved. Consequently, the idea of raising a difficult issue or responding to one that has been raised by someone else becomes less daunting. While communication using whole messages does not always resolve the issue, it opens the door for nonthreatening engagement and therefore increases the chances of reaching a mutually acceptable solution.

## COMPONENTS OF WHOLE MESSAGES

### Observations

These are statements of fact—things that we have experienced, seen or heard.

> *I arrived half an hour late for my appointment.*
> *Katy asked me why daddy doesn't come home any more.*
> *I haven't had a vacation for two years.*
> *I heard that you told them that I was leaving the company.*
> *Tom is starting a new job next week.*

A central feature of whole messages is that our observations are objective and unbiased. We avoid making emotive statements, jumping to conclusions or trying to interpret the other person's motives.

| EMOTIVE STATEMENTS | OBJECTIVE STATEMENTS |
|---|---|
| When you made a fool of me in front of all those people … | When you said that I'm "not very bright" in front of all those people … |
| You're just playing power games with me. | You've become very quiet and uncommunicative lately. |
| You're blaming me because you don't see your son, Adam, very often. | Whenever we talk about Adam, you become quiet and you look upset. |

### Thoughts

These are our perceptions and opinions. When we describe our thoughts, we reveal subjective information about how things are from our point of view.

> *I think you're being very hard on yourself—you're doing your best.*
> *I sometimes wonder if your heart is in the job.*
> *It seems unfair that I work full-time and do most of the housework as well.*
> *I'm not sure if I'm going to be able to cope with all that extra pressure.*
> *I think it would be good if you saw the children more frequently.*

### Feelings

Feelings are statements that describe our emotional response.

> *I feel upset that you made that decision without consulting me first.*
> *I'm so grateful that you've been here for me during this difficult time.*
> *You say your friendship with Marieta is platonic, but I can't help feeling threatened.*
> *I feel relieved that we're finally making progress.*
> *I feel anxious that I won't be able to do a good job.*

### *Needs*

These are statements describing what we would like. It's important that our needs are not expressed as demands, but as requests or preferences.

> *I need some help with this project—do you think you can spare some time for me?*
> *I'd like you to take some more responsibility with doing the housework.*
> *I want you to tell me if you're unhappy with something I have done, rather than withdrawing or brooding.*
> *I'd like you to be more affectionate towards me, and show me that you care.*
> *Could you give me a hand with bathing the kids and putting them to bed?*

> 66 Your closest friends, your mate and your family can't know the real you unless you share all of your experiences. That means not leaving things out, not covering up your anger, not squelching your wants. It means giving accurate feedback about what you observe, clearly stating your inferences and conclusions, saying how it makes you feel, and if you need something or see possibilities for change, making straight-forward requests or suggestions. 99 McKay, Davis, Fanning, *Messages*

When we use whole messages, we make a statement describing our observations, thoughts, feelings and needs (not necessarily in that order). In some situations, we may not need to describe either our thoughts or our feelings because they are implied by the rest of our statement. For this reason, in the examples below we see "thoughts/feelings" displayed as one item. The heading actually implies "thoughts and/or feelings."

> *Sandra is angry that her husband, Matt, rarely makes an effort to talk to her girlfriend, Dianne, when she comes to their home. Sandra had said nothing for weeks (avoidance), until one day she exploded, "You're such a pig! Would it kill you to talk to her?" (alienating message). Not surprisingly, this generated a defensive response from Matt, and a major row ensued.*

Let's take a look at how she might have communicated using a whole message.

**Observations:** Whenever Dianne comes over, you seem to ignore her. Usually you avoid coming into the room and, on the rare occasions that you do, you don't say hello or chat to her.

**Thoughts/feelings:** I think she feels uncomfortable when you act like that and I suspect she thinks you're rude. I feel embarrassed and awkward when you behave that way. It upsets me that you can't be more friendly towards her.

**Needs:** I would like you to make an effort—to say hello and to chat for just a couple of minutes, so that she feels welcome when she comes here.

> *Last night Tom and his girlfriend, Sheila, were with a group of friends. Tom's friend, Ralph, had recently lost his job and was describing how difficult it has been to get up in the morning with no plans and no idea of how he's going to spend the day. Much to Tom's irritation, Sheila made light of parts of Ralph's story and kept relating it to her own experiences.*

**Alienating message:** In the car on the way home, Tom exploded, "Can't you just listen to what someone else has to say? Why do you have to bring everything back to yourself?" Not surprisingly, Sheila became defensive, and the atmosphere became very icy between them.

Let's take a look at how Tom could have communicated, using a whole message.

**Observations:** Sheila, I don't know if you were aware of this, but when Ralph was describing how difficult it's been for him since he lost his job, you interrupted him several times and you kept bringing up your own experiences. In the end, Ralph didn't get a chance to finish his story and he stopped talking.
**Thoughts/feelings:** I felt really uncomfortable. It seemed to me that Ralph was trying to talk about something very personal, and that you were making light of his story and not giving him a chance to finish.
**Needs:** I guess I'd like you to be a bit more sensitive to people's feelings. If someone is telling their story, just let them finish, instead of interrupting them and talking about your own experiences.

> *Ian's sister, Paula, tends to become forceful, almost aggressive, whenever she expresses her opinion, especially if someone says something she disagrees with. Ian would like to be close to her but he often avoids bringing up issues because she is likely to respond badly and he doesn't want the "aggro." As family relationships are important to Ian, he decides to talk to her about this.*

**Alienating message,** "Why do you have to jump down my throat every time I disagree with you? Why can't you accept that people don't have to always see things your way?"
**Observations:** I don't know if you're aware of this, but often when I say things that you don't like or that you disagree with, you get very intense and a bit aggressive in your response. For instance, when I mentioned that Mom and Dad seemed lonely, you became irate and accused me of saying that you don't do enough for them. And last week, when

I mentioned that Kath (daughter) was doing really well at school, you seemed annoyed and said that she's at a private school so why wouldn't she do well … You seem to get upset easily, and I find myself avoiding many issues because I don't want to end up in an argument.

**Thoughts/feelings:** I feel frustrated and disappointed at the way we are communicating, as there are often things that I would like to talk to you about, but I hold back. I think that in the end, censoring what we talk about creates distance between us.

**Needs:** I'd like us to be close and to be able to talk to you honestly without feeling that you're going to get angry if I say something you don't like.

## PRELIMINARY STATEMENTS

Sometimes we feel anxious about raising an issue because we expect that the other person will respond aggressively to what we have to say. Making a preliminary statement acknowledging our discomfort reduces our anxiety and decreases the likelihood of a hostile or defensive response. When the other person understands that bringing up the issue is difficult for us, their perception of threat decreases, and they are therefore less likely to respond defensively. A typical preliminary statement may be:

> ➤ I want to discuss something with you, but I'm uncomfortable about bringing it up. I'm hoping that you are willing to listen with an open mind.
> ➤ I'd like to talk to you about something but I feel anxious that you're going to take it personally or get upset.

Let's take a look at how this can work in practice:

*Whenever Lucy and her husband, Frank, go to dinner at Lucy's parents' place, Frank switches on the television immediately after dinner and watches TV for the rest of the night. Lucy feels upset about Frank's behavior, but has been reluctant to bring it up with him because she doesn't want to have an argument. Finally, she has decided to talk to him about it.*

**Alienating message:** You're so selfish—you do it every time! Is it so hard for you to just sit and talk to them?

**Preliminary statement:** Frank, I want to bring up something that is bothering me but I don't want us to have a fight about this. I'd like you to listen with an open mind and not get annoyed.

**Observations:** Every Friday when we go to Mom and Dad's for dinner, immediately after the meal you sit on the couch and watch TV for the rest of the night.

**Thoughts/feelings:** It upsets me that you make so little effort to talk to them. I think Mom and Dad feel disappointed because it means a lot to them that we come over and they want you to be part of our discussion. When you put on the TV you separate yourself from the rest of the family.

**Needs:** I know that you're not terribly interested in what they have to say, but couldn't you make a bit more effort to talk to them?

Another type of preliminary statement that takes the heat out of a potentially confronting situation is **positive acknowledgment**. This involves starting our communication by acknowledging something positive about the other person or their behavior. For instance:

> *Frank, I really appreciate that you're making an effort with Dianne—it's made the situation much more comfortable. But now I'd like to talk to you about Mom and Dad.*

✳

> *Jolan, you've been so much more flexible since we had our talk, and I think it's been great for both of us. But there are still times when you overreact, such as when I told you that I had to work late on Monday. Are you OK to talk about it?*

✳

> *Kim, you've been meticulous with your record keeping since our last review, which is a great improvement, but I still have some concerns about your telephone manner.*

Starting our communication with a positive statement "lowers the temperature" by reducing the other person's perception of threat. This reduces the likelihood of a defensive response and consequently keeps open the channels of communication. We are far more likely to have constructive communication when people do not feel threatened.

## REVISITING AN ISSUE

Most people are willing to bring up an issue once, but what happens if we need to raise it again? Perhaps you have successfully negotiated an agreement with someone, only to find that over time old habits reemerge? Teenage kids who agree to keep their room tidy sometimes renege after only a few days; employees who agree to stop spending too much time on personal phone calls may fall back into long-held habits; and a husband who agrees to make more of an effort with the in-laws sometimes goes back to watching TV. The reemergence of previous behaviors usually reflects a natural tendency to return to old patterns rather than a deliberate decision to renege. Unless the commitment to change their behavior is strong in people's minds, they often lose sight of it over time.

In these circumstances, many of us make the big mistake of concluding that communication does not work and we give up. "I talked to Sheila and she agreed to change her behavior but after two weeks she's doing it again. Communication gets you nowhere." But Tom is wrong. Good communication does work, but sometimes we need to restate our message—people need to be reminded. "But I don't want to keep reminding her," Tom protests, "It makes me feel bad to have to bring it up again." It is true that many of us feel uncomfortable revisiting an issue that has already been dealt with, but if it remains unresolved, then that is what we need to do. The challenge is to communicate skilfully, so that our reasons for revisiting the issue are clear, and our discussion does not get bogged down in hostile accusations. In situations where people have failed to act on their promises, skillful communication can result in a stronger commitment to do the right thing the next time around.

When revisiting an issue that has already been discussed, it is a good idea to make reference to the earlier agreement, and to point out that the problem has reemerged. If you feel uncomfortable about raising the issue for a second or third time, then acknowledge this in your message.

> *Although Ben agreed to put out the garbage when his mother asked him, an hour later he still hadn't done it. Finally she asked again, and this time he said, "In a minute." Half an hour later, the garbage has still not been taken out. Now his mother is tempted to do it herself, however, she decides that this would set a bad precedent—Ben would simply learn that if he procrastinates, Mom will do it for him.*

**Alienating message:** I can't rely on you for the smallest thing. You expect me to do things for you, but you're not willing to give an inch!

Ben's mom decides to use the situation as an opportunity to practice her communication skills. She makes the following whole message:

**Observations:** Ben, I asked you to put out the trash earlier this afternoon, and you said that you'd do it. I asked you again before, and you said that you'd do it in a minute. Now it's half an hour later and the garbage is still sitting there.

**Thoughts/feelings:** I hate asking you again because it makes me feel like I'm nagging. It upsets me that I have to ask you so many times, but if I don't remind you, it seems that it doesn't get done.

**Needs:** I don't want to have to keep asking you to take out the garbage or keep reminding you of your commitments. I'd like to think that when you tell me that you're going to do something, I can count on you to do it.

> *Lorna has approached her landlord on two occasions regarding the broken hot water system in her flat, and on each occasion he has told her that he will come over the next day to repair it. Now, five days later, he still hasn't come, and Lorna is still without hot water.*

**Alienating message:** This is your responsibility—how many times do I have to ask you? I'm going to get a plumber to repair it and send you the bill!

**Observations:** I've already called you a couple of times about the hot water system, and each time you said that you were going to come over the next day to repair it. But now five days have gone by, and you still haven't come. As you know I have no hot water at all, which means that I can't use the shower, and it's difficult for me to wash the dishes or do the laundry.

**Thoughts/feelings:** I feel very frustrated because it's been almost a week, and I still don't have any hot water.

**Needs:** I appreciate that you're busy, but this matter needs your urgent attention. If you're not able to come immediately, then I'd like your agreement for me to call a plumber, so that it can be repaired as soon as possible.

## RESPONDING TO AN ALIENATING MESSAGE

Even though we may have good communication skills and understand the importance of making our messages reasonable and nonthreatening, often other people do not. So how do you respond when someone talks to you in a threatening, hostile way? It is important to remember that, even if someone disagrees with you or is unhappy with something that you have said or done, you have the right to be treated with respect and you are not obliged to put up with abuse. So a good place to start is with an I-statement describing how you feel and what you want. For example, "Bill, when you speak to me in that angry tone, I feel intimidated and uncomfortable. I'd like to discuss this with you, but I don't want to have an argument or get into personal abuse. Now, we can either talk about it reasonably or else we can put it off until later, after you've cooled down."

# EXERCISE 10.1

For each of the following examples, write down whole messages that convey your observations, thoughts and/or feelings and needs in the following situations. *Sample solutions at the end of the book.*

1. Someone has borrowed a book from you and has not returned it. They have had it for a long time, and when you finally asked about it, they said, "If I can find it." They have never mentioned it again. It's quite precious to you, and you would like it back.

   Observations:

   Thoughts/feelings:

   Needs:

2. When a friend asked you to come to a trivia evening at their child's primary school you were caught off guard and agreed to go. The more you think about it, the more you really don't want to go. You'd like to get out of it but you feel bad about letting them down.

   Observations:

   Thoughts/feelings:

   Needs:

3. Your partner has been extremely irritable lately, and you feel concerned and upset about it. You suspect that she might be under a lot of stress, and you would like to talk about it.

   Observations:

   Thoughts/feelings:

   Needs:

# COMMUNICATION DOS AND DON'TS

In addition to using whole messages there are a number of general rules that can help to make our communication more effective. The following DOs and DON'Ts provide some useful guidelines.

## DO—ASK FOR WHAT YOU WANT

When we do not express our needs clearly, we usually end up feeling angry and resentful. An important aspect of effective communication is to clearly express what we want. This means that we do not drop hints or make vague references and we do not give the other person the silent treatment until they work out that something is wrong. Of course, stating what we want does not mean that we demand that things must go our way—only that we are willing to honestly communicate how things are from our perspective.

Some people insist that others should know what they want—"He should know that I need help with preparing for Sunday's barbecue—why doesn't he offer?;" "She should know that I need some peace and quiet while I'm studying—I shouldn't have to ask;" "He should know that I need special attention when I'm sick—he should have offered to come to the doctor with me." The problem is that other people often think differently to ourselves—they have different needs, different concerns, make different assumptions and focus on different issues. If we don't tell them what we want, very often they don't know.

*If you're not happy about something that someone is doing*
*and you want things to change, tell them.*

> *Rick was feeling frustrated because it was Sunday morning, and Julie was at her computer, working away on the business accounts. Finally Rick asked her, "How long are you going to work on those accounts?" Julie replied, "Oh, I suppose until about 2 o'clock." Rick walked away feeling angry and dejected because it was Sunday, and he wanted to go out with Julie and do something leisurely. Meanwhile Julie was totally engrossed in her work and oblivious to Rick's frustration. Rick stewed all afternoon, until a major argument blew up between them later that evening.*

While Rick blamed Julie for being inflexible and tied to her work, the truth is that much of the problem stemmed from Rick's poor communication. By asking a question ("How long are you going to work on those accounts?") instead of making a statement ("I feel disappointed that you want to stay at home and work—I'd like to go out for brunch") Rick failed to clearly communicate what he wanted. As a result, Julie did not notice his frustration and disappointment. Where there is goodwill in relationships, solutions can often be negotiated, but we need to clearly express what we want.

*Harold is cross with the young people who live next door because they often play their music loudly late into the night. He is annoyed at their lack of consideration and has decided to teach them a lesson. One night Harold put an amplifier against the adjoining wall, and at 2 o'clock in the morning he blasted them with some old-time classics at full volume. "That will teach them," he thinks to himself. Ask Harold whether he'd actually talked to the neighbors and told them that their music was a problem, and he'll tell you, "Well, they sure know now!"*

They may have got the message, Harold, but then again, they may not have—some people aren't aware of their own noise and may not even make the connection. And even if they did get the message, why bring out the big guns and create bad feelings when a reasonable request might have done the same job? As so often happens in our dealings with other people, when we avoid saying what we want, our resentment grows, and we often end up behaving with unnecessary antagonism. Harold is quick to point out that being assertive doesn't always solve the problem. That's true, but it increases our likelihood of getting our needs met and is a good place to start. It is never too late to take firmer action, such as calling the police, calling the landlord or complaining to the local council, but starting with conciliatory communication often saves us the need to do this. It also enables us to avoid the stress and bad will that comes with hostile actions.

## DO—BE WILLING TO SAY NO AT TIMES

Just as people have the right to say no to our requests, we also have the right to say no to requests for things that we do not want to do. Being assertive does not mean that we always put our own needs first. Sometimes we may choose to go out of our way for other people because they are in need and we are happy to help out—good relationships involve making sacrifices and doing things for others at times. However, sometimes it is perfectly appropriate to say no to requests for things that we do not want to do. Learning to say no is particularly important for people who are habitually unassertive.

*Tony has a broad taste in music and has over a thousand CDs in his collection. He was somewhat taken aback when his friend, Sean, looked through his collection and pulled out some CDs that he would like to trade. Sean had brought CDs from his own collection and wanted to swap them with those that he had removed from Tony's shelf. Although Tony doesn't like to trade his CDs, he likes Sean, and he didn't want to disappoint him. So Tony agreed to the swap and then felt annoyed about it for weeks—'That mongrel! Why can't he buy his own CDs?'*

When we agree to do things that we really don't want to do or when we say "OK" when it's really not OK, we feel angry and resentful. That's the price that we pay for not being assertive.

| BELIEFS THAT INHIBIT ASSERTIVE COMMUNICATION | RATIONAL BELIEFS |
|---|---|
| If someone asks me to do something, I should always do it. | If someone asks me to do something, I'm not obliged to do it. It's OK to say no. |
| I should never put my own needs before the needs of others. | It's OK to put my own needs first at times. |
| I should never say or do things that some people may disapprove of. | I have the right to say or do things, even if others disapprove. It's OK to behave in accordance with my own values and beliefs. |
| I shouldn't ask for what I want or people won't like me. | It's OK to ask for what I want. People have the right to say no, but I have the right to ask. |
| I should be like other people— I should try to fit in. | It's OK to be different. There's no reason why I have to think, feel or behave the same way as other people. |
| If someone gives me advice, I should always take it. | It's OK to ignore other people's advice. |
| I am not important—other people matter more than I do. | I am no less important than anyone else. I have the right to say what I think and to ask for what I want. |
| If someone is in trouble, I should always help them out. | It's OK for me to not take responsibility for other people's problems. |

## DON'T—DELAY YOUR COMMUNICATION: DO IT NOW

What do you do when you need to resolve an issue but the idea of communication makes you feel uncomfortable? Procrastinate? Drop hints? Put it in the too-hard basket and hope that you might have the courage to deal with it some time in the future? The desire to escape potentially unpleasant situations can undermine our ability to have healthy relationships with our partner, family members, friends and work colleagues.

Confronting difficult issues now rather than later prevents escalation and reduces stress. Once our issues are out in the open, they can be dealt with, and if our communication is reasonable, very often they can be resolved. While there is no guarantee that communication always gets us what we want, we can be pretty sure that things will stay the same if we do not say anything.

*Nothing changes unless something changes.*

When we delay or avoid communication, issues that need to be dealt with remain unresolved and tensions escalate. When we do finally address these issues, accrued resentment has often distorted their magnitude, leading to angry outbursts.

*Val became upset when she discovered that Sharon, one of her work colleagues, had lent their scanner to someone in a neighboring office. As Val uses the scanner a lot she was particularly annoyed that Sharon had not consulted her first. Instead of politely telling Sharon that she would like it to be returned, Val sulked. She said almost nothing the whole day, except for occasional mutterings under her breath. Finally Sharon asked her whether something was wrong, to which Val angrily exploded, "Why do you just give our things away? Don't I have any rights? Why couldn't you ask me first?" Although it may have been reasonable for Val to feel annoyed, her alienating statements created unnecessary hostility and resulted in icy relations between the two women for the next two weeks. As is often the case, delaying our communication causes tension to escalate and creates unnecessary bad feelings between people.*

If there is an issue that needs dealing with, do it now. The only exception to this rule is in situations where we feel very angry, in which case a cooling off period may be a good idea. Delaying the discussion for a few hours or a few days gives us time to calm down and helps us to see things in a more rational perspective.

## DO—BE HONEST

 When you are honest with people—
- they admire and appreciate you
- they trust you
- they know where you stand
- you can get more of what you want.

Don't you appreciate people giving it to you straight?

<small>ANDREW MATTHEWS, *MAKING FRIENDS*</small>

Most of us are a little dishonest at times. When we tell lies, it is usually because we want to be nice or we want to protect someone's feelings. Sometimes we lie to protect ourselves or to avoid conflict or disapproval, "If I'm honest, she'll get offended;" "If I tell him the truth, he'll get angry." Some people lie in order to try to impress people or to manipulate others into doing what they want.

It might be argued that on rare occasions a white lie or omission can save someone unnecessary hurt or offence. Telling someone that you have a prior engagement when the truth is you just do not want to come to their party or telling a distressed friend that their new unflattering haircut looks fine may occasionally be justifiable. However, in most cases lies create barriers between people; they prevent us from dealing with the real issues and impede others from knowing what we really think and want. Lies break down trust— an essential ingredient for healthy relationships. Once we know that we have been lied to, it is hard to trust that person in the future. While it is important to be kind and tactful and to respect other people's feelings, healthy relationships are based on honest communication. This means that we express ourselves truthfully, without ulterior motives or hidden agendas.

> 66 Being straight means that you tell the truth. You state your real needs and feelings. You don't say you're tired and want to go home if you're really angry and want more attention. You don't angle for compliments or reassurance by putting yourself down. You don't say you're anxious about going to a couples therapist when you feel angry about being pushed to go. You don't describe your feelings as depression because your mate prefers that to irritation . . . Lies cut you off from others. Lies keep them from knowing what you need or feel. 99 McKAY, DAVIS & FANNING, *MESSAGES*

*Mandy has just started dating a man whom her best friend, Rachael, detests (Rachael calls him a "complete jerk"). Because Mandy wants to avoid Rachael's disapproval, she omitted telling her friend about her new boyfriend. At times she was evasive and occasionally she lied to Rachael about who she was going out with. When Rachael eventually discovered the truth, she was furious with Mandy, not because of who she was dating but because she had lied. Paradoxically, Mandy had not been honest with Rachael because she wanted her approval, but in the end lying created distance and disapproval.*

Dishonesty feels like betrayal—it destroys trust and can ruin a friendship. Being assertive means being prepared to tell the truth, even when we know that others won't necessarily approve.

*Laura has poor self-esteem and consequently she tries to boost her image by exaggerating some of her achievements. Over the years Laura has made a number of exaggerated claims, including nonexistent college degrees, famous people she's friends with, impressive jobs she's held and high incomes she's earned in the past.*

The problem with making false or exaggerated claims is that eventually we get found out, and we lose our credibility. Laura stretches the truth because she wants to impress people but the harder she tries, the less impressive she becomes. When we know that someone has been dishonest, they lose our respect—lies push people away.

## DON'T—GET AUTOMATICALLY DEFENSIVE

Perhaps the greatest obstacle to effective communication and problem solving is the tendency to feel threatened and to become defensive when we receive criticism or negative feedback from others. Some people are particularly sensitive and perceive criticism even when none is intended. This tendency usually stems from low self-esteem—

doubts about our own worth put us on the lookout for possible threats to our self-esteem. Core beliefs such as, "If someone criticizes me, then it means I'm not OK" and "Criticism means rejection," make negative feedback from others feel like a life-or-death issue. Consequently, we get defensive or go on the attack. On the other hand, people with healthy self-esteem are much less concerned about criticism or negative feedback. An inherent belief that we are OK enables us to accept negative feedback without feeling threatened.

Just as we appreciate it when other people take our comments on board without becoming defensive, so too do others appreciate it when we are willing to take their comments on board. The ability to listen and respond constructively to criticism is an invaluable quality that helps us to learn about ourselves. It enables us to reach an understanding with other people and to work cooperatively at finding solutions. Ultimately, it helps us to get along with others and to have good relationships.

## DO—VALIDATE

While it may sometimes be appropriate to argue our case when someone is upset or angry about something that we have done, often this just inflames the situation. Trying to prove at all costs that we are right and they are wrong may miss the point—often all people want is to be heard. How would it be if instead of arguing or being defensive, you validated the other person's feelings and concerns? When we validate, we make a statement acknowledging that we can understand how it is from the other person's point of view. (Of course, if you really don't understand, you may need to ask them to explain it first.) If we feel responsible for the situation, we acknowledge our responsibility and if we are genuinely sorry, we apologize. "I can see that it must be very upsetting for you. I'm really sorry."

When we validate a person's concerns, it does not mean that we necessarily see things the same way or that we agree with what they have said. Thus, we do not take responsibility or apologize unless we genuinely believe that we are at fault. However, at a minimum level we state that we can understand how it is from the other person's point of view. For the person who is angry or upset, having one's feelings validated is one of the most satisfying experiences. It can resolve all hurt and resentment, and sometimes enables people to let go of issues that have troubled them for months or even years.

> Since childhood, Sylvia has always believed that her parents loved her younger sister more than they loved her. For years this had been a great source of pain to her and finally, at the age of thirty-eight, she decided to talk about it with her mother. Without blaming or condemning her parents, Sylvia reflected on numerous childhood memories of situations where she believed she had received unfair treatment. She described how unloved or dejected she had felt at times.

While this type of message is likely to be confronting for any parent, Sylvia's mother could either add fuel to the fire by responding defensively or she could help her daughter to resolve the pain of the past by validating her experience. Compare the likely outcomes of the two types of responses below:

**Defensive response:** This is complete nonsense. We loved you both equally—this is all in your mind. You're always looking to blame us for all of your problems.

**Validating response:** Darling, I had no idea how difficult things must have been for you at the time. We were struggling with our own problems and we didn't know much about parenting, so I guess we made lots of mistakes. It must have been very painful for you to feel second-best so much of the time.

Validating can be used for issues (such as in the above example) that have been a sore point for years, as well as for more common issues that arise in our daily life situations:

➤ I know it's frustrating to be kept waiting—I'm so sorry I'm late.

➤ I understand that it's hard for you to feed, bathe and put the kids down on your own, without my help. It must be absolutely exhausting. At the moment things are pretty chaotic at work so I can't leave any earlier, but I'll try to change things when this busy period has passed.

➤ It must have been very upsetting to have been spoken to like that—I'll follow it up with the manager.

## DO—GIVE POSITIVE FEEDBACK

While it is important to communicate our concerns when someone does something that we are unhappy about, it is equally important to communicate our appreciation when they do things that make us feel good. Positive feedback helps to create bonds between people and reinforces behaviors that we want to encourage. When people know that we appreciate certain things, they are more likely to continue doing them. Giving positive feedback may be as simple as saying:

➤ I really appreciate that you're making more of an effort to talk to my friends.

➤ I'm so glad that we're both being more open and honest with each other now.

➤ I can see that you're making an effort to help with the housework—I really appreciate it.

➤ Now that you're not angry all the time, I enjoy spending time with you—it's so much easier to talk to you these days.

➤ I know that you wanted to go to that match—I'm very grateful that you're here.

➤ I like the way that you've become more assertive—it means that I know what you want.

➤ You've been a great friend to me. I'm grateful for your support.

    ❝ A crucial step in making your relationship rewarding is to share your good feelings. A basic law of human behavior is that people are more likely to do things which make them feel good. If your partner does something that makes you feel good, and you would like him to do it more often, reward it! Tell your partner how she made you feel good. ❞ Bob Montgomery, Lynette Evans, *Living and Loving Together*

## DON'T—BRING UP RED HERRINGS

In the middle of an argument or an angry exchange we may sometimes find ourselves bringing up "red herrings"—issues that are not really related to the subject under discussion. Usually these involve past hurts, injustices or disappointments—"What about the time you let me down when I really needed your help?", "How come you've never acknowledged the things that I did well?", "You showed more loyalty to your friends than to me." These past hurts are sometimes marginally related to the current issue and sometimes not at all, but we bring them up to bolster our defences, as if to say, "You're bad, and here's the evidence."

In their book *Really Relating*, Jansen and Newman refer to the "gunny sack" that we carry on our back. The gunny sack is a metaphor for the collection of past hurts and resentments that we carry around with us—"All the angers, resentments, hurts, grievances that we haven't talked about and resolved." These issues may fester silently for years until they finally pour out during a fit of rage in an argument over some other matter.

The problem with bringing up past hurts is that they derail the communication process and impede problem solving. Suddenly we are arguing about peripheral issues and losing sight of the main game. The challenge during any discussion is to stay focused on the current issue. This is not to say that revisiting unresolved issues from the past is a pointless exercise. In some situations talking about past hurts can be healing and worthwhile but the question here is one of timing. It may be worth choosing some time to talk about other unresolved issues, however, it is rarely helpful to raise them in the context of an argument about other things.

## DO—KEEP YOUR COOL

A major disadvantage of anger is that it limits the opportunities for constructive problem solving. Once we lose our cool, people feel threatened and tensions escalate. For this reason, it is important to be aware of our voice and body language, as well as the things we say. Try to set the tone by speaking calmly and reasonably, avoiding alienating messages and not being sidetracked by irrelevant issues. If the tone of the discussion becomes hostile, it is useful to point this out to the other person—"We seem to be getting angry again. Let's try to speak calmly and stay focused on the issue." If the discussion remains heated, it may be best to suggest a cooling-off period, and to return to the issue when tempers have settled down.

## DON'T—WALK AWAY FROM A DISCUSSION

Talking honestly about our thoughts and feelings can make us uncomfortable at times. Some people deal with their discomfort by literally walking away. While this may give them temporarily relief, it does not solve the problem and usually creates new ones. With few exceptions, walking away from a discussion is one the most unhelpful ways of dealing with problems in relationships. Avoiding communication usually stems from beliefs such as, "Talking about it will make me feel uncomfortable, and it's bad to feel uncomfortable," and "If we don't talk about it, the problem will disappear."

In some situations, people deliberately walk away from a discussion to punish the other person—usually a partner or family member. The knowledge that doing this causes frustration to others gives some people a sense of power—"I know that she wants to talk about it, so I'm not going to give her the opportunity!" Of course walking away is totally self-defeating because if problems are not resolved, it is impossible to have satisfying relationships—in the end, no one benefits.

*Over the ten years of their marriage, Justine had often tried to discuss some of her concerns with her husband, Noel. Every time she tried to talk, Noel became annoyed and literally walked out of the room. After years of frustration and unresolved issues, Justine had finally had enough. She packed her bags and moved out, leaving only a short note saying that she couldn't take any more. Noel was devastated. To him the break up came totally out of the blue. "Why didn't she tell me that she was so unhappy?" he asked himself, "If I had known, I would have done things differently." She tried to talk to you, Noel, but you kept walking away, remember?*

Although walking away from a discussion does not always result in the breakdown of a marriage, it does ensure that problems are unresolved and resentment grows. When issues cannot be discussed, relationships invariably suffer.

## DO—ASK FOR CLARIFICATION

Sometimes we get messages that are ambiguous or unclear—someone seems cold and withdrawn; someone appears to ignore us for no reason; someone hints at an issue;

someone hasn't called for ages and we assume that they are probably angry. Misread messages can result in unnecessary hurt, tensions and bad feelings. If you are unsure of the message you are receiving, ask for clarification.

> ➤ You seem very quiet lately. Have I done something to upset you?
> ➤ I haven't heard from you for a long time—is everything OK?
> ➤ When we first talked about the idea, you seemed excited about it, but now you sound less enthusiastic. I'm wondering if you have changed your mind.
> ➤ You seemed keen to see me when we spoke on the phone, but now that I am here, you appear put out. Is something the matter?
> ➤ You have talked about people in relationships needing to take breaks from each other. Are you saying that that is what you would like us to do?

## EXERCISE 10.2

For each of the following situations:

a. Describe what you would probably do if you found yourself in this situation. (Be honest!)
b. For those situations in which you would *not* respond assertively, write down:
   i. the beliefs that might stop you from being assertive
   ii. more reasonable perceptions that would help you to respond assertively.
c. Write down a brief assertive statement that would be appropriate for the situation.

1. A friend asks you to tell a lie to someone on his behalf. You feel uncomfortable with this.
2. The salesman has been serving you for over forty minutes and he has been extremely pleasant and helpful. You have found something that is OK, but you're not really sure. You are aware that you've taken up a lot of his time.
3. You get a call from someone you met while traveling overseas two years ago, and she wants to stay at your place for "a while." You're not too happy about the idea.
4. You have had dinner with friends at an expensive restaurant. You have not had any alcohol, while the others have drunk a lot. Although the alcohol alone comes to over $30 a head, when the bill is being worked out, no one suggests that you should pay less.
5. One of your colleagues at work has a habit of sitting down next to you and talking while you are trying to work.

*Sample solutions at the back of this book.*

6. You have already asked the two people sitting behind you in the theater to stop talking. Now, ten minutes later, they have started talking again.

7. You are watering your front garden when a dog that is being walked by with its owner poops on your nature strip.

8. A group of friends is at your house, and one of them lights up a cigarette. You have a no-smoking policy at your house.

9. The coffee you ordered at a restaurant arrives lukewarm.

10. A friend borrowed $200 from you four months ago and seems to have forgotten about it.

# IN SUMMARY

➤ Effective communication skills enable us to get on with people, solve problems and get our needs met a lot of the time.

➤ Avoidance and alienating messages are the most common cause of poor communication within relationships.

➤ Alienating messages are perceived as hostile and therefore put the other person on the defensive. This reduces the likelihood of successful negotiation.

➤ We are far more likely to get our needs met and to maintain healthy relationships when our communication is conciliatory and is respectful of the needs of others.

➤ Communication techniques that increase our chances of successful negotiation include assertive requests, I-statements and whole messages.

➤ Important ingredients for good communication include respect for the rights of others, clear and honest communication, validating the feelings of other people and positive feedback to others when appropriate.

➤ Poor communication habits include hostile manner or statements, defensiveness, walking away from a discussion, delaying communication and bringing up unrelated issues from the past.

ELEVEN

# Being Happy

Why search for personal happiness? Because you'd damned well better! If you don't achieve some measure of your desires, your goals, your values, who will get them for you?

ALBERT ELLIS

The desire for happiness is the underlying force that motivates many of our decisions and the things we do. Whether we behave selfishly or altruistically, work until we are sixty-five or retire early, enroll in a college degree or drop out of a course, keep the house spotless or neglect the housework, take frequent holidays or stay at home, search for a new relationship or end an existing relationship, have children or choose not to have children, join a gym or join the couch potato club, it is the desire to feel good and to be happy, now or in the future, that underlies most of our behaviors.

Although we all want to be happy, few of us can clearly define what happiness is. Psychologists, like philosophers and sociologists, have struggled with the term. The most widely accepted, yet inadequate definition is: a state of subjective well-being. There is much disagreement about the characteristics of happiness. Some experts argue that happiness is an enduring human trait—an ongoing perception that life is good, meaningful and pleasurable. Others argue that it is a temporary state—that people have experiences of happiness rather than an ongoing sense of being happy. However we choose to define happiness, it does appear that some people are more predisposed towards feeling happy and satisfied with their lives than others.

Since the 1960s, studies examining the issue of happiness have been reported in the research literature. Many sought to measure people's level of happiness and to identify the factors that predict whether or not they feel happy. In the late 1980s, two American social psychologists, David Myers and Ed Diener, analysed the results of international studies across sixteen countries around the world based on the responses of 170,000 people.

They looked at people's ratings of happiness in countries all over the world, and what sort of factors predict whether or not they are happy. One of their surprising discoveries was that the factors that predict happiness are very similar across different countries and cultures. Here is what they found.

## FACTORS ASSOCIATED WITH BEING HAPPY

**Wealth:** There is good evidence for the old cliché "money doesn't buy happiness." People on high incomes tend not to be much happier than those on low incomes. The exception to this is for those who live in poverty, who tend to be much less happy than other people. For instance, in the poorest countries, such as India and Bangladesh, poor people are much less happy than those who are better off. It seems, however, that as long as people have enough to buy the necessities of life, they can be happy, and having a lot more does not make people much happier.

**Age and gender:** These are not related to people's level of happiness. There are happy and unhappy people about equally at every age group and among both men and women. People's race and level of education are also not associated with their level of happiness.

**Work:** This can play an important role in people's level of happiness. Those whose work provides them with a sense of vocation, identity, purpose or connection with others are more likely to feel happy.

**Consuming interests:** These can also contribute to human happiness. Having a passion for something that we do (e.g., golf, gardening, music, writing, tennis, bridge, bowling or dancing) and indulging in it on a regular basis increases the likelihood that we will feel happy.

**Goals:** These can also play a role in people's overall sense of happiness. Having a sense of mission or purpose or working towards something that we consider important, helps us to feel happy.

**Relationships:** One of the strongest predictors of happiness is the quality of our relationships. Close, committed, enduring relationships are associated with higher levels of happiness. People who have intimate relationships are more likely to be very happy than those who have lots of superficial relationships but little intimacy. Being happily married is also a strong predictor of overall happiness, but people who are single tend to be happier than those who are unhappily married.

**Religion:** People who are highly spiritually committed are more likely to be happy than those who have no spiritual commitment. It may be because religious beliefs give people a sense of connection and purpose, which makes their lives meaningful. People with strong religious beliefs also frequently have good social support through "communal fellowship," which may also explain why they are more likely to feel happy.

**Active lifestyle**: Happy people live active, robust lives, and are less focused on themselves than people who are unhappy.

## PERSONAL ATTRIBUTES OF HAPPY PEOPLE

In addition to lifestyle factors, the researchers found that four key personal attributes were associated with higher levels of happiness.

**Good self-esteem**: People who feel good about themselves are more likely to feel happy than those who have poor self-esteem.

**Sense of control**: People who feel in control over the things that happen in their lives are more likely to be happy.

**Optimism**: People who feel optimistic about the future are also more likely to be happy.

**Extroversion**: People who are outgoing and who associate easily with others are more likely to report feeling happy.

The conclusions drawn from this and other research suggest that human happiness is partly determined by our personal characteristics (such as our level of self-esteem, sense of control, extroversion and optimism) and partly determined by the way we live our lives (our work, interests, goals and interpersonal relationships).

Much of the focus of this book has been on our thoughts—knowing ourselves better, identifying the cognitions that that make us feel unhappy (i.e., angry, sad, anxious, depressed, frustrated, worthless) and consciously working towards changing those cognitions. Using the cognitive and behavioral techniques that we have looked at throughout the book can help us to feel better in situations where we might otherwise feel bad. It can also help us to develop more of the traits that are associated with human happiness—a sense of control over our experiences, good self-esteem, optimism and greater willingness to take social risks and connect with people.

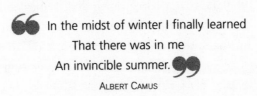

In the midst of winter I finally learned
That there was in me
An invincible summer.
ALBERT CAMUS

## LIFESTYLE

The way we spend our time from day to day, week to week and month to month can have a huge impact on the way we feel. Our lifestyle can determine whether we feel happy or sad, stressed or relaxed, lonely or connected, healthy or ill, bored or stimulated, contented or unfulfilled. The way we spend our time often reflects our beliefs about what we think is important. So for instance, if you spend much of your time on work-related activity, it is probably because you believe that work and the things that it gives you are important. If you spend a lot of time on leisure activity, chances are you believe that having fun is important, and if you spend a lot of time studying, it is because you believe that study and the things that it will ultimately bring you are worth the effort. Sometimes, however, our beliefs fall out of step with the way we live our lives. So for instance, you may believe that your health is important, but actually spend very little time on exercise or healthy lifestyle habits. Or you might believe that relationships are important but make little effort to initiate friendships or spend time with people you like. Or you might believe that having fun is important, but spend very little time on leisure activities or things that you enjoy.

For this reason, it is useful to reflect on the way that we spend our time and ask ourselves whether our lifestyle is consistent with the things that we want. The lifestyle self-assessment questionnaire at the end of this section can help us to look at different aspects of our lifestyle and identify areas that might be worth modifying. Of course, there is no correct way to spend our time. However, it is useful to consider whether our current lifestyle is consistent with the things we believe are important and helps us to achieve the things that we want.

ASK YOURSELF:
➤ How satisfied are you with your current lifestyle?
➤ Does it reflect your beliefs about the things that are important?
➤ Is it conducive to happiness and good health?
➤ Will your current lifestyle bring you the things you want in the future?

For most people, having a balanced lifestyle increases our likelihood of feeling happy. This means spending time and energy on a range of activities and not putting all of our eggs into one basket. As people who have relied too much on any one area of their lives can testify, if we drop our basket (as a result of being laid off, divorce, health problems, financial problems) we can get into all sorts of trouble. Spending our energy on a range of activities is not only a safer bet for the future but also makes our lives richer and more satisfying in the present.

While there are many different types of activity that people find rewarding, a good balance includes spending some time and energy on each of the following areas:

➤ work/regular commitments
➤ interests/leisure activity

- ➤ mental stimulation
- ➤ health maintenance
- ➤ relationships.

## WORK/REGULAR COMMITMENTS

**Question–Do you feel satisfied with the way you spend your time during the week, either at work or doing other things?**

Most people feel good when they are involved in some sort of regular work or activity. Although there is no reason why it should consume five days of every week or fall within certain hours, a commitment to regular activity—be it paid work, voluntary work, education or an interest—can have many benefits. Commitment provides a structure to our day or week and gives us a reason to get up in the morning. Even though we may instinctively prefer to sleep in, the discipline that comes with a regular routine seems to make most of us feel and function better. Work or some regular activity can also provide other benefits—mental stimulation, social contact, enjoyment, a sense of purpose, a sense of achievement, self-efficacy, personal satisfaction and self-esteem. It also reduces our risk of becoming depressed. In fact, satisfying work is one of the key predictors of overall life satisfaction. Of course, work can also be tedious, stressful and soul-destroying, and for some people, resigning or retiring is the most rational and life-enhancing decision they can make. One of the ironies of work is that it can be our greatest source of happiness and satisfaction or it can be a source of misery, stress, isolation, unfulfilled needs and, ultimately, health problems.

Having too much time on our hands or too few interests puts us at risk of unhappiness and depression. People who are not in paid work can experience many of the benefits that come with satisfying work (such as routine, social contact, stimulation, sense of purpose and so on) through participating in activities such as voluntary work, education or regular hobbies. My father is a perfect example. When he retired twenty years ago, Dad joined the local gym. Today, well into his eighties, he still attends the gym every morning, from Monday to Friday. For Dad, the gym provides a structure to his week, a focus for his life, feelings of self-efficacy and achievement, social contact and of course, it helps to keep him fit and stay well.

## INTERESTS/LEISURE ACTIVITY

**Question: What sort of things do you do for leisure/recreation? Do you have enough fun in your life?**

Leisure activities are anything that we do for enjoyment and relaxation. Different people enjoy doing different things. Common leisure activities include sports, crafts, hiking, sailing, movies, eating out, computer games, artwork, roller-blading, writing and dancing. Leisure activities are a source of pleasure and relaxation, and provide an escape from our regular routine. They also provide a counterbalance to the demands and stresses that exist in other areas of our lives. One of the benefits of not being in a work situation is that it gives us more time to participate in leisure activities.

In modern Western countries like ours, watching television is the most popular form of leisure activity. Some people are highly critical of television because of the poor quality of many of the programs and the frequent interruptions of intrusive, inane advertisements on commercial TV stations. Watching TV is also a passive pastime—it draws our attention from other things and discourages social interaction or engagement in more creative or challenging activity. This can particularly be a problem among children, who often watch for several hours a day. My own view is that television has its place—it can be a great source of entertainment, information, relaxation and even mental stimulation. However, like cars and fast food, used excessively or unwisely, it can have an insidious influence on our lives. Excessive TV watching robs us of other, more worthwhile pursuits—we could be reading, talking to people, solving a problem, playing a musical instrument, walking, discussing, entertaining, playing a sport or doing any one of a myriad of other worthwhile activities. Watching indiscriminately also means exposing ourselves to mindless junk and inane commercials—why do that to ourselves when there are so many other, more worthwhile things we could be doing?

> 66 When people say to me, "How do you do so many things?"
> I often answer them,
> without meaning to be cruel
> 'How do you do so little?'
> It seems to me that people have vast potential.
> Most people can do extraordinary things
> if they have the confidence or take the risks.
> Yet most people don't.
> They sit in front of the telly
> and treat life
> as if it goes on forever. 99
> PHILLIP ADAMS

Some people feel guilty when they engage in leisure activity because they believe that they should always be "productive" in their use of time. This comes from rigid beliefs, often learned in childhood, that things that are pleasurable are somehow less valid than those that involve hard work and produce tangible results. Unless we engage in leisure activity with a spirit of indulgence, fun and guilt-free pleasure, it may not be worth engaging at all. The secret is to find a balance.

## MENTAL STIMULATION

### Question: What sorts of things do you do for mental stimulation?

Our brain loves stimulation. For most people acquiring new knowledge, thinking critically, challenging our own ideas and solving problems are among our most satisfying experiences because they exercise our mind. Many activities can give our mind a workout—reading, writing, studying, solving puzzles, working, watching good quality TV programs, listening to the radio, playing games, seeing films, going to the theater and having discussions with other people. In fact, many of us like nothing more than engaging in a good debate with some friends over a meal and a glass of wine. Mentally stimulating activities are enjoyable in themselves and add richness and texture to our lives. Exercising the brain also helps us to retain good mental functioning into our old age. The old saying, "If you don't use it, you lose it" applies to the brain, just as it does to other parts of the body. In addition, activities that affect the "right side of the brain"—things that move us on a "spiritual level," such as music, art, poetry, dance, theatre, meditation or any creative interest—also help us to keep a healthy balance between intellectual and creative parts of our mind.

## HEALTH MAINTENANCE

### Question: How much responsibility do you take for looking after your health?

Earlier in history, physical health was presumed to be largely a matter of chance—if you were lucky you had good health; if you were not so lucky, you were frequently ill or died young. Since medical research made the connection between human behaviors and physical health some half a century ago, we have come to realize the importance of healthy lifestyle choices, such as not smoking, doing regular exercise, maintaining a balanced diet, getting adequate sleep and relaxation, and avoiding excessive amounts of alcohol or drugs. More recently, stress management and supportive social relationships have been added to the list of healthy lifestyle habits. Although there is also an element of luck involved in our physical health (unfortunately, we cannot control our genes), our lifestyle choices can make a huge difference to how well we feel—physically and psychologically—as well as how long we live. Given that most of us already know what we need to do in order to maximize our chances of staying healthy, it is amazing that so many of us don't put these things into practice.

> 66 Knowing what to do is not usually the problem. The elusive goal is translating intentions into action and resolutions into results. The gap between knowing and doing remains a weak link in most of our lives. 99
>
> DAN MILLMAN, *NO ORDINARY MOMENTS*

Whether or not we have the self-discipline to look after our physical health largely depends on our willingness to tolerate frustration. Low frustration tolerance frequently sabotages our desire to stay motivated and achieve our goals because we pursue immediate gratification at the expense of our long-term best interests (see chapter 4). Motivating ourselves to give up self-defeating behaviors, such as smoking, overeating, drinking too much alcohol, abusing drugs or not exercising, requires us to make our physical health a top priority. In addition, we need to set clear goals, make a plan of action and prepare to deal with the obstacles that are likely to arise along the way (see chapter 9).

## RELATIONSHIPS

### Question–How much time do you spend with people you like? Are relationships a priority for you?

Humans are social animals. We enjoy talking to and being with others because that is our nature—we are genetically programmed to affiliate. Although we can be perfectly happy to spend time alone, being by ourselves for too long can sometimes make us feel down. At an instinctive level we like to be with people.

Good relationships provide us with many benefits—both emotional and practical. They satisfy our need for social connection and belonging, help us to feel secure and contribute to feelings of self-worth. They also provide enjoyment, entertainment and mental stimulation. When we are trying to solve problems, other people can give us ideas, useful information, a fresh perspective and sometimes, practical assistance. Several studies have found that strong supportive relationships are beneficial not only for our psychological well-being but for our physical health as well.

There are some interesting differences in the social behavior of men compared to women. In most families, men take little responsibility for maintaining social connections, other than with their partner and immediate family. Women are more frequently responsible for making social arrangements and are more likely to initiate contact with friends. They are also more likely than men to have close friendships with people outside their family unit—usually other women. Although good social support is just as important for men as it is for women, men are generally less inclined to initiate contact or maintain social relationships, and therefore tend to be more dependent on their partner for friendship, intimacy and social support. For this reason, men often have fewer resources to help them cope at times of marital breakup or bereavement. In fact, losing one's spouse often has a more devastating impact on the health of men than of women, largely because of the more limited support that is available to men. While a loving and supportive primary relationship is a wonderful thing to have, relying on one person to satisfy all of our emotional needs is risky—a bit like putting all of our eggs into one basket. A safer and psychologically healthier approach is to develop at least a few close friendships, instead of relying on just one person to meet all of our social and emotional needs.

There are two essential ingredients for maintaining satisfying relationships—time and communication. In other words, we need to be available, both physically and emotionally. Maintaining supportive relationships involves making ourselves available—spending time with people and initiating contact at times. People who lead busy lives may find this difficult. The demands of a stressful job, family responsibilities or a new love interest can cause us to fall out of touch with friends. If we are lucky, we realize the error of our ways in time to do something about it; if not, loneliness, isolation or depression will eventually bring home to us the cost of neglecting our friendships. Sharing a regular activity, such as going to movies, concerts, dinners, sporting events, walks or playing a sport, can provide a structure for ensuring that we stay in touch.

The second ingredient for good relationships is open communication. Self-disclosure—talking honestly about our experiences, thoughts and feelings—is the stuff that connects us to other people. Communication that is consistently polite, formal or "edited" keeps a wall between people, no matter how much we want to connect. Good relationships involve self-disclosure and honest communication. Of course, this does not mean that every conversation should be filled with deep and meaningful descriptions of our innermost feelings. However, it does mean that we are willing to talk candidly, and to disclose our feelings at times. With communication as with everything else, balance is the key.

## HOW BALANCED IS MY LIFESTYLE?

Now that we have looked at different components of a balanced lifestyle, it might be useful to check our own. The following exercise can serve as a guide for reflecting on the various aspects of our lives and may help to highlight areas that could do with some changes. There are five lifestyle categories, and under each of these are ten statements. Read each one and circle a number between one and five to indicate how true that statement is for you. When you have finished, add up the numbers you have circled and write down the total (out of fifty) in the space at the bottom of each category.

## Self-assessment exercise–How balanced is my lifestyle?

For each of the following statements, circle a number to indicate how true the statement is for you.
1 = not true at all, 3 = somewhat true, 5 = very true.

### A. WORK/DAILY ACTIVITIES

1. I feel productive/useful in the way I spend my time during the day.    1   2   3   4   5

2. The work/things that I do during the day are enjoyable.    1   2   3   4   5

3. My work/daily activities suit my personality, interests and temperament.    1   2   3   4   5

4. My work/daily routine is mentally stimulating.    1   2   3   4   5

5. My work/daily routine involves some enjoyable social interaction.    1   2   3   4   5

6. My physical environment during the day is pleasant.    1   2   3   4   5

7. I feel valued by the people around me.    1   2   3   4   5

8. I feel adequately rewarded for the things that I do.    1   2   3   4   5

9. The demands that are made of me are reasonable and manageable.    1   2   3   4   5

10. The time I spend at work/in my daily activities is balanced and leaves me enough time to do other things that I value.    1   2   3   4   5

TOTAL SCORE     /50

### B. HEALTH

1. I make a conscious effort to look after my health.    1   2   3   4   5

2. I do some form of exercise (walking, swimming, etc.) at least four times per week.    1   2   3   4   5

3. I don't smoke.    1   2   3   4   5

4. I drink no more than a moderate amount of alcohol, consistent with guidelines recommended by health authorities.    1   2   3   4   5

5. I eat a balanced and healthy diet.    1   2   3   4   5

6. I avoid eating junk foods and foods that are high in saturated fat.    1   2   3   4   5

7. I do not have a highly stressful lifestyle.    1   2   3   4   5

8. I don't push myself too hard–I make sure I get lots of rest.    1   2   3   4   5

9. Most nights I sleep well and get adequate sleep.    1   2   3   4   5

10. I rarely feel stressed to the point of experiencing physical symptoms.    1   2   3   4   5

TOTAL SCORE     /50

### C. MIND

1. I frequently read material that is thought-provoking.    1   2   3   4   5

2. I often have challenging discussions/debates with others.    1   2   3   4   5

3. I have interests that are mentally stimulating.    1   2   3   4   5

4. I am constantly developing my thoughts, ideas and knowledge.  1  2  3  4  5

5. I actively participate in activities, rather than just observe.  1  2  3  4  5

6. I like to ask questions and think critically about issues.  1  2  3  4  5

7. Much of my entertainment (e.g., TV, films, radio) is thought-provoking.  1  2  3  4  5

8. I frequently partake in activities that move me on a spiritual level.  1  2  3  4  5

9. I am constantly seeking to learn new things.  1  2  3  4  5

10. Many of my daily activities are mentally stimulating.  1  2  3  4  5

TOTAL SCORE        /50

## D LEISURE

1. I pursue hobbies/interests that I enjoy.  1  2  3  4  5

2. I frequently indulge in pleasurable activities.  1  2  3  4  5

3. I have lots of fun.  1  2  3  4  5

4. Watching TV is *not* my main leisure activity.  1  2  3  4  5

5. Some of my leisure activities involve doing things with others.  1  2  3  4  5

6. I take regular holidays and breaks from my usual routine.  1  2  3  4  5

7. When I participate in leisure activities, I can really let go and
enjoy myself.  1  2  3  4  5

8. When I indulge myself, I never feel guilty.  1  2  3  4  5

9. I let go and relax on a regular basis.  1  2  3  4  5

10. I enjoy most of the things that I do.  1  2  3  4  5

TOTAL SCORE        /50

## E SOCIAL SUPPORT

1. I find it easy to self-disclose and talk about my feelings.  1  2  3  4  5

2. I have enough people in my life with whom I share a trusting and
intimate relationship.  1  2  3  4  5

3. I socialize a lot.  1  2  3  4  5

4. I am generally friendly and supportive to others.  1  2  3  4  5

5. I have a good network of social support.  1  2  3  4  5

6. I feel relaxed and comfortable with most people.  1  2  3  4  5

7. I am willing to take risks in initiating friendships.  1  2  3  4  5

8. I spend sufficient time connecting with the significant people in my life.  1  2  3  4  5

9. When I need emotional or practical support, I always have people that
I can turn to.  1  2  3  4  5

10. When I need emotional or practical support, I do not hesitate to ask for it.  1  2  3  4  5

TOTAL SCORE        /50

After completing this exercise, look at your scores for each of the five areas. As a general rule, those areas in which you scored above forty appear to be working well for you—it is likely that they are contributing to a sense of well-being and personal satisfaction. Areas in which you scored between thirty and forty may not be quite as satisfying, and making some changes within those areas could improve your quality of life. Lower scores tend to reflect lower levels of personal satisfaction or possible problems. Scores below thirty often point to areas that may be in need of attention. Making positive changes in these areas could help to improve your quality of life, and ultimately, enable you to feel happier.

The aim of this exercise is to help you reflect on your current lifestyle and identify areas that might be worthy of some attention. If you already feel perfectly satisfied with your current lifestyle, then that is more significant than your scores on this or any other questionnaire, and there is no need to consider making changes. If you would like to reflect on your current lifestyle, the questions in the following exercise are worth reflecting on:

**EXERCISE 11.1**

1. How balanced is your current lifestyle? Are there some areas that are missing out?
2. What sort of changes could you make to enhance your lifestyle?
3. What obstacles will you need to overcome in order to make these changes?
4. What would you need to believe in order to overcome those obstacles?
5. Write a plan of action (see chapter 9) for the things that you need to do to make these positive lifestyle changes.

Whether or not you resolve to make any changes to your lifestyle, remember that the best decisions are those based on rational, considered judgments—as opposed to simply giving into inertia or low frustration tolerance.

> 66 Most of us believe we want change—to improve ourselves, but we carry the weight of inertia—the resistance to change, within us . . . We can get so locked into old patterns that we stick with them even though they clearly don't work any more. 99 DAN MILLMAN, *NO ORDINARY MOMENTS*

## LIVING PURPOSEFULLY—SET LIFE GOALS

We have already seen that setting goals can help us to overcome depression and reduce the likelihood that it will recur (see chapter 8). Setting goals can also help us to solve problems and take control over some of life's challenges (see chapter 9). Finally, setting goals can also help us to create meaningful changes to our lives.

Identifying what we want, making a plan of action and working through it is the means by which we can accomplish many of the things that are important to us. Defining life goals helps us to focus on the things we want, and motivates us to mobilize our resources to work towards them.

> 66 I went to the woods
> Because I wanted to live deliberately
> I wanted to live deep,
> And suck the marrow out of life.
> To put to rest all that was not life
> And not, when I came to die
> Discover that I had not lived. 99
> HENRY THOREAU

Most of us live our lives from day to day. While we sometimes plan for future events—home renovations, next year's vacation, dinners, dentist appointments, job interviews, retirement—most of the time we respond to the pressures and demands of our daily life situations. There is, of course, nothing wrong with this, if the things that we do enable us to feel satisfied. Sometimes, however, it is worth reflecting on whether the current direction of our lives is where we want to go. Have you ever asked yourself, "What is it that I want? What things are important to me? Where do I want to be in five years' time?"

## VISUALIZATION

A good way to clarify the things that are important to us is to visualize our lives at some time into the future—four, five or six years ahead is ideal. The best way to do this is to get someone else to read you this prepared script very slowly, while you sit with your eyes closed and try to picture what is being said. Alternatively, you might record the script onto a tape recorder and then play it back to yourself while sitting in a comfortable chair with your eyes closed. With all visualization and relaxation exercises, the secret is to pace yourself. Speak very slowly, and pause for about ten seconds between each sentence to give yourself time to create and experience the images that you describe. The following is a text that I recommend. You can use it as it is or modify it to make it more personally meaningful to you:

> *Within your mind's eye, see yourself moving forward through time. Perhaps you can see spirals and psychedelic colors and patterns as time flies before your eyes. And now, you find yourself at another point in time, (five) years into the future. Think of what year it is. How old are you now? You are walking towards the place*

*where you live, see it from the outside, and now you walk in the front door, and step inside. How does it feel to be at home? Watch yourself, doing some things around the house. What sort of things are you doing? How do you look? Do you look healthy and well? How do you feel? Is there a bounce in your step? Are you happy with your life? Are you a happier person than you were five years ago? What has changed? What are the good things in your life? Now you can see the people who are important to you at this stage of your life sitting in the loungeroom with you, talking and laughing. Who is there? What are they talking about? How do you feel about the different people who are there with you? Who are your closest friends? Now let your visitors fade away, and see yourself at your place of work or the place where you spend much of your time during the week. Where are you? What are you doing? Is there anyone else there with you? Are you enjoying the things that you do? Now let that scene fade away and see yourself indulging in some leisure activity that you frequently enjoy. What sort of things do you do for fun or relaxation? What are your interests? Look back over your life so far. What do you feel proud of? What are you especially glad to have done? What sort of things give you personal satisfaction? Just allow yourself a little time to enjoy your fantasy. And now, see the passage of time moving backwards, once again in spirals and psychedelic patterns, taking you back to the present time. Feel yourself gently returning to the here and now, back to the room that you're in at this point in time, back to the present moment. And when you feel ready, you can open your eyes.*

After you have taken a little time to think about the images that came to you during this exercise, it is a good idea to write them down. In particular, focus on areas that you would like to work towards.

The following are some of the broad areas in which people often choose to set some of their life goals. You might like to select one or more of these and write down specific changes that you want to make within that area.

When writing down your goals, try to be specific. Avoid vague statements. For instance, not "Have good relationships," but "Have a close, open and honest relationship with my daughter"; not "Improve my health," but "Stop smoking, get my blood pressure down to 140/70;" not "Improve my attitudes," but "Learn to accept myself without putting myself down."

AREAS FOR SETTING LIFE GOALS
➤ health
➤ relationships
➤ attitudes
➤ leisure

➤ knowledge
➤ interests
➤ work
➤ material
➤ spiritual
➤ self-development
➤ other.

Once you have identified your life goals, it may be worth rereading chapter 9 on formulating an action plan to help follow through from intentions to action.

## EXPECTATIONS

*Whether we are happy or miserable*
*depends on our expectations.*
*Not on the things that we have,*
*but on the things we expect.*

In nearly every way, our lives are easier and more comfortable than they were for people of previous generations. Technological advances and economic growth in the last few decades have given us access to material goods that our grandparents would not have dreamed of. We own houses, cars, televisions, mobile phones, iPods, computers, DVD players and fancy equipment for home entertainment. We take more vacations than people of previous generations, and we go overseas more often. We own devices that save us time and energy—washing machines, dishwashers, refrigerators, vacuum cleaners and microwaves. Most of these things have made our lives easier and freed us from the tedious aspects of domestic life. In addition, we have more opportunities than our predecessors—to study, travel, change careers, move, develop our talents, indulge our passions and even to leave an unhappy marriage. With all of these new-found freedoms and creature comforts, one would think that life in the new millennium would be happier than in any previous period in history. Yet there is little evidence of increased happiness—in fact, some sections of the community are less happy now than in the past. This is the paradox of the twenty-first century. Depression is currently the fourth leading cause of disability in the United States and is expected to rise to second place (after heart disease) by the year 2020. Drug abuse, loneliness, youth suicide and divorce are increasingly common symptoms of personal unhappiness and social alienation. While many factors, including urbanization, unemployment and changing social values, have contributed to these problems, an important but often unacknowledged factor is our changing expectations.

It was the ancient stoic philosopher Seneca who first pointed out the role that our expectations play in determining our level of happiness. In 50 AD, Seneca observed that people who are dissatisfied with their lives often have unrealistic expectations about how things should be. Today, with the mass media promoting tantalizing images of fame, success, beauty, romance, popularity and wealth, the perceived gap between our own lives and those of the people we compare ourselves with has never been greater. Consequently we are more likely to feel dissatisfied with our lot than ever before. We have so much, yet we expect so much more. Because we tend to compare our lives with those of other people, we are left with the impression that we are somehow missing out—that our lives are not good enough the way they are.

> *Comparing yourself with idealized images of others*
> *is guaranteed to make you miserable.*

People living in modern Western countries often have unrealistic expectations about how things should be. We want to retain our youthful looks for ever, and we become despondent and desperate as we discover that we have little control over the aging process. We expect to have perfect friendships and so we become easily disillusioned when friends and family members fail to live up to our expectations. We expect to have well-paid, stimulating and satisfying work and so we feel frustrated and dissatisfied because we still have not found the perfect job. We expect to be married or in a committed relationship and so we feel desolate and despairing because we have not found our ideal mate. We want to have perfect children and happy harmonious families and we feel disappointed when ours do not live up to our expectations. We want to own an attractive home with lots of material comforts and we want to accomplish lots of important things. In short, many of our expectations leave us feeling unsatisfied with what we have.

> *Unrealistic expectations lead us to believe that we're missing out.*
> *That the lives we are living are, somehow, not good enough.*

## CHANGING OUR EXPECTATIONS OVER TIME

As we move through the various stages of our lives, new circumstances constantly challenge us to modify our expectations. One of the greatest challenges is in relation to aging. Over the course of our lives we will need to change our expectations in relation to our appearance, and our physical and mental abilities. Age brings with it a series of physical changes—our skin starts to sag, and wrinkles appear, our hair thins and goes gray, our thighs and tummy get bigger, and a lot of flabby bits appear where they never used to be; our eyesight, hearing and memory deteriorate; and even our sense of smell and taste decline. None of this is in itself a problem, as long as we modify our expectations along the way. With the passage of time, we also need to adjust to the changing stages of life—from childhood to adolescence, adulthood, parenthood, working life, retirement and old age. With each new stage come new challenges, responsibilities and rewards. Recognizing that life is composed of a series of stages, and adjusting our expectations as each new stage unfolds, helps us to make smooth transitions over the course of our lives. Unrealistic expectations or failing to modify our expectations over time can leave us feeling frightened, angry or depressed.

*A good example to illustrate how our expectations affect our perceptions of whether things are good or bad is the changing price of gasoline. When gas first went up to $2 per gallon in 2000, the public was horrified—we had been used to paying less than $1.50, so the new price felt exorbitant. However, as the price climbed to over $3 in 2005, $2 per gallon suddenly sounded incredibly cheap. If by some good fortune we managed to find gas at $2.60 per gallon, it felt like we had snared a bargain. What would have previously seemed outrageously expensive now seemed cheap. Although $2.60 per gallon is still $2.60 per gallon, it feels like less. It is not the price that we pay, but our expectation of what the price should be, that determines whether we believe we are being fleeced or getting a bargain.*

66 A Chinese peasant celebrates because the abundant rice crop harvested this year will be sufficient to feed his family over the coming winter. In another part of the world, an American businessman contemplates suicide after the net worth of his assets has fallen from $27 million to just $7 million. He will be depressed for years. It is all about expectations. 99

## CONDITIONAL HAPPINESS—WAITING FOR THE RIGHT CIRCUMSTANCES

Many people believe that they could be happy, if only they were able to overcome a particular obstacle to their happiness—a rotten job, an obstinate child, an unpaid mortgage or an unhappy marriage. As a result, we focus on our difficulties and postpone our happiness, assuming that one day, when all of our problems have been resolved or we have achieved some important goal, then we will be able to sit back and be cheerful.

➤ When I finish my studies, then life will be so much easier.
➤ When I find the right job—something that makes me feel fulfilled.
➤ When I move out of home, then I'll feel much happier.
➤ When I'm earning enough to feel financially secure, I'll be able to relax.
➤ When I meet the right man, then I'll be happy.

➤ When I have children, I'll feel fulfilled—it's hard to be happy when your biological needs aren't met.

➤ When the children finally leave home, then I'll be able to relax at last.

➤ When I finish writing this book, then maybe I'll get a life.

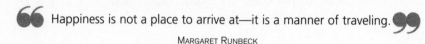 Happiness is not a place to arrive at—it is a manner of traveling. 
MARGARET RUNBECK

Waiting for things to fall into place before we can feel happy is a precarious strategy for two reasons. Firstly, we miss the opportunity to fully experience and enjoy the present moment—to feel good now. And that is a pity because today is the only chance we will ever get to experience today. Remember the saying, "This is not a dress rehearsal—it's the real thing"? Postponing our happiness to some future time means that we miss out on today. And once today has passed, it's gone, and we don't get another chance to have it again. Secondly, when we make our happiness conditional on solving our problems, we may never be happy, as problems will always be with us. As some are resolved, new ones emerge—that is the nature of things. The challenge is not to expect that all of our problems should disappear but to fix what is fixable, accept what we cannot change and focus on all the many good things that we already have.

## IT'S WHAT WE FOCUS ON

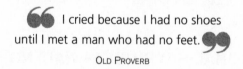 I cried because I had no shoes until I met a man who had no feet. 
OLD PROVERB

Making a conscious effort to redirect our focus from thoughts that make us miserable to the thoughts that make us feel good can make a big difference to the way we feel.

| THOUGHTS THAT MAKE US FEEL MISERABLE | THOUGHTS THAT MAKE US FEEL HAPPY |
|---|---|
| All the things that have gone wrong | All the things that have gone right |
| Injustices | Our good fortune |
| Rejections | People who care about us |
| Our failures | Our achievements |
| Our shortcomings | Our strengths and qualities |
| Things we've missed out on | Things that we've been lucky enough to have or experience |
| What we've lost | What we've gained |
| Other people's faults | Other people's qualities |

We have already seen that having unrealistic expectations and focusing on the things that we believe are missing from our lives contributes to our own unhappiness. The reverse is also true—having reasonable expectations and being in the habit of acknowledging all the good things that we have makes us feel fortunate and satisfied. Everyone has both positive and negative aspects in their lives—achievements and failures, pleasures and disappointments, losses and gains, illnesses and recoveries. The secret is to focus a little more on all the good things that we have. We take so much for granted! Although we may not realize it, there is much to celebrate, if only we open our eyes.

One way to stay mindful of all the good things we have is to write a daily gratitude list. This involves taking five minutes each morning or evening to think of all the things that we have that we can feel grateful for. Gratitude has long been the domain of prayer—most religions urge followers to express gratitude for the things that they have, including good health, a roof over one's head and food on the table. Gratitudes do not need to exclusively focus on big-ticket items. We can learn to appreciate every positive aspect of our lives, no matter how small—an outstanding task finally accomplished, an invitation to dinner, a fascinating program on TV, the affections of our pet, the sunshine beaming through our window, the sweet, curious questions of a child. Keeping a daily gratitude list need only take up a few minutes a day, and can make a huge difference to the way we feel. For example, these are the gratitudes that I wrote down this evening:

*I feel grateful for:*
1. *The laughter that I shared with Sue on the phone this evening.*
2. *The pleasure of reading today's newspaper.*
3. *The revived energy and sense of well being that I felt after my morning walk.*
4. *The gradual healing of a wound—a problem that has troubled me is fading.*
5. *Mom is feeling better.*
6. *That phone call that I had been putting off has now been made.*
7. *The peace of mind that I am experiencing right now.*
8. *My ability to think and write today.*
9. *The progress that I've made on my book.*
10. *Living in a T-shirt—Spring's great weather.*

*Don't ignore the small pleasures.*
*When you add them together,*
*they are the things that make life fantastic.*

**EXERCISE 11.2**

Write down a gratitude list for today. Record the things that are going well in your life, the things that you enjoy or appreciate, and the things you are lucky enough to have. Repeat this exercise every day for a week, and see how you feel. Consider making this a lifelong habit.

# IN SUMMARY

➤ Research from studies around the world suggests that people who have satisfying work, absorbing interests, close supportive relationships or religious affiliation are more likely to be happy than those who don't. Personal attributes of people who describe themselves as happy include good self-esteem, optimism, extroversion and a sense of being in control.

➤ A lifestyle that balances regular commitments with leisure activity, mental stimulation, social interaction and health maintenance is also conducive to psychological well-being.

➤ Setting and working towards goals can help us to achieve life-enhancing changes and is a satisfying process in itself.

➤ Unrealistic expectations are a common cause of unhappiness. It is often useful to identify and challenge some of the expectations that limit our ability to be happy. It is also important to modify some of our expectations as we get older, and as our life circumstances change.

➤ Focusing on the good things that we already have, rather than the things we are missing out on, can help us to feel happy. A daily gratitude list is a useful way of maintaining this focus.

# Solutions to Exercises

*These are sample solutions to the exercises. There are no definitive answers.*

## EXERCISE 2.1

1. Personalizing: I should be a perfect mother. I am totally responsible for my children's lives and happiness.
2. Filtering: I should always sound intelligent and socially progressive. I should never say anything silly. Everyone must think highly of me.
3. Labeling, black-and-white thinking: Not having a degree means that I'm not clever enough. I must have a college degree in order to be OK.
4. Predicting catastrophe: A restructuring means that I will lose my job. If I lose my job, the consequences will be disastrous, and I will never find another one.
5. Filtering: Everything that I have done is useless, and all of my life experiences have been bad.
6. Black-and-white thinking: My performance must be perfect—otherwise it's a complete disaster.
7. Predicting catastrophe: A pain in the abdomen must mean cancer. It's better to avoid situations than to face possible problems.
8. Mind reading: People must be looking at me and thinking there is something wrong with me.
9. Labeling; overgeneralizing: I should have gone ahead and established my own business. Not establishing a business means that I am a failure. Not achieving this particular goal means that I have never achieved anything worthwhile.
10. Comparing: I should achieve the same level of wealth as my friends.
11. Labeling; filtering: He should behave in the way I think is right. Certain behaviors mean that he is totally unacceptable as a person.
12. Jumping to negative conclusions: If some money has been withdrawn from my account without my consent, it means someone is trying to cheat me.
13. Black-and-white thinking: Unless our marriage is perfect, it's no good and it won't work.
14. Labeling, jumping to negative conclusions: If I had problems in my previous job, it means I am no good and will continue to have problems in other jobs.
15. Comparing; shoulds: I should achieve the same level of success as my peers.
16. Personalizing; mind reading: He must be helping out because he is disgusted with me.

## EXERCISE 3.1: PRACTICE LOGICAL DISPUTING

### The neglected birthday

DISPUTE: Not making a fuss about my birthday doesn't mean that he doesn't care about me. Birthdays are important to me but not to him—he has different priorities and values to me. He shows me he loves me in other ways.

POSITIVE ACTIONS: Talk to him. Tell him that birthdays are important to me, and I'd like to feel special on this one day of the year. Tell him what I would like for my next birthday.

### The frustrated public servant

DISPUTE: It's disappointing that I didn't achieve very much today, but I can't change what has been. What I can do is organize myself better so that I'm more productive tomorrow. Most people have occasional days when they're not very productive, and so do I. Although I prefer to be productive, having a slack day is unlikely to result in catastrophic consequences.

POSITIVE ACTIONS: Set clear goals for tomorrow. Prepare what I am going to work on, so that I can get straight into it first thing in the morning. Learn from the experience and avoid falling into the same traps in the future.

### The forgotten breakfast arrangement

DISPUTE: I prefer to be reliable and I nearly always am, but it's human to occasionally make mistakes. I don't know why I forgot on this occasion but I didn't do it on purpose—she knows that. As long as I explain how sorry I am, chances are she'll understand. I have been a good and loyal friend over the years, and it's unlikely that she'll write me off on the basis of one oversight.

POSITIVE ACTIONS: Apologize profusely. Perhaps send her a bunch of flowers with a note reiterating how sorry I am.

## EXERCISE 3.2: PRACTICE BEHAVIORAL DISPUTING

1. Speak up in class as often as possible. Observe whether there is any evidence that people think badly of you for speaking up.
2. Take as many flights as possible. Even though you might initially feel anxious, observe that you don't collapse or go mad, and nothing terrible happens.
3. Speak your own mind as often as possible. Observe whether there is any evidence that people like you less if you don't always agree with them.
4. Stop procrastinating—make decisions. Observe whether there was a right or wrong decision. Notice that even when you don't make the best decision, the consequences rarely lead to disaster.
5. Take social risks—approach people at conferences. Notice that people usually respond if you take the first step and that even if they don't, no disastrous consequences follow.

6. Once you have done a reasonable job on your essay, stop and hand it in. Set yourself a time limit. Observe that not being a perfectionist does not make a huge difference to the end result, and frees you to be productive on other things.

7. Make yourself get up in the mornings and exercise. Observe that there is no evidence that getting up early to exercise is too difficult.

8. Challenge yourself to be alone at times. Do things by yourself—go for walks, to the movies, to a coffee shop. Take a vacation at a spa on your own. Observe that it's not awful to be alone at times.

## EXERCISE 3.3: PRACTICE GOAL-DIRECTED THINKING

1. Does demanding that my mother shouldn't be there help me to enjoy my party? Getting upset about my mother's presence won't change the fact that she's there, but will spoil the evening for me. I want to have a good time at my party. I don't need to worry about the fact that she's there. It doesn't need to be my problem and it's not worth getting upset about.

2. Does giving him the cold shoulder help us to have a good relationship? Not speaking might punish him but it also creates tension in our relationship and makes us both feel bad. I want us to be happy together. Not communicating whenever I feel upset does not help us to have a good relationship. It's better to talk about it so that he understands how I feel.

3. Does telling myself that I shouldn't have come help me to feel good or do well in my exam? I'm here now—I may as well try to relax and enjoy the movie. In retrospect I can see that it wasn't a great idea to come, but telling myself that I shouldn't be here doesn't help with my exam preparation and only makes me feel bad. It's not worth worrying about it now—just relax and enjoy the movie.

4. Does focusing on her behavior help me to enjoy my work? Focusing on her unethical behavior doesn't change the situation. It stops me from enjoying my job and distracts me from what I'm meant to be doing. I've chosen not to say anything to her or my boss, so the best thing for me to do is not worry about it. She's not my problem.

## EXERCISE 5.4

**1. Someone you considered to be a friend was not available to help you when you needed them.**

ACTIONS: Communicate—tell your friend how you feel (see chapter 10).

BELIEFS: My friends should always be available when I need them. They should behave towards me as I would towards them. If they don't, they are horrible and deserve my utmost condemnation.

DISPUTE: It's disappointing that she was not there for me when I needed her, but I accept that this is one of her limitations. She has enough likeable qualities for me to want to keep our friendship, even though I have learned that I can't always count on her support.

## 2. Your partner has behaved very rudely in a social situation.

ACTIONS: Communicate. Explain how you feel, and why the behavior upset you (see chapter 10). Perhaps negotiate that the next time you socialize with people he doesn't like, he need not come along.

BELIEFS: He should always behave appropriately in social situations. It's awful when he doesn't. I am responsible for the way that he behaves. People will think badly of me.

DISPUTE: I need to talk to him about his behavior and negotiate a solution but ultimately I am not responsible for him. It is unlikely that people will dislike me because of his behavior.

## 3. A friend is constantly late. You have made a lunch date with her and have been kept waiting for over an hour.

ACTIONS: Communicate. Tell her how you feel and what you would like (see chapter 10). Perhaps in future, bring a book with you; arrive late yourself; don't make further social arrangements with her unless others are also going to be present.

BELIEFS: Everyone should have the same values as I do. It's very bad to be kept waiting.

DISPUTE: This is who she is. If the friendship is worth keeping, I may need to accept this aspect of her behavior and find ways to avoid getting bored or angry.

## 4. Someone keeps putting their garbage in your paper recycling bin when you leave it out for collection.

ACTIONS: Talk to the neighbors. Try to identify who is doing it, and then speak to them directly. Put a sign on your recycling bin.

BELIEFS: People should always do the right thing. It's awful when things like this happen.

DISPUTE: Although most people do the right thing, some people don't. I don't like it, but I can accept it. I am doing what I can to resolve the problem.

## 5. You told someone something in confidence and now you learn that they have told others about it.

ACTIONS: Communicate (see chapter 10).

BELIEFS: People should always do the right thing. Anyone who betrays my confidence is a terrible person and deserves my contempt.

DISPUTE: It's disappointing but I've learned a lesson. Although I can trust some people, I can't trust everyone. This person has some nice qualities but on this occasion she has let me down. I don't have to hate her for this.

**6. You are extremely inconvenienced by some ridiculous bureaucratic procedure imposed by a particular government organization.**

ACTIONS: Communicate (see chapter 10).

BELIEFS: Things should proceed easily and smoothly. Bureaucratic rules and procedures should benefit members of the public. They should be simple and efficient, and it's awful that they're not.

DISPUTE: I have tried to negotiate a simpler solution but I have not been successful. Bureaucratic organizations often have cumbersome, silly rules. I don't like it, but I can accept it. It is a pain in the neck but it's not a disaster.

**7. Owing to staff cutbacks at a telecommunications company you are kept waiting on hold for half an hour each time you try to call them.**

ACTIONS: Try to call at less busy times. Keep yourself occupied with other tasks while waiting for a response. Use email or written correspondence whenever possible. Check out the competitors and consider changing to another company, if practical.

BELIEFS: The service should be prompt and efficient. It's awful to be kept waiting. They should put customers before profits.

DISPUTE: Being on hold a pain in the neck but it's part of the modern world we live in. I don't like it but I can stand it. Getting upset over something I cannot control only makes me feel bad and doesn't solve the problem.

**8. You have been substantially overcharged by a tradesman.**

ACTIONS: Communicate (see chapter 10). Explain why you believe the bill to be excessive and suggest a compromise fee. Contact the Better Business Bureau for advice. Consider sending what you regard to be reasonable payment.

BELIEFS: I am being ripped off. My perspective is the correct one. It's terrible to be overcharged.

DISPUTE: I've learned a lesson—in future I need to clearly negotiate the fee before I start. I have done what I can. Are my expectations reasonable? Perhaps it's not as outrageous as it sounds. For my own peace of mind, it may be better to just pay the bill and let it go this time.

**9. The company you work for has a ruthlessly exploitative policy towards its employees.**

ACTIONS: Communicate specific grievances to the relevant people (e.g., HR manager, management). Look for another job.

BELIEFS: It's a terrible situation, and I don't have a choice—I have to put up with this.

DISPUTE: My health—both psychological and physical—is number one. No job, no matter how high-status and well-paid, is worth jeopardizing my health. I have choices—I don't have to put up with this.

### 10. Someone is rude to you for no reason.

ACTIONS: Communicate or ignore them, as appropriate.

BELIEFS: If I am nice to other people, they should always be nice to me. It's awful if they're not. Rude behavior is personal.

DISPUTE: I prefer people to treat me courteously, and most of the time they do, but I can stand it if on occasions some people do not. People behave badly for all sorts of reasons, and often it's more about them than me. I don't have to take this personally.

## EXERCISE 6.4

### 1. Eve is anxious about going to a social function where she won't know anyone.

THOUGHTS/BELIEFS: I may end up standing by myself all night. People might look at me and feel sorry for me. They might think I have no friends or that I am a loser. If I am at a social function, I must be seen to be talking to people and having a good time. It's bad to be seen alone.

DISPUTE: Chances are I'll end up talking to people for at least part of the night—that has been my experience to date. Even if I am on my own for some or all of the night, it's unlikely that people will think badly of me for that. Most people can relate to not knowing anyone at a social function. Even if I stood on my own, and some people thought I had no friends, that's too bad. It's not my problem. At worst it may be a boring night, but it's unlikely to be a disastrous night.

POSITIVE ACTIONS: Tell the hostess that I don't know anyone—ask her to introduce me around. Offer to take plates of savories around to the guests. Move out of my comfort zone—make an effort to go up and talk to people. Perhaps take a friend with me. If I'm totally bored, I can go home after a couple of hours.

### 2. Beatrice feels anxious about running late for a doctor's appointment.

THOUGHTS/BELIEFS: This is bad. I may miss my appointment. They will be vexed with me. I should always be punctual. It's bad to be late. The consequences of arriving late are likely to be disastrous.

DISPUTE: I know from past experience that even when I am running late, I am never excessively late, and it's never a disaster. The worst possible thing that might happen is that I may miss my appointment, and I will have to pay for this one and make another appointment. That would be inconvenient but it would not be the end of the world. I could cope with it, if it should happen.

POSITIVE ACTIONS: Pull up for a moment, call the doctor's office on my cell and let them know that I'm running a bit late. Relax.

### 3. Kim is anxious about having to give a speech to a large audience of professional people.

THOUGHTS/BELIEFS: They are professionals—they might know more than I do. They will see how nervous I am. They will think I'm incompetent. I might do a bad job or I might even fall apart. I must do a brilliant job. It would be awful if I didn't. Because they are professionals, they know more than I do. It would be awful if they could see that I was nervous or if they didn't think I was any good.

DISPUTE: Just because they are professionals, doesn't mean they are knowledgeable in my area. I have enough expertise on the subject to do a good presentation. I prefer to do a great speech and I'll do my best, but even if it's not brilliant, the consequences are unlikely to be disastrous. Even if I look nervous, that's OK. Many people get nervous when they're giving a speech. It's highly unlikely that I'll fall apart or that the audience will think that I'm incompetent. I have never fallen apart or done a terrible speech in the past. At worst, it may not be a great presentation but it won't be a disaster.

POSITIVE ACTIONS: Prepare thoroughly. Practice the speech in front of my friends. Record it onto a tape recorder and listen to it a few times.

### 4. Rick is anxious about having to make a potentially unpleasant phone call.

THOUGHTS/BELIEFS: He'll probably hate me. He might get aggressive. This might be very unpleasant. Everyone must like and approve of me. I should avoid conflict/disapproval at all costs. If he became aggressive, it would be awful, and I couldn't stand it.

DISPUTE: I don't know how he will react—he may or may not react badly towards me. I prefer to be liked (and many people do like me), but I accept that not everyone has to like me. It's OK if some people don't like me. I prefer to avoid conflict, but I am willing to risk conflict and I can cope with it if it should arise.

POSITIVE ACTIONS: Plan what I'm going to say—make some brief notes to jog my memory. Do it now—don't procrastinate.

### 5. Fay feels anxious about having to confront her neighbors about their dog, which is constantly barking.

THOUGHTS/BELIEFS: They will not like me if I complain. They might be hostile towards me. I should avoid the possibility of conflict with my neighbors. If they became aggressive, it would be awful, and I couldn't stand it.

DISPUTE: They have been friendly towards me in the past. I have no evidence that they will respond badly to me. If I communicate in a conciliatory way, chances are they will be reasonable. Even if they are not reasonable, I won't like it but I will stand it. It's important that I say something. If I don't communicate, they won't know that I have a problem.

POSITIVE ACTIONS: Plan what I'm going to say. Do it now.

## 6. Jeremy is anxious about an approaching job interview.

THOUGHTS/BELIEFS: They may ask me questions that I won't be able to answer. I may come across poorly or make a total fool of myself. I may not get the job. I should perform really well. I should be able to impress them. I should get the job. It would be awful if I performed poorly or didn't get the job.

DISPUTE: I'd like to do well, and I'll do my best, but if I don't do a fantastic interview, it will be a learning experience and not a disaster. It would be great to get the job, but if I don't, I can accept that. This is not a do-or-die situation. I may need to go to several job interviews before I am successful. That's part of the process for most people.

POSITIVE ACTIONS: Prepare thoroughly. Read up about the company. Prepare answers to some of the possible questions that they might ask.

## 7. Clive feels anxious about having to return some goods to the shop.

THOUGHTS/BELIEFS: They may feel put out by my request for a refund. They may not like me. They may end up being very unpleasant. People should always be nice to me. It's awful when people are rude or unpleasant. It's wrong for me to return goods to the shop.

DISPUTE: I have the right to return goods to the shop. They have the right to say no, but I have the right to ask. They may be perfectly reasonable. I know from past experience that when I expect the worst I am often pleasantly surprised. Even if they refuse to give me a refund, I will lose nothing by trying. I prefer people to be nice to me but I can cope even if they are not.

POSITIVE ACTIONS: Do it now. Don't procrastinate.

## 8. Olivia feels anxious because her daughter has slept in and may miss her flight for the vacation that she had planned.

THOUGHTS/BELIEFS: Jenny might miss her flight. It will be an absolute disaster if she does. This is my responsibility.

DISPUTE: It will be unfortunate if Jenny misses the flight, but if she does, chances are she will be able to get on another one. Other people also sometimes miss flights and, as far as I know, they always end up getting other flights. At worst, she may need to wait around for hours for the next available flight. It will be a hassle, but she will manage. Jenny is twenty-two years old—it is her responsibility to get up in time to catch her flight. I can do what I can to support her but I am not responsible for her in this situation.

POSITIVE ACTIONS: Help her get ready. Drive her to the airport.

# EXERCISE 10.1

## 1. Someone has borrowed a book and has not returned it.

OBSERVATIONS: Pam, I lent you my copy of *The Road Less Traveled* in September last year, and when I asked you about it a few weeks ago, you said that you don't recall whether you still have it.

THOUGHTS/FEELINGS: The book is very precious to me, and I'm feeling rather upset at the possibility of not getting it back.

NEEDS: I'd really appreciate it if you had another look and made a special effort to find it.

## 2. You agreed to go to the trivia evening, but now you don't want to do it.

OBSERVATIONS: Jo, you remember I agreed to go to the Trivial Pursuit night at St Joseph's last Saturday?

THOUGHTS/FEELINGS: I feel bad about saying this, but I really don't want to go. At the time, I thought it was really nice of you to invite me, so I didn't want to be a bad sport. In retrospect, I wish I had been more honest with you.

NEEDS: I'm really sorry about backing out of it at this stage but I hope that you'll understand.

## 3. Your partner has been very irritable lately.

OBSERVATIONS: Ken, you seem to be very irritable lately. You have been getting upset about fairly minor issues, like when the paper didn't arrive on Thursday, and when Johnny didn't wash his hands before dinner. You've also been pretty uncommunicative with me in the last few weeks.

THOUGHTS/FEELINGS: I'm wondering if there's something wrong? Perhaps you're under a lot of stress at the moment? It really worries me when you're like this.

NEEDS: I'd like us to be able to talk about things and support each other if there's a problem—would you like to talk about it?

# EXERCISE 10.2

## 1. A friend asks you to tell a lie to someone on his behalf. You feel uncomfortable with this.

BELIEFS: If someone asks me to do something I should always do it. She will disapprove of me if I say no. I should never do things that might disappoint my friends.

DISPUTE: It's OK to say no to requests for things that I don't want to do, even when the request comes from a friend. It's not really fair for her to put me in this position. If she is a good friend she will respect my right to say no.

ASSERTIVE STATEMENT: Jane, I really don't feel comfortable lying to Toby. I feel bad about saying no because you're a close friend and I care about you. I hope you'll understand why I'm not able to help you with this.

## 2. The salesman has been serving you for over forty minutes and he has been extremely pleasant and helpful. You have found something that is OK, but you're not really sure. You are aware that you've taken up a lot of his time.

BELIEFS: If a salesperson gives me good service I am obliged to buy something. He will be annoyed if I don't buy anything. It's important for him to like me.

DISPUTE: He gave me very good service, but he was doing his job. People who work in sales frequently have customers who spend a lot of time but don't buy anything. That is a normal part of their experience. I am not obliged to buy something if I haven't found what I want. Chances are he won't be annoyed but if he is, that's not my problem. I can acknowledge the good service without having to buy anything.

ASSERTIVE STATEMENT: You've been very attentive and helpful and I really appreciate it. Unfortunately, I still haven't found anything I really want. Thank you for all your help.

### 3. You get a call from someone you met while traveling overseas two years ago, and she wants to stay at your place for "a while." You're not too happy about the idea.

BELIEFS: If someone asks me to do something, I should always say yes. She won't like me if I say no. Everyone must like me.

DISPUTE: I have the right to put my own needs first. I am not under any obligation to put her up. It's OK to say no if it doesn't suit me. If she doesn't like me that's too bad. I can cope with that.

ASSERTIVE STATEMENT: I'd be happy for you to stay for a day or two while you are looking for accommodation, but it really doesn't suit me for you to stay here for more than a couple of days.

### 4. You have had dinner with friends at an expensive restaurant. You have not had any alcohol, while the others have drunk a lot. Although the alcohol alone comes to over $30 a head, when the bill is being worked out, no one suggests that you should pay less.

BELIEFS: I shouldn't speak up or they'll think that I'm stingy. I should just go along with what other people expect. It's tacky to stand up for your rights when you're dealing with money.

DISPUTE: As the alcohol contributed to a major part of the bill, it is reasonable for me to not pay as much as everyone else. Speaking up is unlikely to cause people to disapprove of me, but if someone does, I can live with it. It's not going to make any difference to my life. It's OK for me to stand up for my rights, whether I am dealing with money or any other issue.

ASSERTIVE STATEMENT: As I've had no alcohol tonight, I'm going to put in my share, minus the drinks. I hope that's OK with everyone.

### 5. One of your colleagues at work has a habit of sitting down next to you and talking while you are trying to work.

BELIEFS: Asking him to leave is likely to offend him. I should never say anything that might offend people. I should never put my own needs before the needs of others. It's better to put up with it than to risk the possibility of his disapproval.

DISPUTE: It's OK to put my own needs first in this situation. It is appropriate for me to tell him that I'm busy–it's better to be honest than to feel resentful.

ASSERTIVE STATEMENT: Bill, I hope you'll excuse me. I really have a lot of work that I need to get on with.

### 6. You have already asked the two people sitting behind you in the theater to stop talking. Now, ten minutes later, they have started talking again.

BELIEFS: Asking once is OK, but asking a second time might make them mad. It's not OK to make the same request a second time. They will think I am a pest if I ask again–they might be rude or abusive to me.

DISPUTE: It's OK for me to ask again. Some people need to be reminded about their noise because they are oblivious to the people around them. If I ask politely, I'm unlikely to get a hostile response, but if it happens, I'll deal with it.

ASSERTIVE STATEMENT: I'm sorry to ask you again, but it's still a problem. Would you mind not talking during the film?

### 7. You are watering your front garden when a dog that is being walked by with its owner poops on your nature strip.

BELIEFS: If I say something, he'll get aggressive. People don't like being told what to do. It's better to say nothing.

DISPUTE: Dog owners have a responsibility to clean up after their dogs. It's reasonable for me to ask him to clean up the mess, as it affects me. He knows that it's his responsibility. If I ask him nicely, he is unlikely to be rude or aggressive, however, even if he is, I can handle it.

ASSERTIVE STATEMENT: Excuse me, your dog just did its business on my nature strip. Would you mind cleaning up the mess?

### 8. A group of friends are at your house, and one of them lights up a cigarette. You have a no-smoking policy at your house.

BELIEFS: I shouldn't say anything because these are my friends. She won't like me if I ask her to smoke outside. When it comes to friends, I should put my own needs last.

DISPUTE: It's perfectly valid for me to ask her not to smoke in my house. These days, smokers are aware of other people's rights and are used to being asked not to smoke. It's highly unlikely that asking her not to smoke in the house will cause any bad feelings.

ASSERTIVE STATEMENT: Karen, would you mind going out on the balcony while you're smoking?

### 9. The coffee you ordered at a restaurant arrives lukewarm.

BELIEFS: Asking them to replace it with a hot cup of coffee will cause an inconvenience to the staff. I should never say anything that might inconvenience the staff, especially if they are busy. My needs are not that important.

DISPUTE: I am paying for the coffee—it's reasonable to expect to get what I paid for. It may be a slight inconvenience to them, but it's inconvenient to me to get lukewarm coffee. My needs matter, and it's OK for me to ask for what I want.

ASSERTIVE STATEMENT: Excuse me. This coffee is lukewarm. Would you mind getting me a hot cup of coffee?

## 10. A friend borrowed $200 four months ago and seems to have forgotten about it.

BELIEFS: Asking people to repay their debt is tacky. She might think that I am tight. She won't like it and she may not like me as a result.

DISPUTE: It's OK to ask her to repay the money that she borrowed from me. The money was lent on the understanding that it would be repaid, so it is not unreasonable to expect this. It is unlikely that she will dislike me for bringing it up, but if she does, that reflects poorly on her. If our friendship relies on me bailing her out and being totally submissive, it is not a very healthy friendship.

ASSERTIVE STATEMENT: Ruth, remember you still owe me $200 from when we went to the club? It's been four months now since I lent it to you, so could you arrange to pay it back?

# Recommended Reading

## Anger

Beck, AT (1999). *Prisoners of Hate: The cognitive basis of anger, hostility, and violence,* HarperCollins Publishers, NY.

Nelson, M & Finch, AJ (1996). *Keeping Your Cool: The anger management workbook,* Workbook Publishing, Ardmore, PA.

Schiraldi, GR & Hallmark-Kerr, M (2002). *Anger Management Source Book,* Contemporary Books, USA.

Potter-Efron, R & Potter-Efron, P (1995). *Letting Go of Anger,* New Harbinger Publications, Oakland, CA.

## Anxiety–general

Bourne, E (1998). *Healing Fear: New approaches to overcome anxiety,* New Harbinger Publications, Oakland, CA.

Bourne, E (2000). *The Anxiety and Phobia Workbook,* New Harbinger Publications, Oakland, CA.

Kennerley, H (1997). *Overcoming Anxiety: A self-help guide using cognitive behavioral techniques,* New York University Press, NY.

Page, AC (2002). *Don't Panic: Anxiety, phobias and tension,* ACP & Media 21, Sydney.

## Depression

Aisbett, B (2000). *Taming the Black Dog: A guide to overcoming depression,* HarperCollins, Australia.

Burns, D (1999). *The Feeling Good Handbook,* Plume Books, NY.

Emery, G (2000). *Overcoming Depression: A cognitive behavior protocol for the treatment of depression,* New Harbinger Publications, Oakland, CA.

Gilbert, P (1999). *Overcoming Depression: A step-by-step approach to gaining control over depression,* Oxford University Press, NY.

McQuaid, J & Carmona, P (2004). *Peaceful Mind: Using mindfulness and cognitive behavioral psychology to overcome depression,* New Harbinger Publications, Oakland, CA.

Parker, G (2004). *Dealing with Depression: A commonsense guide in the mood disorders,* Allen & Unwin, Sydney

Tanner, S & Ball, J (1998). *Beating the Blues,* Doubleday Books, Sydney.

Wright, JH & Basco, MR (2001). *Getting Your Life Back: The complete guide to recovery from depression,* Free Press, NY.

Yapko, M (1997). *Breaking the Patterns of Depression,* Doubleday, NY.

## Effective communication

Burns, D (1999). *The Feeling Good Handbook*, Plume Books, NY. Part IV on communication.

McKay, M, Fanning, P & Paleg, K (1994). *Couple Skills*, New Harbinger Publications, Oakland, CA.

McKay, M, Davis M & Fanning, P (1995). *Messages,* New Harbinger Publications, Oakland, CA.

Paterson, RJ (2000). *The Assertiveness Workbook*, New Harbinger Publications, Oakland, CA.


## General books

Antony, M & Swinson, R (1998). *When Perfect Isn't Good Enough: Strategies for coping with perfectionism*, New Harbinger Publications, Oakland, CA.

Barlow, DH & Rapee, RM (2001). *Mastering Stress—A Lifestyle Approach*, American Health Publishing, Dallas, TX.

Burns, D (1999). *The Feeling Good Handbook*, Plume Books, NY.

Butler, G & Hope, T (1995). *Manage Your Mind*, Oxford University Press, NY.

Csikszentmihalyi, M (1990). *Flow: The psychology of optimal experience*, Harper & Row. NY.

Greenberger, D & Padesky, CA (1995). *Mind Over Mood: Change how you feel by changing the way you think,* Guilford Press, NY.

McKay, M, Davis, M, & Fanning, P (1997). *Thoughts and Feelings*, New Harbinger Publications, Oakland, CA.

Seligman, ME (1991). *Learned Optimism*, Alfred A. Knopf, Inc., NY.


## Generalized anxiety disorder

Copeland, M (1998). *Worry Control Workbook*, New Harbinger Publications, Oakland, CA.

Craske, M, Barlow, D, & O'Leary, T (1992). *Mastery of Your Anxiety and Worry,* Oxford University Press, NY.

Leahy, R (2005). *The Worry Cure: Seven steps to stop worry from stopping you,* Harmony, NY.

White, J (1999). *Overcoming Generalized Anxiety Disorder,* New Harbinger Publications, Oakland, CA.


## Happiness

Niven, D (2000). *The 100 Simple Secrets of Happy People*, HarperCollins, NY.

Seligman, M (2002). *Authentic Happiness: Using the new positive psychology to realize your potential for lasting fulfillment*, Free Press, NY.

Sharp, T (2005). *Happiness Handbook: Strategies for a happy life,* Finch Publishing, Sydney.

## Meditation/relaxation

Brantley, J (2003). *Calming Your Anxious Mind: How mindfulness and compassion can free you from anxiety, fear and panic*, New Harbinger Publications, Oakland, CA.

McQuaid, J & Carmona, P (2004). *Peaceful Mind: Using mindfulness and cognitive behavioral psychology to overcome depression*, New Harbinger Publications, Oakland, CA.

Wilson, P (1985). *The Calm Technique*, Greenhouse Publications, Melbourne.


## Obsessive compulsive disorder

Baer, L (2000). *Getting Control: Overcoming your obsessions and compulsions*, Plume Books, NY.

De Silva, P & Rachman, S (1998). *Obsessive-Compulsive Disorder: The facts*, 2nd edn, Oxford University Press, NY.

Foa, EB & Wilson, R (2001). *Stop Obsessing: How to overcome your obsessions and compulsions*, Bantam Books, NY.

Grayson, J (2003). *Freedom from Obsessive Compulsive Disorder: A personalized recovery program for living with uncertainty*, Penguin, NY.

Hyman, B & Pedrick, C (1999). *The OCD Workbook: Your guide to breaking free from obsessive compulsive disorder*, New Harbinger Publications, Oakland, CA.

Schwartz, J (1996). *Brain Lock: Free yourself from obsessive compulsive disorder*, HarperCollins, NY.

Steketee, G & White, K (1990). *When Once Is Not Enough—Help for Obsessive Compulsives*, New Harbinger Publications, Oakland, CA.


## Motivation

Bliss, EC (1984). *Doing It Now: A twelve-step program for curing procrastination and achieving your goals*, Bantam Books, NY.

Knaus, WJ (1998). *Do It Now!: Break the procrastination habit*, J. Wiley, NY.

Montgomery, B (1987). *The Truth About Success and Motivation*, Lothian Books, Melbourne.

Roberts, MS (1995). *Living Without Procrastination: How to stop postponing your life*, New Harbinger Publications, Oakland, CA.


## Panic attacks

Aisbett, B (1999). *Living With It: A survivor's guide to panic attacks*, HarperCollins, Australia.

Bassett, L (1997). *From Panic to Power: Proven techniques to calm your anxieties, conquer your fears and put you in control of your life*, Harper Perennial, NY.

Fox, B (1999). *Power over Panic*, Shakti River Press, Saratoga, CA.

Silove, D & Manicavasagar, V (2001). *Overcoming Panic: A self help guide using cognitive behavioral techniques,* New York University Press, NY.

Zuercher-White, E (1999). *Overcoming Panic Disorder and Agoraphobia*, New Harbinger Publications, Oakland, CA.

**Relationships**

Beck, A (1989). *Love is Never Enough*, Harper & Row, NY.

Bireda, M (1990). *Love Addiction: A guide to emotional independence*, New Harbinger Publications, Oakland, CA.

Christensen, A & Jacobson, N (2000). *Reconcilable Differences,* Guilford Press, NY.

Jansen, D & Newman, M (1989). *Really Relating*, Random House, Sydney.

Lamble, J & Morris, S (2000). *Side by Side—How to Think Differently About Your Relationship*, Finch Publishing, Sydney.

Markman, H, Stanley, S & Blumberg, SL (2001). *Fighting for Your Marriage*, Jossey-Bass Inc. Publishers, San Francisco.

Montgomery, B & Evans, L (1995). *Living and Loving Together*, Nelson, Melbourne.

Nelson-Jones, R (1999). *Creating Happy Relationships: A guide to partner skills*, Cassell, NY.

Spring, J (1997). *After the Affair: Healing the pain and rebuilding trust when a partner has been unfaithful*, HarperCollins, NY.

**Self-esteem**

Firestone, RW, Firestone, L & Catlett, J (2002). *Conquer Your Critical Inner Voice*, New Harbinger Publications, Oakland, CA.

Fennell, M (2001). *Overcoming Low Self-esteem: A clinically proven step-by-step program to recovering on your own,* New York University Press, NY.

McKay, M & Fanning, P (2000). *Self-Esteem*, New Harbinger Publications, Oakland, CA.

McKay, M & Fanning, P (1999). *The Self-Esteem Companion*, New Harbinger Publications, Oakland CA.

Schiraldi, GR (2001). *The Self-Esteem Workbook*, New Harbinger Publications, Oakland, CA.

**Social phobia**

Antony, M & Swinson, R (2000). *The Shyness and Social Anxiety Workbook: Proven techniques for overcoming your fears*, New Harbinger Publications, Oakland, CA.

Butler, G (2001). *Overcoming Social Anxiety and Shyness: A self-help guide using cognitive behavioral techniques*, New York University Press, NY.

Hope, D, Heimberg, RG, Juster, HR & Turk, CL (2000). *Managing social anxiety: A cognitive behavioral therapy approach,* Oxford University Press, NY.

Rapee, RM (1998). *Overcoming Shyness and Social Phobia*, Jason Aronson Inc., Northvale, NJ.

**Trauma**

Herbert, C & Wetmore, A (2001). *Overcoming Traumatic Stress: A self-help guide using cognitive behavioral techniques*, New York University Press, NY.

Schiraldi, G (2000). *The Post-Traumatic Stress Disorder Source Book*, McGraw-Hill/Lowell House, Chicago.

Smyth, L (1999). *Overcoming Post-Traumatic Stress Disorder*, New Harbinger Publications, Oakland, CA.

## PSYCHIATRISTS AND PSYCHOLOGISTS

Psychiatrists are doctors who have undergone additional training to specialize in the treatment of psychological disorders. They have expertise in diagnosing disorders and may prescribe drugs for treatment, if appropriate. To make an appointment with a psychiatrist, you may need to get a referral from your family doctor.

Psychologists specialize in a wide range of areas, including counseling and clinical psychology, organizational psychology, health psychology, sports psychology and forensic psychology. Some psychologists specialize in treating a range of psychological disorders, while others provide counseling to help mentally healthy people feel and function better. Psychologists cannot prescribe medication. Not all psychologists use CBT, but many do (before making a first appointment, you can ask what type of therapy they use). You do not need a doctor's referral to visit a psychologist.

### Psychologists referral service

The American Psychological Association is the main professional body for psychologists in the United States. It operates a referral service for people who would like to locate a psychologist in their area. (You can specifically ask for a psychologist who practices CBT.) The service can be accessed by calling 1-800-964-2000. Alternatively, the service can be accessed via the Internet at: *www.apa.org*.

# Index